DECODABLE BOOK

Harcourt

SCHOOL PUBLISHERS

Copyright © by Harcourt, Inc.

All rights reserved. No part of this publication may be reproduced or transmitted in any form or by any means, electronic or mechanical, including photocopy, recording, or any information storage and retrieval system, without permission in writing from the publisher.

Requests for permission to make copies of any part of the work should be addressed to School Permissions and Copyrights, Harcourt, Inc., 6277 Sea Harbor Drive, Orlando, Florida 32887-6777. Fax: 407-345-2418.

STORYTOWN is a trademark of Harcourt, Inc. HARCOURT and the Harcourt Logo are trademarks of Harcourt, Inc., registered in the United States of America and/or other jurisdictions. Printed in the United States of America

ISBN 10 0-15-364109-6
ISBN 13 978-0-15-364109-1

1 2 3 4 5 6 7 8 9 10   179   17 16 15 14 13 12 11 10 09 08

Ordering Options
ISBN 10-0-15-364212-2
ISBN 13 978-0-15-364212-8

If you have received these materials as examination copies free of charge, Harcourt School Publishers retains title to the materials and they may not be resold. Resale of examination copies is strictly prohibited and is illegal.

Possession of this publication in print format does not entitle users to convert this publication, or any portion of it, into electronic format.

Contents

Bridget, Please Don't Fidget

by Guadalupe V. Lopez

illustrated by Anne-Sophie Lanquetin

Bridget is six. She likes to run and play.

Today, Bridget cannot run and play. Today, Bridget is in a wedding. There is little time for fun.

Madge fixes Bridget's lace dress.

"Stand still, Bridget. Please don't fidget,"

says Mom. Bridget stands for a long time.

Ginger tames Bridget's curls.
"Sit still, Bridget. Please don't fidget,"
says Mom. Bridget sits for a long time.

At the church, the wedding song starts. Bridget wants to race.
Yet, she walks at a slow pace. She walks for a long time.
6

Next, they all drive to a big hall. A band plays on the stage. Mom gives Bridget a gentle nudge. "Let's dance, princess."

Bridget walks out to dance. Bridget does
not fidget. She dances for a long time.

The Dodge River Race

by Guadalupe V. Lopez   illustrated by Betsy Snyder

Winter is here. The forest sparkles with
snow. Dodge River has turned to ice.
It is time for the big ice race.

10

Forest animals line the edge of Dodge River.
They twist and fidget. When will the race start?
Who will win?

Last winter, Midge Rabbit was the champ. She can't wait for the race to begin. Here she is in her lace cape.

At last, the animals are set to race. Madge Turtle is the judge. She waves the flag and yells "Go!"

13

Ginger Otter had a slow start. Roger Fox is in the lead.

Roger Fox is at the finish line first! Roger is the champ!
"Hurray for Roger!" everyone calls.

"Thanks!" says Roger Fox. "Let's all go to my place
and eat the prize—this large fudge cake!"

Cinder Hills

by Amy Collier   illustrated by Cindy Revell

Trace does not live in a big town. His home is in a small place called Cinder Hills.

Cinder Hills is a simple town with a slow pace. People never rush. Trace always has a smile on his face.

19

Each morning, Trace eats in peace. Then he runs in the center circle of the park.

Trace likes to ride bikes with his pal Spencer.
They race up the hill to the school.

21

Then Trace and Spencer ride down the
cement road until they reach the big oak tree.

22

Time for a snack! They sit in the shade and eat rice cakes and apple slices.

That night, Trace thinks about the nice day he had
in the best place around – Cinder Hills!

24

Bridget, Please Don't Fidget
Word Count: 130

High-Frequency Words	Decodable Words*			
does	a	dress	let's	please	starts
don't	all	drive	likes	princess	still
gives	and	**fidget**	little	race	tames
out	at	fixes	long	run	the
says	band	for	**Madge**	she	time
there	big	fun	Mom	sit	wedding
they	**Bridget**	**gentle**	next	sits	yet
to	**Bridget's**	**Ginger**	not	six	
today	cannot	hall	**nudge**	slow	
walks	church	in	on	song	
wants	curls	is	pace	**stage**	
	dance(s)	lace	play(s)	stand(s)	

*Words with /j/ *g, dge* appear in **boldface** type.

The Dodge River Race

Word Count: 135

High-Frequency Words

animals
are
everyone
go
here
my
of
says
they
to
was
who

Decodable Words*

a	eat	has	let's	she	wait
all	**edge**	her	line	slow	waves
and	**fidget**	hurray	**Madge**	snow	when
at	finish	ice	**Midge**	sparkles	will
begin	first	in	Otter	start	win
big	flag	is	place	thanks	winter
cake	for	it	prize	the	with
calls	forest	**judge**	Rabbit	this	yells
can't	Fox	lace	race	time	
cape	**fudge**	**large**	River	turned	
champ	**Ginger**	last	**Roger**	Turtle	
Dodge	had	lead	set	twist	

*Words with /j/ *g,dge* appear in **boldface** type.

Cinder Hills

Word Count: 123

High-Frequency Words

about	to
always	town
around	
does	
down	
live	
night	
of	
people	
school	
they	

Decodable Words*

a	**circle**	Hills	on	runs	that
and	day	his	**pace**	rush	the
apple	each	home	pal	shade	then
best	eat	in	park	simple	thinks
big	eats	is	**peace**	sit	time
bikes	**face**	likes	**place**	**slices**	**Trace**
cakes	for	morning	**race**	slow	tree
called	had	never	reach	small	until
cement	has	**nice**	**rice**	smile	up
center	he	not	ride	snack	with
Cinder	hill	oak	road	**Spencer**	

*Words with /s/c appear in **boldface** type.

MW00514585

TAROT
Book of Shadows

Jennifer & Richard ShadowFox

Schiffer Publishing Ltd

4880 Lower Valley Road · Atglen, Pennsylvania 19310

Dedication

For Taylor and Nolan

Copyright © 2010 by Richard and Jennifer ShadowFox
Library of Congress Control Number: 2009943909

All rights reserved. No part of this work may be reproduced or used in any form or by any means—graphic, electronic, or mechanical, including photocopying or information storage and retrieval systems—without written permission from the publisher.

The scanning, uploading and distribution of this book or any part thereof via the Internet or via any other means without the permission of the publisher is illegal and punishable by law. Please purchase only authorized editions and do not participate in or encourage the electronic piracy of copyrighted materials.

"Schiffer," "Schiffer Publishing Ltd. & Design," and the "Design of pen and ink well" are registered trademarks of Schiffer Publishing Ltd.

Designed by RoS
Type set in Tiranti Solid LET/Garamond Premier Pro
ISBN: 978-0-7643-3487-0
Printed in China

Schiffer Books are available at special discounts for bulk purchases for sales promotions or premiums. Special editions, including personalized covers, corporate imprints, and excerpts can be created in large quantities for special needs. For more information contact the publisher:

Published by Schiffer Publishing Ltd.
4880 Lower Valley Road
Atglen, PA 19310
Phone: (610) 593-1777; Fax: (610) 593-2002
E-mail: Info@schifferbooks.com

For the largest selection of fine reference books on this and related subjects, please visit our web site at
www.schifferbooks.com
We are always looking for people to write books on new and related subjects. If you have an idea for a book please contact us at the above address.

This book may be purchased from the publisher.
Include $5.00 for shipping.
Please try your bookstore first.
You may write for a free catalog.

In Europe, Schiffer books are distributed by
Bushwood Books
6 Marksbury Ave.
Kew Gardens
Surrey TW9 4JF England
Phone: 44 (0) 20 8392-8585; Fax: 44 (0) 20 8392-9876
E-mail: info@bushwoodbooks.co.uk
Website: www.bushwoodbooks.co.uk

Acknowledgments

We would like to thank our families and friends for their love and support:

Our loving parents: Doris, Virginia, Nolan and Richard.

Our wonderful siblings: Dan and Susan, Ron and Marcia, Steve and Linda, and Tom.

Our lifelong friend, Angela.

Our fantastic editor, Dinah.

And to Pamela Colman Smith, who created a standard of imagery that we can only hope to stand in the shadow of.

Contents

1

Foreword

We would like to welcome you to the fascinating world of the Tarot. There is an infinite amount of knowledge associated with the Tarot available; it is a ceaseless cultivation, blending experience with knowledge.

It is interesting and relevant to ponder over Dorothy's different perceptions of Professor Marvel in the film, *The Wizard of Oz*. When Dorothy first encounters him in the film's depicted real world, known geographically as Kansas, she trusts and believes him, with emphatic naiveté. Later in her dream perception of him as the Wizard of Oz, she begins to see him as arrogant and self-aggrandizing, and then she turns him into a put-on, a phony. It's her dream, remember. So why did Dorothy have different perceptions of Professor Marvel, and Professor Marvel as Dorothy's Wizard of Oz?

Auntie Em... well, being a Christian woman, might be a clue to the answer. What we choose to believe in and what we are told we should believe in are often parallel concepts, and by that we mean they aren't allowed to intersect. In the beginning, depicted as a charlatan and a traveling con man, Professor Marvel still gave Dorothy the best possible advice. Returning as the Wizard, shortly after the, "pay no attention to that man behind the curtain," line was delivered, Professor Marvel again gives the best possible counsel. In her dream, Dorothy stripped away how religion defines a "spiritual advisor" and found that the truth and sincerity were still there.

In general principle we all live in our own realities, and our relationships with individuals with whom our realities overlap are more enjoyable – and as a result are longer lasting. We call this phenomenon compatibility, although the dictionary's definition of compatibility doesn't require common interests or beliefs; it merely states "capable of existing or living together in harmony." Tragically, humans have a propensity to demand, by strength of majority, power or control that we relinquish our individual ability to believe what we choose, or face ridicule, ostracization, and even violent repercussions.

The "Reading of Tarot Cards" is synonymous with fortune telling and often viewed as evil, or a way to con people out of their money. The truth is, while there are those that exploit the trust of the public for profit, it really isn't fortune telling, and there isn't anything evil about it. Fortune telling is defined by the dictionary as predicting the future; in contrast the reading of Tarot cards offers insight into what outcome your current path will have. Ponder the paradox that if one has predicted the future, then one is powerless to change it, or the prediction was false, but if one has seen the outcome of their current path of action, they may alter their course if they choose.

The key element of a Tarot card reading is the question; it defines the purpose of the reading. If one doesn't know the question, then one will have a difficult time making sense of the answer. Actual case in point: An individual lays the cards out in a Celtic Cross spread without asking a question. In the Crown position is the Lovers card and in the outcome position is the Death card. Within the next two weeks after the reading, the person who the reading was for learned of a possible divorce in the family and experienced the death of a beloved family pet.

Either of the events could have been foretold by the how the cards appeared in that reading, so without the question, the reading was moot. What gives the cards their insight is not knowledge that exists on the terrestrial plane, that we are aware of. But once you have experienced it, your perceptions of the Universe around you will never be the same again. In this world we are offered a choice between the staunch inflexible absolutes of science, and the harshly intolerant dogma of religion, and both are required to understand the significance of the other, but yet they are in conflict and cannot bond all that we know together.

2
A Short History
of the Tarot

It doesn't take very long to discover that the origins of the Tarot are a debatable topic among historians. However, verifiable historical records have led the charge of common consensus to the early fifteenth century, about 1420, in Northern Italy. This belief revolved around a card game which was said to be antecedent to the modern game of bridge. The Visconti-Sforza deck, hand painted in the 1450s for the Visconti-Sforza family, the rulers of Milan at the time, is the oldest deck from which intact cards still exist. It is believed that a deck was commissioned for Duke Filippo Maria Visconti of Milan in 1420, but no remains can be found.

Carte da Trionfi, which means a deck of cards with triumphs added, was the first known reference to the deck of cards used for playing the game associated with the cards we now know as Tarot. The name was changed to Tarocchi around 1530, later evolving into the word Tarot. The origins of the word Tarocchi or why it came to be associated with these particular types of cards is unknown. One belief is that it might have been derived from the Taro River, which runs through Northern Italy and would have had locale significance. It is believed the first paper mills were located there and used the river to turn the wheels of these first mills.

After being invaded, Milan was under the control of Charles VIII of France from 1499 until 1535. It is this event that is accredited with exposing France and Switzerland to Carte da Trionfi, and in turn, eventually led to a series of decks of similar design, which were created during the sixteenth century, and came to be known as the Tarot of Marseilles. The oldest known deck to still exist of the Tarot of Marseilles style of deck is the Jean Noblet Tarot, which was printed in Paris in the mid-seventeenth century.

Prior to the Tarot of Marseilles decks, the trumps, or Major Arcana, did not have numbers, only their imagery, making historical collection of complete decks an uncertainty. For example, in the afore mentioned Visconti-Sforza Tarocchi deck that was recovered only twenty of the twenty-two cards in the Major Arcana were found. The Devil and The Tower have never been located. Some believe they were included but never found, while others believe they were never part of the original deck; and unless the two cards are found, this is a question that more than likely will never be resolved. Current reproductions include the cards, and the deck is available with or without numbers.

There were a number of different decks published throughout the fifteenth and sixteeth centuries, as it seemed everyone wanted to get in on the game. Most notable from the 1400s, and also of Italian creation, was the Sola Busca Tarot deck, which also came to be known as the Ancient Enlightened Tarot. However, from the standpoint of the imagery on the trumps, only the Fool resembles the traditional archetype. The remaining twenty-one Major Arcana are depictions of legendary warriors with no correlation to the symbolism of the Visconti or any of the other known decks of the Carte da Trionfi, or Tarocchi decks of this era.

It is nonetheless significant in that it was a seventy-eight card deck with twenty-one trumps, numerically marked by Roman numerals. This is consistent with the twenty-two cards in our Major Arcana today in that the Fool was included in the deck and bears the zero. But in the game, the deck was designed for it and was regarded as a wild card, and was not a trump card. The Minor Arcana were named as the familiar Swords, Wands, Cups, and Pentacles (Coins), but unlike every other known deck of the era, there was imagery depicted on the pip cards. This makes it the first known deck with imagery on all seventy-eight cards.

It seems yet undeniable, but without absolute proof, that these beautiful cards in these most elaborate decks were being used for more than just playing a game in the three centuries that followed their original creation in the early fifteenth century. After all, there are numerous historical references to ordinary playing cards being used for divination during this period known as the Renaissance. In the late 1700s, a Parisian man, who was to become known as the first professional Tarot reader, commissioned the first Tarot deck to be used solely for divination, and what truly could or might be, became reality.

By reversing his last name in 1767, Jean-Baptiste Alliette became known only as Etteilla, and Tarot reading became fact. An alchemist, astrologer, and occultist, Etteilla claimed as his own ideas from a Swiss Freemason, who was now living in Paris, Court de Gebelin, and began to weave an intricate, but unsubstantiated, web connecting the Tarot to Egypt, by asserting that the Tarot was in fact hieroglyphs that told the story of creation and other secrets of the universe. In 1788, he began teaching his theories, and formed a study group that he named the "Society of the Interpreters of the *Book of Thoth*."

In 1909, 500 years after the Visconti-Sforza, Pamela Colman Smith, under the commission of Arthur Edward Waite, brought to life what would prove to be the most recognizable and popular Tarot deck that has ever been produced. Known originally as the Rider-Waite deck, it is a 78-card deck with illustrations on all 78 cards. Miss Smith, the artist, received a meager sum for her efforts, and until recently, very little recognition. Now that the deck's centennial has arrived, readers and historians have adapted to calling the deck the Waite-Smith Tarot to honor the deserving Smith.

The Waite-Smith Tarot is a product of the Hermetic Order of the Golden Dawn's philosophy, or more specifically Arthur Waite's view of it told through the art of Pamela Colman Smith. In actuality, it is merely a journey or a path if you will, to personal fulfillment. It begins with the Fool, and through the combined will of nature, the trials and tribulations of diligence, and the precise combination of the elements, one will achieve the World. The Waite-Smith Tarot's imagery is the standard by which all other decks are judged. Its symbolism defines the Tarot, as it was, and most likely, as it will be.

One extremely significant aspect of the Waite-Smith deck was that it marked a shifting away from the unsubstantiated Ancient Egyptian *Book of Thoth* heritage. It was a cleansing for the Tarot, a release from the aura of historical uncertainty. Then in 1944, Aleister Crowley, a man whose name became synonymous with the occult in the early twentieth century, delivered his vision of the Tarot in the sublimely enigmatic Thoth Tarot. The artist, Lady Frieda Harris, spent five years working on the project, which was completed in 1943, at times while World War II raged literally right outside her door.

The project was originally expected to take three months, but extensive collaboration, which was defined as up to eight designs for each of the cards in the deck, submitted for Crowley to choose from, made for a much more formidable endeavor. A controversial deck perhaps, but by Crowley's standard of controversy, and given the attempted connection to the Egyptian Pharaoh God Thoth by Etteilla in the eighteenth century, the stated controversy surrounding the deck is actually fueled by the self-proclaimed "wickedest man alive" legend of Aleister Crowley more than anything else.

Relatively indisputable is the fact that the Tarot cards first appeared in Northern Italy in the early fifteenth century as a card game called Carte da Trionfi, later known as Tarocchi, and eventually Tarot. The concept of adding a fifth suit to the already existing four-suit deck, specifically for a game that involved trumps, seems perfectly logical. Since this was the time of the Renaissance, and the arts were making an overwhelming resurgence, why not make this fifth suit, the trump suit, more artistic and character driven than the other four?

But what about the events that came before that first Visconti deck?

The idea of cards starts with paper, and China in the second century C.E. is said to be first. They are believed to have created what has been referred to as money cards used for transactions and playing card games. There would be little or no resemblance between the Ancient Chinese games and those of latter Western Europe, but we would still be on the trail of cards, made of paper, with objects of some type painted or printed on them. From there the trail led to the Middle East and the Islamic Mamluk deck which contained suits, but due to prohibitions against painting living imagery would have only symbols and inanimate objects. The time frame for the Mamluk deck would be near the end of the first millennia.

The earliest known record of playing cards in Europe was when they were banned in Bern, Switzerland, in 1367. There are later records of bans in France and Italy over the next fifteen years. That leaves about a half of a century to the first known Tarot deck. It is unlikely that more detailed historical records will ever be discovered, given the human tendency to destroy when conquering, or in the name of righteousness, or while practicing censorship. The mystery surrounding the Tarot cards is destined to be "an open to interpretation" proposition. The plot thickens when you raise the question of divination and the Tarot.

Without factual evidence, the answer to the question of when the Tarot cards were first used for divination can be nothing more than an educated guess. So let's take a look at the question of when divination might have been first practiced in any form. The great religions of the world and all their many branches have sacred books just full of divinations, under the guise of prophecy. That means several thousand years by way of mythical interpretation that some form of divination has existed. It cannot exist strictly within the confines of religious dogma and nowhere else, which would be like a country without gravity.

Everybody who believes that the Great Pyramid of Egypt was a tomb, raise your hand! In all of the known tombs where actual sarcophagi were found, they also found hieroglyphics all over the walls, and these hieroglyphics were all translated to be spells and incantations. That makes a connection to mysticism and spirituality, which in turn makes a connection to divination. Not by implication that hieroglyphics are the so-called *Book of Thoth*, giving forth the secrets of the universe through the images. It does infer a belief system that runs parallel to those who would have an interest in divinity.

It simply stands to reason that divination has existed as far back as communication, perhaps in the simple warning: "If you don't run from the beasts of the forest, they will kill you and eat you." The ability to understand consequences is a necessary tool of survival, and risk is a natural aspect of survival, making the knowledge of when to take a risk something that we would naturally want to know. The answer to the question regarding when the Tarot cards were first used for divination is quite simply: the very first time a person with a divining spirit ever saw them and imagined the possibilities in them.

3
Frequently Asked Questions *about the* Tarot

Will I be a Witch if I Read Tarot Cards?

Do you mean, will you feel a strange desire to portray Margaret Hamilton's character in, *The Wizard of Oz?* Or do you mean, will you feel a sudden inexplicable desire to hang around costume shops admiring the pointy hats? Perhaps you are wondering if you will suddenly feel more attached to nature, become more interested in organizations that are socially conscious, and realize that some of the most benign people on Earth are in fact Pagans and Wiccans, otherwise known as Witches.

Tarot card reading is about divination, which is prevalent, in some form, in every known religion in the world. The word Witch isn't a description of what a person does; it is a description of what a person believes. There aren't any stipulations assigned to Tarot reading, except perhaps in the more minute mental cavities; there are only the levels of competence and mastery that a reader must earn. Very similar to an ordained member of the clergy, a witch studies, learns, and becomes proficient in many different areas of the craft. Divination is only one part, as are Herbalism, History, and Astronomy. Resist the temptation to fall victim to labels and misinformation that rain down upon you on a daily basis. Don't fall victim to the stereotypes of Hollywood; that sort of witchcraft is for the movies only, and doesn't exist outside a movie set.

Are Tarot Cards Evil?

The dictionary clearly states that evil is something that is, or would be, harmful or injurious to someone. Tarot cards do not have any power to put curses or spells on anyone, and if a person is reading alone or consulting with a professional reader, they aren't in contact with, or summoning, "evil" spirits. Evil is found in the hearts of those who seek power or control over others. They hide it from others by pointing at those they envy or fear and say, "They are why your life is so bad, they are the evil."

"We are oft to blame in this, - / 'Tis too much proved - that with devotion's visage/ And pious action we do sugar o'er/ The devil himself."
~Polonius, Shakespeare's *Hamlet*,
Act 3, Scene 1

It doesn't take a great leap to realize that evil is a dangerous word. It isn't used to define harmful behavior like hunting a species to extinction, or toxic waste dumping; no, what it is used for is to define an enemy. The evil is hiding within the heart of the one who points out the evil for everyone to hate, in the name of righteousness. There isn't anything evil in the Tarot cards, or the people who read them. The cards are a tool. A knife is also a tool – it can be used to prepare food, to create beautiful carvings, and in a surgeon's hands it can even be used to heal. A knife can also be used to torture and kill; yet we do not refer to a knife as being evil. It comes down to whose hands the tool is in to determine what their usage will be.

There are Pentagrams on Some of the Cards. Aren't They the Sign of the Devil?

If the devil does exist, he would do better to market

himself with a more original symbol than a five-pointed star within a circle. On "The Devil" card in the Smith-Waite Tarot deck, there is an inverted star at the top between the horns, and that certainly looks incriminating. The Devil card represents hedonism, self gratification, and the inverted star is actually depicting an imbalance or disharmony as a result.

The Pentacle or Pentagram is probably one of the most maligned and misunderstood symbols in history, and in more recent times, feared. There is a difference between the two – the Pentagram is the drawing or creation of the symbol, and the Pentacle is an actual item, sometimes worn as a charm on a necklace, ring, etc. Although its exact origins are unknown, we do know that it predates Christianity and possibly even Judaism.

The five-pointed star in the upright position has been used by the European Churches to symbolize the five wounds of Christ, and by the Hebrews to represent the first five books of the *Torah*. In the times of the Old Testament, the Pentagram was the first and most important of the Seven Seals, the amulet that contained the Seven Secret Names of God. Earth based religions such as Wicca use the Pentacle or Pentagram to symbolize the five elements: Earth, Air, Water, Fire and Spirit. It is used as the symbol of the Order of the Eastern Star, the female counterpart to the Masonic Order. In the mid 1960s, the Church of Satan adopted the Pentagram and inverted it so that it appeared as a goat or a horned man/devil. The inverted Pentagram is sometimes referred to as the Sign of Baphomet. In some Wiccan traditions, initiates are required to wear the inverted Pentagram as a part of their training, but we must stress here that Wicca and Satanism are in NO way connected in any way, shape, manner, fashion or form.

We can assure you that as it appears on the Tarot cards it is in reference to the five elements, Earth, Air, Fire, Water, and Spirit, not with the devil, or with devil worship. Although it has been used by many cultures, or subcultures, over the history of humankind, it existed long before anyone had ever heard of the devil. Nevertheless, if you find that you are uncomfortable with the Pentacle symbol, there are a number of different decks available with different suit names, such as Coins instead of Pentacles.

Do You Have to be Psychic to Read Tarot Cards?

Reading the Tarot cards is primarily about interpretation. Compare it to a person who was alive 1,000 years ago. What would they do if they heard a cell phone ring? Being psychic is to be sensitive to elements of information that enters your conscious thought process by means other than your five senses. There are people who seem to be more gifted than others, which really isn't any different than a musical prodigy. Just because they seem to be exceptional with limited effort, it doesn't mean that others can't play exceptionally well with a lot of effort. It's a matter of acknowledgment when it comes to the messages we all receive in a psychic method.

To become more acquainted with your psychic abilities, start by paying attention to thoughts that come to you without influence from your five senses. Try keeping a journal with your impressions, writing down all that you can think of about the when, where, and what that may have triggered the thought. Be sure to date your entries so that you can follow up from time to time to see which ones did and did not occur.

Can I Use the Tarot Cards to Make Someone Fall in Love With Me?

Since Tarot cards are not an object of influence, they cannot effect the actions of anyone, or change the outcome of any event. Furthermore, you can't bend or break another person's will to choose whom they love with any methodology, be it substance or incantation, regardless of what you might hear or read. The Tarot cards can be very helpful in guiding you through the different stages of love or romance, but your questions must center on only what you can affect change upon, and that is yourself.

When you are dealing with "Love Spells" in the magickal sense, you are dealing with a substance and/or an incantation that will change the way you are perceived by others, and the change takes place with you, not with them. If you have your eye on someone, and they have given you hope but no promises, ask the cards, "What can I change about me that will raise his/her level of interest in me?"

I'm Afraid of the Death Card. Will Someone Die if it Shows up in a Reading?

The Death Card almost never refers to actual death; rather, it is a card of change. Death doesn't always have to mean physical death – it can also mean the death of a situation, such as moving, or the death of a relationship, such as losing your job or divorce. Change isn't always a bad thing; it just is.

Can I Read the Tarot Cards for Myself?

The only potential problems lie in your subjectivity. People sometimes tend to see only what they want to see, and not what is actually there. If you can detach yourself from your present situation enough to interpret the cards and the message within, objectively, then you most certainly can read for yourself.

4

Choosing a Deck, Choosing a Book, Learning the Cards

Tarot cards are strong in symbolism, and it is strongly recommended that you begin with a more traditional deck. The Smith-Waite Tarot is the quintessential Tarot deck and a popular choice for beginners. However, if your Tarot journey began when you found yourself attracted to the imagery of a particular deck, or once you became interested in the Tarot, you found yourself drawn toward the imagery of a particular deck, don't take this attraction lightly. Your affinity for a specific Tarot deck is not adventitious. Your feelings, your very organic aspect of emotion, is intrinsic to your connection to the Tarot, and you will soon begin to realize that your feelings exist beyond the shallow depths of personal preference, and are in fact an unequivocally accurate guide through the forest of uncertainty and ambiguous purpose that lies between you and the destiny of your dreams.

Many decks today are available with companion books that can help make learning with a nontraditional deck a less complicated process. There is an abundance of resource material available and the more you explore, the more confident you will feel. We have included a section on resources and recommended reading at the end of this book. We also recommend that you check your local library for a vast selection of titles. If your interest runs deep, you will soon find that there are more than a singular set of rules, and you may have to rely on a consensus of beliefs, as well as your own feelings, to properly interpret the story that you have spread out before you. There are Tarot apprentices and accomplished readers, and many that fall in between, but regardless of rhetoric and varnish, boastfulness and grandeur, there are no complete Tarot readers. Accept all the offerings of knowledge that you are able to, and allow your feelings to decide the relevance and significance as it applies to the art of reading the Tarot.

There is a belief that it is bad luck, or just not a good idea, to purchase your first deck, and that it should be acquired as a gift from someone. In all probability this custom is the result of the practice of reading Tarot cards having primarily been a passed-down tradition within families, and is more of a ceremonial tradition than an effective enhancement to reading the cards. There are, however, two significant customs that we feel will have an effect on your readings, and we enjoin you to follow them. The first traditional custom being the initial bonding of the devices that combines to tell the story.

1. You should be the first person to touch each card in the deck once the package has been opened.
2. The second rule you should adhere to is that you should never read from the deck of someone who is currently deceased, unless they gave the deck to you, and preferably before they died.

Also, a sense of humor is a valuable tool, as it resets your emotional barometer.

Beginning Exercise: Take each card from your deck individually and write down what you see and how it makes you feel. Describe each object you feel is a symbol, and any character action that you feel is symbolic, then compare to your book.

5
The Environment, Your Intentions, *and* Your State of Mind

Getting the right atmosphere, needing the necessary ambiance, and creating the perfect mood are all acceptable approaches if you enjoy them. Make the room dark and spooky and read by candlelight if you like, but remember the difference between the theatrical and what is truly essential to a reading. If you start out by designing the perfect setting, which is lengthy and time consuming to prepare, you run the risk of becoming overly dependent upon it. The only elements that are truly essential are the cards, a realistic question, and the concentration of the reader. You do want to be comfortable and relaxed, preferably in a familiar environment when you are starting out. You may find that sitting in a chair at a table is comfortable, or sitting or kneeling in front of a coffee table, or perhaps reclining on pillows on the floor is what you prefer. Over time, as you become more familiar with the cards, and the flow of the reading begins to smooth out, you may find that you feel comfortable reading in a number of different positions and settings. Again, and it is worthy of repeating, the Tarot Trinity of cards, question and concentration are essential – anything less will not provide accurate results, and anything more is superfluous. At this point we must ask you to be thoughtful of what it is you are seeking by learning to read the Tarot.

If it is your belief that this would make a great way to amuse your friends at parties, be strongly cautioned that you are toying with the lives of people that you care about. If the subject of your "party time" reading has a sincere belief in what you are telling them, but at the same time you are not reading with sincerity in your heart, the consequences could be devastating. A Tarot card reader has an obligation to the person for whom they are reading, and it is not to amuse or impress them.

Aside from your sincerity, your state of mind is important. You should not be experiencing a peak of emotion, such as anger, sorrow, or even elation. You must be relaxed, perhaps even serene when you read. This goes doubly so if the reading is directly connected to the emotions you are feeling. Take a walk, if it is raining, or soak in a warm bath for a while. Imagine the emotion is washing away with the rain, or swirling down the drain. You need your feelings to be clear to interpret the cards, and that is difficult if you are already feeling something strongly.

As you hold the cards in your hand, with your environment prepared and distractions eliminated, close your eyes, take a deep breath in, and then slowly let it out. With your eyes still closed, say out loud, "I am ready, and I am going to read now," then open your eyes and shuffle the cards. There are no absolutes for shuffling, you may rifle, bridge, or lay them all face down on a table and swirl them around, whatever your personal preference may be. As a general rule we do not allow others to shuffle or touch our personal decks.

Intermediate Exercise: Write the card identifier on one side of an index card, then turn it over and write what it signifies on the other side. Make one index card for each card in your deck, then look at the identifier and try to remember the Significator.

6
The Celtic Cross Spread

A "spread" is a pattern in which you lay out the cards, and there are a myriad of different spreads to read from, and countless books to help you learn them. A spread can be as simple as a single card, or a three-card spread, all the way up to the Rahdue's Wheel, which utilizes all 78 cards of a standard Tarot deck.

Here is a look at what we would call our signature spread. We didn't invent it, but it is our predominant choice when doing a reading, unless otherwise requested by the Querent, or the person asking the question.

Known as the Celtic (Kel-tic) Cross, not to be confused with a Boston Celtic (Sel-tic), it is a ten-card spread with a Significator. It provides the right amount of detail to answer a question, but it doesn't overwhelm. If you are reading with a Significator card you will want to find it and pull it from the deck, before you shuffle the cards, and place it face up in the center of what will become your cross.

Once the cards are thoroughly shuffled, begin laying them out, face down, beginning with the one position following the pattern sequentially until you reach the ten position. Then turn the cards over, again starting with one and going in order until you reach the tenth card.

As you shuffle and lay out the cards there will be various abnormalities such as reversed cards in the spread, or cards that pop out while you are shuffling. We consider these to be of significance, so make a mental note of them when they occur and refer to them during and after the reading to see what additional information they carry with them. Place any cards that pop out back in the deck and continue to shuffle.

This is a general overview of the positions of the Celtic Cross.

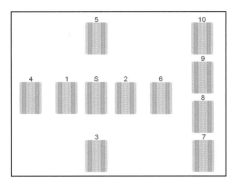

(S) Significator – Who or what the question is about.
(1) First Position – The heart of the matter.
(2) Second Position – Opposing or reinforcing factor.
(3) Third Position – Starting point or hidden influence.
(4) Fourth Position – The recent past.

(5) Fifth Position – Conscious influence, goal, or alternate future.
(6) Sixth Position – Upcoming influence or defined alternative.
(7) Seventh Position – How the Querent feels about the situation.
(8) Eighth Position – Outside influence or how others feel.
(9) Ninth Position – Hopes and fears, ideals, or personal demon.
(10) Tenth Position – Where the current path will lead.

What follows is a more detailed look at the positions of the Celtic Cross:

(S) Significator
This card is specifically chosen by the reader in advance of the reading, and should be done prior to shuffling the cards. There can actually be multiple perspectives in regards to Who or What the question is about.

Usage
For example, you might be seeking insight about some important information – news perhaps – and you are waiting to hear from someone. You might choose the Eight of Wands if your question is about the status of the news. However, if you are awaiting news about a new job you have applied for, you might choose the Three of Pentacles. If your question is about your mother, as another example, you might choose the Empress or the Queen of Cups.

The Significator card has no actual bearing on how you read the cards that have been placed into the spread, but what it does do is bring the question out in its specificity. It gives it focus, and this becomes important if the possibility of ambiguity exists, and in truth, we mean by this within the reader or Querent. The cards know what they are talking about.

(1) First Position

What actually is at the heart of the matter is relative to how the person asking the question feels about the situation. The heart is considered the emotional aspect of a human being by reference; thusly, the brain would be responsible for the question while the heart would have the stake in the outcome.

Usage

This becomes especially important for the reader because the brain, which asks the question, has no actual stake in the outcome, and brains are often strong protectors of the heart, giving off false and misleading indicators. In order for the reader to interpret, for example, good news, the reader needs to know exactly what the heart of the matter views as good news.

(2) Second Position

Called the Cross, this card weighs heavily on the overall outcome of the reading, viewed within the context of the entire reading.

Usage

If, for example, the question is about romance and you find a favorable card in this position, but in the Tenth Position, the Outcome Position, you find a much less favorable card, this tells the reader that the goal described by the question is obtainable, but something, or perhaps someone, is blocking the path. Through the interpretation of the other position cards, the reader can find the key to unlocking the outcome. If as a result of a question about romance, the Outcome card is favorable, but the Crossing Card is not, then the goal is obtainable but there is a pitfall that must be avoided to achieve it. The reader should be able to identify the possible mistake or wrong decision so that it can be avoided.

There are some that say you do not interpret reversed cards in this position as reverses, but as if they were right side up. We feel this puts limits on the readers access to pertinent information, and the reasons why are quite obvious. If the interpretation of the card is intended to be that of a card placed right side up then most assuredly that is the way you will find it. So we adamantly disagree.

(3) Third Position

The third position explains where "it" began, or how things came to arrive at this question. Quite possibly the origins might not be known by the Querent, and could even be the result of a past-life event.

Usage

The card that falls into this position is a key element to the overall reading if it is properly interpreted. The reader must distinguish between what lies at the heart of the matter, as defined by the First Position card, and what the truth of the matter is, which is defined here. As stated above, what lies in the heart of the Querent provides insight into the emotional stake the Querent has, but because of unknown events or denial, might be questioning from a different perspective than the truth.

Let's look at how this could show up in a reading. A woman asks if her husband is having an affair. The First Position card is The Lovers reversed, which is a pretty straightforward indication that the woman's emotional stake is the possible infidelity of her husband. Then in the Third Position, you find the Queen of Wands reversed, and now you have a different picture all together. At this point, it would be somewhat apparent that this woman might very well feel jealous every time a woman even speaks to her husband. Keeping in mind that this is only two cards of the entire ten card spread and other factors might come in to play, the husband may actually be having an affair, but the reader now has insight that the Querent could not or would not give.

(4) Fourth Position

This position represents the recent past, and can often describe an event that has raised the question the Querent has asked.

Usage

If we stay with the example we used to describe in the Third Position above, leaving The Lovers reversed in the First Position and the Queen of Wands reversed in the Third Position, and add the Eight of Swords upright in the Fourth Position, the possibility that the woman asking the question has no real basis for her suspicions has just been further reinforced. The possibility that it is all in her head is now greater. To show the importance of reading all the cards in the context of the entire spread we will try reading a different card into the Fourth Position, changing only the one card, and see how the story of the woman's husband changes.

Now in our example reading we find the Six of Cups upright in the Fourth Position. This could very well validate the woman's suspicions in that it points toward the possibility of a recent contact from a past love. That was in fact a fork in the road we just passed, and it should be abundantly clear that every card has tremendous weight on the reading, but at the same time the significance of a single card depends entirely on the sum of the weight of all the cards that fall into the spread.

(5) Fifth Position

This is often referred to as The Crown, or the Crowning Card. How it effects the overall reading can vary in many ways, and the card in this position is perhaps the most likely to cause the reader to misinterpret the situation. This at the very least could lead to a poor reading, and quite possibly some very bad advice.

Usage

To describe this fragile position we will continue with our suspicious wife from above. We have The Lovers reversed in the First Position, the Queen of Wands reversed in the Third Position, and the Six of Cups upright in the Fourth Position. Our interpretation so far is that we have a jealous woman with quite possibly a legitimate concern. In the Outcome Position, the Tenth Position, we find the Two of Cups reversed. This strongly indicates that the end of a relationship is the outcome of the current path. In the Crowning Position is the Ten of Cups reversed which is an indicator of divorce.

Before we show you what could go wrong here, there are two things to point out. The first is the number of Cups in the reading so far. This would be very important to take note of because the Cups indicate love is present, and the more cups the stronger the love. The second aspect to be aware of is that we have a high number of reversed cards. A high number of reversed cards often indicate that all is not as it appears to be. We will say more about these two anomalies in just a moment.

The mistake that is too easy to fall into is that the Crowning Card in this case is reinforcing the Outcome card which could lead the reader to believe that the husband is having an affair and the end result, without alternative, will be a breakup, or separation, and divorce. In contrast, it is possible that the reversed Ten of Cups could actually be describing a conscience influence, where the woman actually causes the breakup by confronting her husband with unfounded accusations. The Ten of Cups can also describe family disharmony, and an argument over a non-existent affair would certainly qualify. As we mentioned before, the number of Cups is important for the reader to consider in the overall reading. It is highly likely with the presence of the three Cups, and there quite possibly could be more

as we progress through the reading, that the love in the relationship moves both ways. The husband does in fact love the wife and is not interested in having an affair, but persistent suspicions will eventually destroy the relationship, making the Outcome true. The number of reversed cards reinforces the interpretation that the woman is predisposed to jealousy and the husband hasn't had an affair. There are always alternatives, and it is the responsibility of the reader, professional or someone just entrusted by a friend, to move delicately around the decisions of another person's life.

(6) Sixth Position

In this position we are actually looking at a moment in the future where the Querent will either consciously or subconsciously make a choice, and most assuredly a choice will be made. It is important to remember that deciding to not choose is in itself a choice as well. The card in this position will define how the path to the outcome will be altered or reinforced.

Usage

A card such as the Eight of Wands or Page of Wands indicating a message will mark the choice. It could be the Page of Swords or The Chariot describing a journey or travel that will affect the choice. Realistically, any card in the deck could fall into the Sixth Position, which can make it as problematic to interpret as the Crown, or Fifth Position Card. There will be challenging moments of interpretation and obviously card familiarity will make it easier, but never guess, or force yourself to remember if you are unsure what a card or position means. Always have a reference available when you read and don't hesitate to consult it when you are unsure. There aren't any bonus points for memorization.

(7) Seventh Position

You may hear this position referred to by some as The Self Position. It is a look at how the Querent perceives themselves in the given situation, or in an aspect that relates to the situation.

Usage

If you find The Hanged Man card in this position it describes the Querent as feeling like they make all the sacrifices, but it doesn't define them as a self-sacrificing person. The sacrifices may very well be seeds planted to yield a reward at some time in the future. If you were to find Justice reversed here, it would be an indication that they feel as if they have been treated unfairly, or perhaps manipulated, and that may be true, and it may not. The Six of Pentacles would reveal them to envision themselves as generous and giving, and it's possible they are, but also possible they are not. Quite often, how a person perceives themselves is an ideal, something they strive for, or maybe just wish they were, knowing full well they aren't.

In the Ninth Position we will show you a Trinity of Truth by combining the First, Seventh and Ninth Positions to define the person behind the question.

(8) Eighth Position

The position defining statement, "how others feel and outside influence," used to describe this position is almost redundant because people are often influenced by the feelings of others. The statement stands because not everyone with feelings puts them on display, which means it is possible that the Querent has no awareness of an influence upon them. They may be being influenced on a subconscious level, or it may very well be that a key element to the question that was asked revolves around someone's unknown feelings.

Usage

To give you an example of this we can use a question that is often asked; "do they feel the same way about me as I do about them?" The Eighth Position plays a key role in interpreting the cards in a spread when this question is asked because, although that may be all the Querent says when they ask, it is really an if-then question. There is always a reason they want to know now, for example: Querent Mary says, "Bob asked me out, but I really like Steve. I would go out with Bob if I knew that Steve wasn't interested in me. Does Steve feel the same way about me that I do about him?" The question centers around Steve, making Bob the outside influence that might show up in this position or another possibility, such as Steve having a girlfriend might be revealed here.

(9) Ninth Position

The strongest influence on a person is in fact their own hopes and fears, and the demons that reside within. The Ninth Position holds the last card before the Outcome card, and that is for a good reason. More often than not, what blocks a desired Outcome, or puts the Querent on the path to an undesired one, emanates from inside them. It is significantly more difficult to be objective with oneself, and once love becomes an element of the equation, it becomes impossible.

Usage

A significant majority of Tarot readings are done in the interest of love, because this is where we are the weakest and most vulnerable to others, and we are looking for an advantage that will help us find bliss and avoid heartache.

As we mentioned prior, the First Position, Seventh Position, and Ninth Position combine to form a Trinity of Truth. The heart of the matter, how the Querent feels about the situation, and what they hope for or fear, provide the keys to understanding the Querent. This in turn brings in to focus why the question was asked, and knowing the purpose of the question defines the path to the answer.

For the sake of example we will describe the cards in these three positions as part of a fictional reading.

The question posed from our Querent is: My husband and I don't seem to be getting along; doesn't he still love me? In the First Position is the Seven of Swords upright, which generally represents something operating beneath the surface, out of view. In the Seventh Position we find Death upright. Here lies a possible pitfall, in that jumping on the "Querent believes that the relationship is over" conclusion would be a common mistake for even an experienced reader to make. What this card means in this reading is that the Querent has noticed a dramatic change in her husband's behavior, and it is the Eight of Cups reversed in the Ninth Position that brings everything into focus. What we have now is the understanding that this woman is concerned that there is something that her husband is not telling her because she has noticed a sudden change in his behavior. The Eight of Cups reversed falling to the Ninth Position indicates that she is actually the one who has changed. She has a fear of staying the same, a dislike for the routine and the traditional. She reinvents herself fairly often, leaving behind her former self, and it is a distinct possibility that her husband hasn't adjusted to the latest change, for one reason or another. The question implies that the husband might not be being a good husband, but after looking at the Trinity of Truth we can see that the woman's standards of love might exceed reasonable expectation.

The answer is unlikely to fit the question since the question is actually an attempt at deflecting responsibility, not an actual concern for the relationship.

(10) Tenth Position

Commonly referred to as the Outcome Position, it is better described as the culmination of the Querent's current direction of travel. The card that falls here will describe the outcome of their current course of action, but be absolutely convinced that if it represents the desired outcome, they can destroy it with a single bad choice.

Usage

There is an old story, often told to young Tarot readers, of a Tarot woman who was visited by a young man with a question. He had a very important interview the next day, and if it went well it would change his life. He asked the woman to read for him to reveal the outcome of this significant event in his life. He was prepared for the interview, knowledgeable in the field, had worked hard to get to this opportunity, and the cards were favorable for the young man. In the Outcome Position was the Nine of Cups upright, a sure sign that he was on the right path. In the Crossing Position was the Knight of Wands, it had come up reversed, but the reader was of the school that taught that Crossing Cards were always read upright, which made the card a reinforcement, not an opposing factor. The woman told the young man that there was nothing standing in his way, the job he was interviewing for was going to be his. When you reverse the Knight of Wands you get impatience and egotism, and the cards were true to their word. The young man lost his patience when he wasn't told he had the job within the first few minutes, puffed out his chest and called the interviewer an idiot for not seeing how great he was.

Who is to say that the young man would have acted differently without the reading, or if the card had been interpreted differently? Actually, who is to say that the story is even true? But it makes a point that we felt we needed to make. You don't have to believe in the Tarot to make it work, but if you empower it by utilizing it as a tool to help guide you on your path, then don't underestimate its ability to express exactly that which is necessary to achieve your goals. It does not suffer from the human margin of error, so we say: As they fall, so shall they be read!

(C) Clarifier

We often build a bridge from the Outcome Position to the Crown in the Fifth Position, and it's called a Clarifier. After you have placed the Tenth Card, place an Eleventh Card directly between the Crown and Outcome Cards, and directly over the Sixth Position card. The Fifth Position card can represent an external or internal influence, or the difference a choice will make. The Sixth Position Card can represent a external or internal influence that has not yet taken effect, or a choice to make.

Usage

A hypothetical example of how the Clarifier might assist in the interpretation would be if you have a current external influence, represented by a Court Card, and the Clarifier is The Moon, then the influence could be hiding something which might be the difference between the Outcome and an alternative. You would need the context of the entire reading to remove the "could be" from that sentence. The Fifth Position, Sixth Position, and Outcome are the What, What if, and Why, of the Reading – in other words, the whole point of the reading. If the previous example was reinforced by context, we would know the who and the what, but without the Clarifier we would not have known why.

7
Creating Your Own Spreads

There are numerous books with hundreds of spreads on the market, and even books on how to create your own spreads. There really isn't a trick to creating your own spread; it is just a matter of determining exactly what your question is, and exactly what information you wish to gain from your reading. This is another area where your Tarot journal will come in handy. Write down as much information about the current situation as possible, and then write down the questions that you have. After review, put your questions in (as much as possible) a sequential order so that you are able to more easily follow the flow of events.

Here's an example: Sally and John have been dating for just over a year, and in the last weeks, John seems to have become more distant. Sally is concerned; she really likes John and doesn't want to end the relationship. She has attempted to talk with him about this on several occasions, and he replies that nothing is wrong and everything is fine.

Sally needs to design her own spread to find out what's really going on.

First, she needs to establish her question, which is "Why is John being so distant?" That is, at best, a vague question, and will garner a vague answer. Let's turn it around a bit, and put the focus more on Sally—and rephrase as: "Is there something I

am doing that is causing John's distance?" This is a little better, but still not quite what we're looking for. Let's try "What can I do to bring closeness back into my relationship with John?"

Sally takes out her notebook and starts to write what she wants to know:

1. The Situation/Significator
2. How does John view Sally in this relationship?
3. How would John like to view Sally in this relationship?
4. What Sally can do to improve the relationship
5. The Outcome

1st Position – Situation:

Here you can use a Significator card to represent the current dynamics. A suggestion would be the 3 of Swords or the 4 of Cups, depending on how time sensitive Sally feels the situation is.

2nd Position – How John views Sally in this relationship:

The card pulled is the 9 of Pentacles reversed. The regal lady in this card is generally shown as self-sufficient and independent. Reversed, however, she is clingy, overly dependent and unable to make any decisions with outside help. This might offer a major clue as to what is bothering John – he feels that Sally is leaning too heavily on him.

3rd Position – How John would like to view Sally in this relationship:

The card pulled is the Queen of Wands. This Queen is strong willed and independent,

fiery and outspoken. Perhaps John is feeling the burden of having to make all the decisions in the relationship.

4th Position - What Sally can do to improve this relationship:

The card pulled is the Ace of Wands. Initiative and action is what this card is all about, and the message is clear – John wants Sally to step up and make some decisions of her own. This could be as simple as replacing "I don't know, what do you want to do?" with "I heard about a great new restaurant; let's try it out!"

5th Position – Final Outcome:

The card pulled is the Page of Cups. A good card in this position, this indicates that if Sally becomes a little more assertive, this relationship can be saved. However, if Sally chooses not to become more assertive, the chasm between them could possibly widen. Remember, when phrasing your question, state exactly what you want to know. A vague question will bring an even vaguer answer. Remember to phrase the question so that you and your behavior are the focus. Even under the best of circumstances, yours is all that you have absolute control over, and it is possible that by changing yours, you can have the happy outcome you are hoping for.

8
The Tarot Book of Shadows Legend

Introduction to the Legend

In reading books about Tarot, you will see the word *correspondence* throughout. This word is used to associate a particular Tarot Attribute, or quality, with something outside the Tarot world, and to give the reader additional information for each card.

For example, let's use the King of Wands. Some of the words to describe this card could be: male, passionate, charismatic, full moon, fire, sun, summer, midday, intense, rigid. This defines a charming man who is passionate and intense, who may have strong views and is willing to voice them. It *also* utilizes the correspondences of Gender, Character Trait, Key Word, Lunar Phase, Element, Astrology, Physical Property, and Quadruplicity. Think of correspondences as friendly mnemonics to help you remember the meanings and symbolism behind each card you see before you. There are many correspondences to be found between the Tarot and other disciplines, and all work together to weave a wonderful web of information and understanding. The ones listed, along with their descriptions, are among the most commonly referenced.

There are a number of different systems of attributions, or correspondences. Some may seem different than what you may see here, others may not. If you find an unfamiliar correspondence here that you wish to incorporate into your own readings, there are many good resources to be found at your local library or on the Internet for further study. There may be groups that meet in your area dealing specifically with that subject. On the other hand, if a correspondence holds no interest for you, merely go on to the next one and use what feels right for you.

Not every category of correspondence will apply to each card; however, we have made every effort to be as thorough as possible. Do you need to master every discipline associated with the Tarot in order to be a good reader? No. However, the more you learn, the more information you have to draw upon, and more information equals a better, more complete reading. You may wish to start a companion journal to use with this book in order to record your own observations and ideas. As a side note, you will occasionally see the word magick throughout the text. This is not a misprint. Aleister Crowley is originally credited with adding the k at the end to differentiate it from stage, or illusion based magick. This is a topic of some debate; however, for our purposes, we'll use it.

Alchemical Quality

The Alchemical Motto:
Solve Et Coagula (Latin: Separate and join together)

Alchemy is such a multifaceted science/art that it defies description. These are the definitions provided by the *American Heritage Science Dictionary*:

> Alchemy: A medieval philosophy and early form of chemistry whose aims were the transmutation of base metals into gold, the discovery of a cure for all diseases, and the preparation of a potion that gives eternal youth. The imagined substance capable of turning other metals into gold was called the Philosophers' Stone.

> *Our Living Language*: Because their goals were so unrealistic, and because they had so little success in achieving them, the practitioners of alchemy in the Middle Ages got a reputation as fakers and con artists. But this reputation is not fully deserved.
> While they never succeeded in turning lead into gold (one of their main goals), they did make discoveries that helped to shape modern chemistry. Alchemists invented early forms of some of the laboratory equipment used today, including beakers, crucibles, filters, and stirring rods.

They also discovered and purified a number of chemical elements, including mercury, sulfur, and arsenic. And the methods they developed to separate mixtures and purify compounds by distillation and extraction are still important.

Alchemy is rooted in the belief that there are four basic elements, which are Air, Fire, Water, and Earth, and three basic principles, which are Salt, the Contractive Force of Nature; Sulfur, the Expansive Force of Nature; and Mercury, the Integrative Force of Nature, conjoining Salt and Sulfur. The famous sixteenth-century alchemist Paracelsus aligned those three principles as Salt representing Earth, Sulfur representing Air, and Mercury representing Water. He considered Fire to be an intangible force, and therefore did not include it. The three principles have also been associated with the concept of Spirit, Body, and Soul, as well as the Holy Trinity. This type of sacred chemistry encompassed many other fields of study, including astrology, medicine, physics, mysticism, and spiritualism, and is first known to have been practiced in the ancient civilizations of Mesopotamia.

In relation to the Tarot, the alchemical properties are assigned according to the element of the **Suit**:

Swords – Hot and Wet
Wands – Hot and Dry
Cups – Cold and Wet
Pentacles – Cold and Dry

Alchemical Symbol

The Alchemical Symbols are:

Air   *Water*

Fire   *Earth*

Animal Energy

The Animals are among our greatest teachers, each having a unique lesson to share with those perceptive enough to see. Shamans, or Medicine Men and Women, from many different belief systems have worked with animal energy from the beginning of time, and understand that we are all connected on the Mother Earth. Animals can come in the form of totems or animal guides. We have assigned an animal to each of the Major Arcana, one which best embodies the lesson, or the spirit, of the card.

Area of the Body

The attributions of the area of the body that are assigned to each of the Major Arcana are inspired by *777 and other Qabalistic Writings of Aleister Crowley*, by Aleister Crowley. (See Resources and Recommended Reading.)

Associated Illness

The attributions of the illness assigned to each of the Major Arcana are inspired by *777 and other Qabalistic Writings of Aleister Crowley*, by Aleister Crowley. (See Resources and Recommended Reading.)

Astrological Correspondences

Western Astrology is the discipline that is the most accessible. Horoscopes appear daily online, in our emails, and are a regular column in our newspapers. Most people can rattle off their Sun Sign and its qualities at a moment's notice, but not everyone has actually had a Natal, or birth, chart done professionally. Generally believed to have originated in Mesopotamia around 2300 BC, this combination of art and science studies Astrological moments. This is mapping a diagram of what position all the planets were in at an exact moment in time from an exact position on the face of the Earth, such as a birthday or a specific event.

The Houses

This diagram is divided into twelve sections, or Houses, each governing a different aspect of life:

1st House is the House of Self. The Tarot card assigned to this house is the Emperor.
This is the most powerful house in the chart. The first house is ruled by the Ascendant, or Rising Sign, and shows how the subject is perceived by others. It can also indicate the appearance and physical condition of the body.

2nd House is the House of Money and Possessions. The Tarot card assigned to this house is the Wheel of Fortune.
This house tells how the subject feels about material gain and wealth, and gives insight to a favored lifestyle.

3rd House is the House of Communication. The Tarot card assigned to this house is the Magician.
This house governs the way you communicate with others, written and verbal. It also influences intellect, and gives insight as to the educational background.

4th House is the House of Home, the safe refuge from the outside world. The Tarot card assigned to this house is the Empress.
This house also rules family life, and the golden years of the subject's life.

5th House is the House of Pleasures and Creativity. The Tarot card assigned to this house is the Devil.
This house governs love affairs, gambling, and everything done purely for pleasure. It also shows creative interests and other manners of self expression.

6th House is the House of Health and Well Being. The Tarot card assigned to this house is Temperance.
This house governs health and service to others. Information about general health issues can be found here.

7th House is the House of Marriage and Partnerships, be they legal or work-related. The Tarot card assigned to this house is the Lovers.
This house shows how well the subject blends his/her personality with others.

8th House is the House of Death and Regeneration. The Tarot card assigned to this house is Death.
This is the house of change and transformation. It also governs inheritances, and is considered the house of the psychic.

9th House is the House of Mental Explorations. The Tarot card assigned to this house is the Hermit.
This house governs the higher mind and learning. Philosophy and religious studies are found here, along with the public expression of ideas.

10th House is the House of Career and Ambition. The Tarot card assigned to this house is the Chariot.
Planets found in this house may give indication of what the true career should be, along with possible aptitudes.

11th House is the House of Hopes and Wishes. The Tarot card assigned to this house is the Star.
This house governs friendships, and determines whether or not you play well with others. It is also the house of idealism.

12th House is the House of Self-Undoing, Sorrows and Secrets. The Tarot card assigned to this house is Judgment.
This house is also called the House of Karma. Look to see what planets are found in this house; it may contain a key to a life lesson. This house governs the desire to look behind the mask to see what truly lies beneath.

You can create a Tarot spread based on these houses, using one card for each house.

The Planets

We learned the names of the planets in elementary school, but most of us did not learn about their associations until later, perhaps while studying Mythology. Pluto is included here, even though it is no longer technically considered a planet.

 The Sun, although it is a star and not a true planet, is the most powerful influence and the basis of the Astrological chart.

 The Moon governs intuition, emotions and the unconscious. While the active Sun represents your will, the passive Moon represents your instinct.

 Mercury is the planet of communication and reason, named for the ancient Messenger and Psychopompus of the Gods. Mercury governs intellect, and the amount of personal energy you possess.

 Venus is the planet of love and pleasures. Venus rules the ability to be affectionate and appreciate beauty. The chart placement can also affect charisma.

 Mars is the red planet of war, governing physical energy, aggression, and sex drive. It also indicates initiative, personal drive, and ambition.

Jupiter is considered the planet of luck, success and generosity. It also affects sense of humor, extravagance and honesty. This is the planet of optimism and exuberance.

Saturn has long been associated with Father Time, and is the planet of discipline, responsibilities, and obligations. It also governs limitations and restrictions.

Uranus is the planet of change and changeability, surprises and sudden events taking strange turns. It also governs the spark of human genius and ingenuity.

 Neptune governs mysteries and illusions, both the external and the internal ones we sometimes try to escape. It also affects spiritual and artistic endeavors.

 Pluto was the last planet in our known solar system up until its demotion in 2006, and it symbolizes death and rebirth, destruction and regeneration.

Planetary Aspects

An aspect is the relationship between two planets and how many degrees they are in your chart. The major aspects were plotted by Claudius Ptolemy in the second century, and are considered the most powerful in the birth chart. Some aspects you may find in an Astrological chart are:

Conjunction – 0 degrees(°) apart
This means two planets are in the same degree in the same sign, or at the very least within 10 degrees of each other. This is the most powerful aspect in astrology.

Trine – Two Planets that are 120° apart
This is a favorable aspect.

Opposition – Two Planets 180° apart
This isn't a very harmonious aspect, often causing discord.

Sextile – Two Planets 60° apart
This is another favorable aspect, bringing opportunity, but you have to work a little harder to see the fruit of your labors.

Square – Two Planets 90° apart
This is a very challenging aspect, placing obstacles in your path and teaching lessons. This is an area that generally shows where you need the most work spiritually.

Quincunx – Two Planets 150° apart
Mildly unfavorable; this can indicate areas of health concerns.

Semisquare – Two Planets 45° apart
Another mildly unfavorable influence; can sometimes indicate tension in the chart.

Sesquisquare – Two Planets 135° apart
Somewhat adverse, similar to the semisquare in influence.

Semisextile – Two Planets 30° apart
Mildly favorable.

Elements

The following elements are also taken into account when calculating an astrological chart:

Imum Coeli (I.C.)
The bottom of the heavens, usually the 4th house cusp. Indicates family relations and home.

Medium Coeli (M.C.)
The Midheavens, the point directly overhead in the chart, usually the 10th house cusp. This emphasizes career, public ambitions and relationships with superiors.

Lunar Nodes

The Lunar Nodes point out areas of imbalance in the Astrological chart.

North Node
The point of interception between the Moon's orbit and the ecliptic, which is the plane of the Earth's orbit. The North Node indicates areas of opportunity for spiritual growth.

South Node
The point of interception between the Moon's orbit and the ecliptic. The South Node usually points out areas where the subject is naturally talented or gifted.

Part Of Fortune
Found by subtracting the Sun's position from the Ascendant and Moon positions in degrees. It is usually indicative of fortunate circumstances. The placement of the Part of Fortune in a chart indicates where life's successes will be found.

Direct
Viewed from the Earth, the planet appears to be rotating in the direction it is moving in its orbit.

Retrograde
When viewed from the Earth, the planet appears to be rotating backwards in relation to the direction the planet is traveling in its orbit.

Zodiac Signs

The twelve signs of the Zodiac are based upon star constellations, and are separated by Quadruplicity, which denotes whether the sign is Cardinal (Aggressive and Active), Fixed (Stable and Rigid), or Mutable (Passive and Changing).

Here are the twelve signs of the Zodiac, along with the dominate phrase associated with the sign, ruling planet, and background information about the constellation itself.

♈ (Glyph)

Aries
(AIR-eez) March 21st to April 19th

This constellation known as the Ram by the Babylonians, Egyptians, Persians, and Greeks, was a constellation of considerable importance in ancient times. The sun passed through it at the Vernal Equinox, which was when the Earth renewed after winter, giving it the distinction as the first sign of the new year. As a result of precession (the wobble in the Earth's rotation), the Sun now passes through Aquarius at the Vernal Equinox. However, Aries is still considered to be the beginning of the Astrological year. Aries the Ram was given as a gift by Hermes to the children Helle and Phrixus. It was later sacrificed, and its golden fleece stolen by Jason and the Argonauts.

Duality	☿	Masculine
Triplicity	△	Fire
Quadruplicity		Cardinal (Aggressive and Active)
Gemstones		Diamond, Opal
Flowers		Honeysuckle
Ruling Planet	♂	Mars, named for the Roman God of War
Cities and Countries		Denmark, England, Florence, France, Germany, Leicester, Lithuania, Marseilles, Naples, Palestine, Richmond, Verona
Colors		Red, all shades
Animals		Sheep, especially Rams
Trees		All thorn bearing trees
Part of the Body		The Head
Polarity or Opposite Sign	♎	Libra
Lucky Day		Tuesday
Lucky Numbers		1, 9
Dominate Phrase		"I Am"
Symbol		The Ram
Herbs		Cayenne, Pepper, Mustard, Capers
Metal		Iron
Tarot Cards		The Emperor, Queen of Wands
Tarot Suit		Wands
Vedic Sign and Symbol		Mesha, the Ram

 (Glyph)

Taurus
(TORR-us) April 20th to May 20th

This constellation has been associated with a bull for over 5,000 years. Since ancient times Bulls have been worshipped as symbols of strength and fertility. The ancient Egyptians worshipped the bull of Memphis, Apis. A real bull was believed to be Osiris. The Israelites worshipped the Golden Calf. The constellation takes its name from the Greek Tauros, meaning "the Bull." The legend states that Zeus, who was in love with the beautiful Europa, daughter of Agenor, King of Phoenicia, disguised himself as a beautiful white bull to entice Europa. While playing at the water's edge, Europa's attention was caught by the majestic beast. The Bull, Zeus, then knelt before her as she approached it. She climbed upon its back, wreathing flowers around its horns. Springing to its feet, the bull took off into the sea and swam to Crete, where Zeus made Europa his mistress.

Duality	♀	Feminine
Triplicity	▽	Earth
Quadruplicity		Fixed (Stable and Rigid)
Gemstones		Emerald, Sapphire
Flowers		Rose, Poppy, Daisy, Violet
Ruling Planet	♀	Venus, named for the Roman Goddess of Love
Cities and Countries		Capri, Cypress, Dublin, Greece, Hastings, Ireland, Leipzig, Lucerne, Mantua, Palermo, St. Louis, Switzerland, Tasmania
Colors		Pastel colors, particularly pale blue, pink and green
Animals		All Cattle
Trees		Apple, Cypress
Part of the Body		Neck, Throat
Polarity or Opposite Sign	♏	Scorpio
Lucky Day		Friday
Lucky Numbers		6, 4
Dominate Phrase		"I Have"
Symbol		The Bull
Herbs		Spearmint, Cloves, Sorrel
Metal		Copper
Tarot Card		King of Pentacles
Tarot Suit		Pentacles
Vedic Sign and Symbol		Vrishaba, The Bull

Gemini ∏ (Glyph)

(JEM-eh-nye) May 21st to June 21st

The twins, Castor and Pollux, were only half brothers. Pollux was none other than the immortal son of Zeus. Pollux's sister was the woman whose face launched a thousand ships, the lady known as Helen of Troy. The twins became Argonauts sailing with Jason in the quest for the Golden Fleece. As the myth goes, Castor was killed on one of the Argonauts' raiding trips, and Pollux was so upset by his brother's death that he asked Zeus to allow him to die with his brother, even though he was immortal. Zeus, moved by Pollux's love for his brother, placed them side-by-side in the heavens.

Duality	♂	Masculine
Triplicity	△	Air
Quadruplicity		Mutable (Passive and Changing)
Gemstones		Agate, Emerald
Flowers		Lavender, Myrtle, Fern
Ruling Planet	☿	Mercury, named for the Roman Messenger of the Gods
Cities and Countries		Armenia, Belgium, Iceland, London, Lower Egypt, Melbourne, Plymouth, San Francisco, Sardinia, Tunisia, USA, Wales
Colors		Yellow
Animals		Brightly colored talking birds, butterflies, monkeys
Trees		All nut bearing trees
Part of the Body		Hands, Arms, Lungs
Polarity or Opposite Sign	♐	Sagittarius
Lucky Day		Wednesday
Lucky Numbers		5, 9
Dominate Phrase		"I Think"
Symbol		The Twins, Castor and Pollux
Herbs		Aniseed, Caraway, Marjoram
Metal		Mercury
Tarot Card		The Lovers, Knight of Swords
Tarot Suit		Swords
Vedic Sign and Symbol		Mithuna, The Couple

Cancer
(CAN-ser) June 21st to July 22nd

(Glyph)

Karkinos in Greek, Cancer in Latin. According to Greek mythology the crab was sent to distract Hercules when he was fighting with the monster Hydra. After biting Hercules on the toe, Hercules crushed the crab under his foot, and as a reward for its sacrifice, Hera (wife of Zeus), placed it among the stars. It was also associated with the term "the Asses' Crib" or "the Asses' Manger." There are two stars named "the Asses" (Asini) in the constellation of Cancer. Most ancient sources agree on these asses being placed in the sky by the Greek god of wine and ecstasy, Dionysus.

Duality	♀	Feminine
Triplicity	▽	Water
Quadruplicity		Cardinal (Aggressive and Active)
Gemstones		Moonstone, Pearl, Alexandrite
Flowers		White Rose, Larkspur
Ruling Planet	☽	The Moon, which governs Intuitions
Cities and Countries		Algeria, Amsterdam, Berne, Holland, New York, New Zealand, North and West Africa, Paraguay, Scotland, Tokyo, Venice
Colors		Silver, Sea Green
Animals		All those with shells
Trees		All trees, especially those rich in sap
Part of the Body		The Breasts, Stomach
Polarity or Opposite Sign	♑	Capricorn
Lucky Day		Monday
Lucky Numbers		3, 7
Dominate Phrase		"I Feel"
Symbol		The Crab
Herbs		Tarragon, Verbena
Metal		Silver
Tarot Card		The Chariot, The Lovers
Tarot Suit		Cups
Vedic Sign and Symbol		Karkata, The Crab

♌ (Glyph)

Leo
(LEE-oh) July 23rd to August 22nd

The first on the list of Hercules' labors was the task of killing the Nemean Lion, and this is thought by some to be how it earned its place in the heavens. However, there is much speculation and many theories that favor a much earlier date than Greek mythology. The fact that in and about the year 10,500 BC the constellation of Leo would have risen (lunging perhaps) precisely due East at sunrise and the Sphinx (with the actual date of construction being factually unknown) being built facing specifically due East, is believed to be more than a coincidence. Still others see a date of around 4,000 BC when there was a shift in beliefs from moon worship to sun worship that was represented by Leo (The Sun), at this time being directly overhead, killing Taurus (The Moon) as it tried to escape below the horizon. It would remain invisible for forty days after which it would rise again on March 21st to announce the Spring Equinox.

Duality	♂	Masculine
Triplicity	△	Fire
Quadruplicity		Fixed (Stable and Rigid)
Gemstones		Ruby, Carnelian
Flowers		Sunflowers, Marigold, Passion Flower, Celandine
Ruling Planet	☉	The Sun, the center of our known solar system
Cities and Countries		Chicago, Czech Republic, Damascus, Hollywood, Italy, Lebanon, Los Angeles, Madagascar, Madrid, Prague, Romania, Syracuse
Colors		Gold, Orange
Animals		All Cats, especially big cats
Trees		Citrus trees, Palm, Olive
Part of the Body		The Heart, Back, Spine
Polarity or Opposite Sign	♒	Aquarius
Lucky Day		Sunday
Lucky Numbers		1, 7
Dominate Phrase		"I Will"
Symbol		The Lion
Herbs		Rosemary, Rue, Peppermint
Metal		Gold
Tarot Card		Strength, King of Wands
Tarot Suit		Wands
Vedic Sign and Symbol		Simha, The Lion

Virgo **ℳ** (Glyph)

(VER-go) August 24th to September 22nd

The Virgin in Latin; the Greek name was Parthenos. Of the twelve constellations of the Zodiac, Virgo is the only female figure. It has been attributed to many female deities over history. She may have been Isis, wife and sister of Osiris, and the Egyptian protectress of the living and the dead and the principal Mother Goddess. She may have also been identified with the Babylonian Goddess Ishtar. As well as Astraea, the Roman Goddess of justice, in which case she is depicted holding the scales of justice from the adjacent constellation Libra. Also Demeter, the Greek Goddess of the harvest, is usually depicted holding an ear of wheat. The most popular association might be with the Goddess, Dike, which also means justice. Dike (daughter of Zeus and Themis) was the final Goddess to give up on humanity and leave Earth.

Duality	♀	Feminine
Triplicity	▽	Earth
Quadruplicity		Mutable (Passive and Changing)
Gemstones		Sardonyx, Sapphire, Agate
Flowers		All brightly colored small flowers,
Ruling Planet	☿	Mercury, named for the Roman Messenger of the Gods
Cities and Countries		Boston, Brazil, Corinth, Crete, Greece, Heidelberg, Lyons, Paris, Somerset, Strasbourg, Toulouse, Turkey, West Indies
Colors		Green, Navy, Blue, Brown
Animals		All domestic pets, in particular Cats and Dogs
Trees		All nut bearing trees
Part of the Body		The Nervous System, Intestines
Polarity or Opposite Sign	♓	Pisces
Lucky Day		Wednesday
Lucky Numbers		5, 3
Dominate Phrase		"I Analyze"
Symbol		The Virgin
Herbs		Cardamom, Marjoram
Metal		Mercury, Nickel
Tarot Card		The Hermit, Knight of Pentacles
Tarot Suit		Pentacles
Vedic Sign and Symbol		Kanya, The Virgin Daughter

Libra (Glyph)

(LEE-bra) September 23rd to October 22nd

Libra is Latin for "the Balance" or "the Scales," from the equivalent Greek word Zygos. This constellation, commonly associated with Themis, the Greek goddess of justice whose attribute was a pair of scales, was once thought to be part of the constellation of Scorpius, and referred to as "the Claws of the Scorpion." Some 4,000 years ago, the sun passed through this constellation on September 21st, also known as the Autumnal Equinox. Like the Spring Equinox, it is a day of balance, where the night and day are of equal length. The glyph (written symbol) for Libra was the ancient Egyptian symbol for the setting sun, which was regarded as the doorway between two worlds.

Duality	♂	Masculine
Triplicity	△	Air
Quadruplicity		Cardinal (Aggressive and Active)
Gemstones		Opal, Sapphire, Jade
Flowers		Roses, Hydrangeas
Ruling Planet	♀	Venus, named for the Roman Goddess of Love
Cities and Countries		Argentina, Austria, Canada, Charleston, China, Copenhagen, Frankfurt, Japan, Johannesburg, Leeds, Lisbon, Tibet, Vienna
Colors		Blue, Lavender
Animals		Snakes, Lizards, all small reptiles
Trees		Almond, Cypress, Ash
Part of the Body		The Lower Back, Kidneys
Polarity or Opposite Sign	♈	Aries
Lucky Day		Friday
Lucky Numbers		6, 9
Dominate Phrase		"I Balance"
Symbol		The Scales
Herbs		Mint, Cayenne
Metal		Copper
Tarot Card		Justice, Queen of Swords
Tarot Suit		Swords
Vedic Sign and Symbol		Thula, the Balance or Weight

Scorpius

M (Glyph)

(SKOR-pee-us) October 23rd to November 21st

Latin for "the Scorpion," Skorpius, this is one of the original six signs of the zodiac, among the oldest constellations known. Although the Sun takes nine days to traverse Scorpius, most of that time is spent in neighboring Ophiuchus, the only constellation that the Sun enters that is not a part of the zodiac. According to myth, Scorpius was sent to kill the mighty hunter Orion. By some accounts, the scorpion would chase Orion across the heavens, but it could never catch him, for the scorpion was so placed that it would rise in the east only after Orion had safely disappeared over the western horizon. Still others claim that "The Mighty Hunter" was actually felled by Scorpius.

Duality	♀	Feminine
Triplicity	▽	Water
Quadruplicity		Fixed (Stable and Rigid)
Gemstones		Opal, Topaz
Flowers		Rhododendron, Geranium
Ruling Planet	♇	Pluto, the Ancient Roman God of the Netherworld
Cities and Countries		Cincinnati, Halifax, Korea, Liverpool, Milwaukee, Morocco, New Orleans, Norway, Savannah, Syria, Uruguay, Washington DC
Colors		Crimson, Burgundy, Maroon, Deep Red
Animals		Insects, Crustaceans
Trees		Blackthorn, bushy trees
Part of the Body		The Genitals
Polarity or Opposite Sign	♂	Taurus
Lucky Day		Tuesday
Lucky Numbers		2, 4
Dominate Phrase		"I Desire"
Symbol		The Scorpion
Herbs		Witch Hazel, Aloe, Catmint
Metal		Steel, Iron
Tarot Card		Death, King of Cups
Tarot Suit		Cups
Vedic Sign and Symbol		Vrishchika, The Scorpion

Sagittarius
(sadge-ih-TAIR-ee-us) November 23rd to December 21st

(Glyph)

This sign is often considered to be Chiron the Centaur, half man, half horse. Sagittarius holds a drawn bow, not in character with Chiron who was known for his kindness and wisdom. Some say that Chiron was created to guide Jason and the Argonauts as they sailed on the Argo. Still others have associated the archer with a mythological satyr by the name of Crotus. Satyrs were creatures depicted as having the body of a man, tail of a horse, and the legs (or horns) of a goat. Satyrs were normally wild, warring, lustful beasts. Like Chiron, the satyr Crotus was said to be of a peaceful nature. In mythology, Crotus is credited with the invention of the bow, was considered to be the swiftest of the forest, and accomplished in his musical skills.

Duality	♂	Masculine
Triplicity	△	Fire
Quadruplicity		Mutable (Passive and Changing)
Gemstones		Blue Topaz, Turquoise, Onyx
Flowers		Carnations, Holly, Narcissus
Ruling Planet	2	Jupiter, the planet of Good Fortune
Cities and Countries		Acapulco, Australia, Avignon, Budapest, Chile, Hungary, Naples, Nottingham, Saudi Arabia, Singapore, South Africa, Spain, Toledo
Colors		Purple, Dark Blue
Animals		Horses, and hunted animals, such as Deer
Trees		Mulberry, Oak, Birch
Part of the Body		The Liver, Hips, Thighs
Polarity or Opposite Sign	♊	Gemini
Lucky Day		Thursday
Lucky Numbers		6, 7
Dominate Phrase		"I See"
Symbol		The Archer
Herbs		Cinnamon, Sage, Aniseed, Dock, Balsam, Bilberry
Metal		Tin
Tarot Card		Temperance, Knight of Wands
Tarot Suit		Wands
Vedic Sign and Symbol		Dhanus, the Bow or Weapon

Capricornus
ꑣ (Glyph)

(kap-reh-KOR-nuss) December 22nd to January 19th

Carpricornus (Capricorn) is usually translated as the "The Sea Goat" or the "Goat Fish," although the name literally means horned goat. The "Goat Fish" is said to relate to the story about the god Pan, who while fleeing the monster Typhon, jumped into the Nile. While his top half, which was still above water, remained that of a goat, the part of him that was submerged became a fish tail. This is an ancient constellation, and was one of the earliest members of the zodiac. It is also believed to have once combined with Aquarius to form the constellation know as "The Ibex," or "Horns of Ibex."

Duality	♀	Feminine
Triplicity	▽	Earth
Quadruplicity		Cardinal (Aggressive and Active)
Gemstones		Garnet, Turquoise, Amethyst
Flowers		Ivy, Pansy, Carnation
Ruling Planet	♄	Saturn, the planet of Discipline
Cities and Countries		Afghanistan, Albania, Bosnia, Boston, Brussels, Bulgaria, Delhi, Ghent, India, Mexico, Mexico City, Montreal, Oxford
Colors		Dark Green, Gray, Black, Brown
Animals		Goats, animals with cloven hooves
Trees		Pine, Elm, Poplar, Willow
Part of the Body		The Bones, Joints, Knees
Polarity or Opposite Sign	♋	Cancer
Lucky Day		Saturday
Lucky Numbers		2, 8
Dominate Phrase		"I Use"
Symbol		The Goat
Herbs		Hemp, Comfrey, Hemlock
Metal		Lead, Silver
Tarot Card		The Devil, Queen of Pentacles
Tarot Suit		Pentacles
Vedic Sign and Symbol		Makara, The Alligator or Shark

Aquarius 〜〜 (Glyph)
〜〜

(ah-KWAIR-ee-us) January 20th to February 18th

Aquarius is known as Ganymede, "Cup-Bearer to the Gods," in Greek mythology. Ganymede is also the name given to Jupiter's largest moon, which is larger in diameter than the planet Mercury. The constellation of Aquarius seems to have represented water in a number of ancient cultures. For example, in Egypt it was thought to cause the Nile to give forth its annual floods. The night sky, in June, would show Aquarius at its zenith as waters of the Nile would start to rise. Interestingly, as viewed from Earth, Aquarius resides in the sky near Delphinus (dolphin), Cetus (the sea monster), and Pisces (fish).

Duality	♂	Masculine
Triplicity	△	Air
Quadruplicity		Fixed (Stable and Rigid)
Gemstones		Amethyst, Aquamarine
Flowers		Orchids
Ruling Planet	♅	Uranus, named for the Ancient Greek Sky God
Cities and Countries		Buenos Aires, Ethiopia, Finland, Hamburg, Helsinki, Iran, Israel, Moscow, Poland, Russia, Salzburg, Stockholm, Sweden, Syria
Colors		Electric Blue, Turquoise
Animals		Large Birds, especially those capable of long flight
Trees		All fruit trees
Part of the Body		The Shins, Ankles, Circulatory System
Polarity or Opposite Sign	♌	Leo
Lucky Day		Wednesday
Lucky Numbers		1, 7
Dominate Phrase		"I Know"
Symbol		The Waterbearer
Herbs		Those with sharp flavors, such as Pepper and Chilies
Metal		Aluminum, Uranium
Tarot Card		The Hierophant, The Star
Tarot Suit		Swords
Vedic Sign and Symbol		Kumbha, The Jug or Pot

Pisces

ℋ (Glyph)

Pisces
(PIE-seez) February 19th to March 20th

This sign is called Ichtyes ("the fishes") by the Greeks, "Pisces" being the Latin translation. According to Greco-Roman mythology, Aphrodite and her son, Heros, in order to escape the pursuing monster Typhon, transformed themselves into fish. The pair tied their tails together to insure that they wouldn't be parted during their escape. Aphrodite and Heros, who escaped the monster's wrath, were given their fish-like images in the heavens, thus commemorating the time Typhon nearly overran Olympus. Later cultures equated the two fish with the Biblical story of the miracle of the fishes and the loaves.

Duality	♀	Feminine
Triplicity	▽	Water
Quadruplicity		Mutable (Passive and Changing)
Gemstones		Aquamarine, Moonstone
Flowers		Water Lily, Jonquil, Poppy
Ruling Planet	♆	Neptune, named for the Ancient God of the Sea
Cities and Countries		Alexandria, Dublin, Gobi and Sahara Deserts, Jerusalem, Lisbon, Normandy, Portugal, Samoa, Scandinavia, Seville, Warsaw
Colors		Pale Green, Turquoise
Animals		Fish, mammals that live in water
Trees		Fig, Willow, all trees growing near water
Part of the Body		The Feet
Polarity or Opposite Sign	♍	Virgo
Lucky Day		Friday
Lucky Numbers		2, 6
Dominate Phrase		"I Believe"
Symbol		The Two Fish
Herbs		Lime, Chicory, Mosses, Saccharin
Metal		Platinum, Tin
Tarot Card		The Moon, Knight of Cups
Tarot Suit		Cups
Vedic Sign and Symbol		Meena, The Fishes

The tabled correspondences for the zodiac signs are inspired in part by the very wonderful and informative book *Parker's Astrology – The Definitive Guide to Using Astrology in Every Aspect of Your Life* by Julia and Derek Parker.

The Astrological Associations that are used in conjunction with the Tarot cards were originally defined by the Hermetic Order of the Golden Dawn, a group that furthered the study of Occult Science, Western Philosophy, and Ceremonial Magick. It is not a religion in itself, although religious and/or spiritual ideas are highly regarded. The Order places great emphasis on tolerance for all paths of belief, and women are given the same rights and positions as men. Originating in England during the late 1800s, past members included Pamela Coleman Smith and Arthur Edward Waite, the creators of the Smith-Waite Tarot deck; the poet William Butler Yeats; the actress Florence Farr; and Aleister Crowley, the self-described wickedest man alive.

We generally ask for a date of birth when doing a reading to discern two things: the Sun Sign, and the numbers for the personal year, personal month, and life path (See the section on Numerology). For example, after learning some Astrology basics, it may not come as a surprise to you to learn that the fidgety young woman talking nonstop while waiting for her reading is a Gemini. You will know that the ruling planet is Mercury, a planet associated with high energy and communication, and that one of the not-so-good traits of that particular sign is an inability to finish projects once they are started. So before the reading has even begun, you have established a small bit of information about your querent, or the person asking the question, and that tidbit may shed some light on the reversed 7 of Pentacles you see in the spread before you.

9
Astrological Quadruplicity

A Quadruplicity is the astrological way of saying "group of four" referring to whether a sign is:

Cardinal, meaning aggressive and creative. The Cardinal signs of Aries, Cancer, Libra, and Capricorn tend to be assertive and strong willed. These are natural leaders.

Fixed, meaning rigid and unchanging. The Fixed signs of Taurus, Leo, Scorpio, and Aquarius are primarily concerned with maintaining the status quo.

Mutable, meaning passive and adaptable. The Mutable signs of Gemini, Virgo, Sagittarius, and Pisces adjust more easily to change.

Attribute

The Four **Attributes** are:

Intellectual (Swords - Air)
Spiritual (Wands - Fire)

Emotional (Cups - Water)
Physical (Pentacles – Earth)

For example, the High Priestess is considered to be a card of the Subconscious. Therefore, the Attribute would be Emotional, which corresponds with the Element of Water, which also corresponds with the Direction West and the Suit of Cups.

Blood Type

In Japan during the 1930s, the concept of blood type affecting personality type was formed. The four major blood types – A, B, AB, and O – were assigned personality traits, and became as popular as the American horoscopes for determining everything from productive employees to potential mates. Matchmaking companies often used blood typing to eliminate possible marriage combinations that simply would not work due to personality conflicts, and the phrase "What's your blood type?" became as popular a pick-up line as "What's your sign?" The Rh factor did not play a role in affecting the personality type.

As with many superstitions and urban legends, this one was debunked by modern science. It is still used in Japan, but mostly as an icebreaker in conversation or as a fun party game. Blood typing by personality, however, is making a surprise comeback in recent news – not as a dating tool, but as a dietary guideline for optimal health.

Because the blood types and matching personalities were divided by four, the temptation

to assign Tarot suits as well was irresistible. Thusly:

Type O Blood – Swords

Positive Qualities – Leader, intuitive, focused, daring, motivated, initiator, ambitious, confident
Negative Qualities – Controlling, manipulative, arrogant, insensitive, vain, ruthless, domineering, cowardice

Type B Blood – Wands

Positive Qualities – Individualist, creative, passionate, optimistic, extraverted, flexible, goal oriented, loyal friend

Negative Qualities – Sloppy, self centered, irresponsible, forgetful, over confident, brash, boastful, tactless

Type AB Blood – Cups

Positive Qualities – Charming, spiritual, intuitive, empathetic, free spirit, original, social butterfly
Negative Qualities: Scattered, flighty, indecisive, aloof, contradictory, unforgiving, critical, spoiled

Type A Blood – Pentacles

Positive Qualities – Conservative, smart, desires to please, patient, reserved, conscientious, trustworthy, animal lover

Negative Qualities – Perfectionist, obsessive, stubborn, self conscious, doesn't handle stress well, overly sensitive, easily offended

Celtic Tree Year

The Celtic Tree Year is a topic of heated debate. Some say it was created by Druids, who believed that each tree had specific magikal qualities. They supposedly preserved this knowledge in a secret alphabet known as the Ogham, named for the Celtic God of Poetry. Others say it is a product of the imagination of Robert Graves, scholar and author of The White Goddess, a collection of (in his own words) "a historical grammar of the language of poetic myth."

The calendar is based upon the 13 lunar cycles of the year. December 23rd is widely considered to be the day in the "year and a day," or the equivalent of the extra day in the leap year. This day is not included in the calendar.

Whichever way you believe, it makes for interesting reading, and we have included it here for that reason. It is your decision whether to take it into consideration when planning your workings. Included are the dates, corresponding tree along with the Gaelic translation, the inherent qualities or characteristics, and the symbol and Tarot card associated with it.

Dec. 24 - Jan 20 – Birch (Beth)

Qualities – Rebirth, fertility, creativity, healing, protection

Celtic Symbol – The White Stag
Tarot Correspondence – The Empress

Jan 21 - Feb 17 – Rowan (Luis)

Qualities: Personal power, astral travel, success
Celtic Symbol – Green Dragon
Tarot Correspondence – The Chariot

Feb 18 - Mar 17 – Ash (Nuin)

Qualities – Self improvement, intuition, prophecy, spiritual knowledge
Celtic Symbol – The Sea Horse
Tarot Correspondence – The Hanged Man

Mar 18 - April 14 – Alder (Fearn)

Qualities – Divination, Intuition, Prophecy, Defense, protection
Celtic Symbol – The Hawk
Tarot Correspondence – The Fool

April 15 - May 12 – Willow (Saille)

Qualities – Healing, growth, protection, female energy. love, fertility
Celtic Symbol – The Serpent
Tarot Correspondence – The Moon

May 13 - June 9 – Hawthorn (Uath)

Qualities – Male energy, business decisions, protection, strength
Celtic Symbol – The Chalice
Tarot Correspondence – The Magician

June 10 - July 7 – Oak (Duir)

Qualities – Protection, strength, good fortune, success, endurance, growth
Celtic Symbol – The White horse
Tarot Correspondence – The Sun

July 8 - Aug 4 – Holly (Tinne)

Qualities – Protection against evil, good luck, wisdom, courage, dreams
Celtic Symbol – The Cat
Tarot Correspondence – The Emperor

Aug 5 - Sept 1 – Hazel (Coll)

Qualities – Wisdom, protection, creativity, divination, meditation
Celtic Symbol – The Salmon
Tarot Correspondence – The Hermit

Sept 2 - Sept 29 – Vine (Muin)

Qualities – Passions, ambitions, fertility, money, death and rebirth
Celtic Symbol – The White Swan
Tarot Correspondence – The Hierophant

Sept 30 - Oct 27 - Ivy (Gort)

Qualities – Releasing negativity, healing, protection, removing addictions, dreams
Celtic Symbol – The Butterfly
Tarot Correspondence – Strength

Oct 28 - Nov 24 – Reed (Ngetal)

Qualities – Contacting the dead, spirit guides, energy work, divination
Celtic Symbol – The White Hound
Tarot Correspondence: The High Priestess

Nov 25 - Dec 22 – Elder (Ruis)

Qualities – Renewal, cycles, protection against negativity, creativity
Celtic Symbol – The Black Horse
Tarot Correspondence – The Star

Character Trait

The Character Trait is that which sums up the intrinsic nature of the energy of the Suit:

Swords – Restlessness
Wands – Passion
Cups – Healing
Pentacles – Hibernation

Color

In Traditional Witchcraft, the colors associated with the Four Direction are:

North – White
South – Red
East – Yellow
West – Blue-Green

It is important to take into consideration that the Celts had different color associations. In Celtic magick the Correspondences are:

North – Black
South – White
East – Red
West – Gray

We have included both colors as a reference for each card.

Direction

The four basic points on a compass are referred to as the Cardinal Direction: North, South, East, and West. There is a great deal of symbolism in these, as outlined by various cultures and religions throughout history.

In Wicca, the Four Direction are often referred to as the Watchtowers, with the Regents standing guard at each.

In Buddhism, they are the Four Heavenly Guardians.

In Japan, they are known as the Four Heavenly Kings.

In Native American symbolism, the Four Direction are found in the Medicine Wheel, the journey each of us takes to find our path in this life.

Element

Also called the Triplicities in Astrology, the Elements are as follows:

Air – Represents thought and communication
Fire – Represents action and energy
Water – Represents emotion and the subconscious
Earth – Represents the physical and steadfast

Elemental

Paracelsus, the Swiss occultist (b.1493, d.1591), is credited with being the first to write about Elementals, or Nature Spirits believed to inhabit the four elements. These are not ensouled beings; rather, they are each a part of the collective soul and thus not individuals. The Elementals are:

Slyphs – The Spirits of Air
Salamanders – The Spirits of Fire
Undines – The Spirits of Water
Gnomes – The Spirits of the Earth

Elemental Counterchange

This particular symbolism was introduced by the Golden Dawn as the concept of assigning each of the four elements and all their possible combinations with the sixteen Court Cards. They are determined by Rank and Suit, or Element.

They are then further divided into type of Counterchange:

Pure, which corresponds to the Fixed signs of the Zodiac, Aquarius, Leo, Scorpio, and Taurus. This Counterchange is determined by an identical Rank and Suit or Element, such as Air. Using, for example, the King of Swords – the Kings are always represented by Air, and Swords are represented by Air.

Compound, which corresponds to the Cardinal signs of Libra, Aries, Cancer, and Capricorn. This Counterchange is either wholly masculine or feminine in gender. An example of this would be the King of Wands. The King is Air, and the Wands are Fire, both masculine.

Complex, which corresponds to the Mutable signs of Gemini, Sagittarius, Pisces, and Virgo. This Counterchange is a mixture of masculine and feminine energies, such as the Knight of Pentacles as Fire of Earth. The Knight is represented by Fire, which is masculine, and Pentacles, which are feminine in gender.

Elemental Counterchanges work with the concept of Force and Form. In the Court, Force and Form take the shape of Element (Suit) and Rank. Four of the court cards have only one element; the other twelve are a combination of two.

Think of Force as one of the Elements – Air, Fire, Water, or Earth, which correspond to the suits of Swords, Wands, Cups, and Pentacles. Think of

Form as the container which holds the Force, in this case the ranks of King, Queen, Knight, and Page. So to use a literal example, if you have a bottle of wine, the wine becomes the Force or Element, and the bottle becomes the Form which contains and shapes the Force.

The Elemental Counterchanges are determined by Element and Rank, and then it is your job to figure out how one tempers the other. The Elemental Counterchanges are as follows:

The Kings are always Air, representing Intellect. The Kings correspond to the Fixed signs of the Zodiac:

King of Swords: Air of Air (Pure)
He is the most cerebral King, and also the most emotionally distant.

King of Wands: Air of Fire (Compound)
He is outgoing and charismatic, but thinks before he acts.

King of Cups: Air of Water (Complex)
He is the fatherly type, dispensing good advice and an ear for listening.

King of Pentacles: Air of Pentacles (Complex)
He is the combination of intellect and potential, a good businessman.

The Queens are always Water, representing Intuition. The Queens correspond to the Cardinal signs of the Zodiac:

Queen of Swords: Water of Air (Complex)
She allows her head to rule her heart, and may seem indifferent to her emotions.

Queen of Wands: Water of Fire (Complex)
She is passionate and fiery, a good businessperson with a flair for high drama.

Queen of Cups: Water of Water (Pure)
She is the governed by emotions rather than intellect, and is nurturing and psychic.

Queen of Pentacles: Water of Earth (Compound)
She is emotion tempered with practicality, and a good household manager.

The Knights are always Fire, representing Motion. The Knights correspond to the Mutable signs of the Zodiac:

Knight of Swords: Fire of Air (Compound)
He is consumed with fighting the good fight, the champion of the weak and oppressed.

Knight of Wands: Fire of Fire (Pure)
Fools and the Knight of Wands rush in where angels fear to tread, he knows no boundaries.

Knight of Cups: Fire of Water (Complex)
He puts his passion into emotion, the most charming and disarming of all the knights

Knight of Pentacles: Fire of Earth (Complex)
He moves slowly, his Fire being slowed and dampened by the practical and predictable Earth.

The Pages are always Earth, representing Potential. The Pages are not assigned to a particular Quadruplicity; they are instead assigned a Season:

Page of Swords: Earth of Air (Complex)
Spring – She has the potential of intellect and communication

Page of Wands: Earth of Fire (Complex)
Summer – She has the potential of action and purpose

Page of Cups: Earth of Water (Compound)
Autumn – She has the potential of opening up emotionally

Page of Pentacles: Earth of Earth (Pure)
Winter – She has the potential to manifest reality

Elemental Ruler or King

Working with Hermetic Magick often involves requesting the aid of the Elemental Kings, who are actually non-gendered ensouled beings that govern each plane. The Elemental Kings are:

King Paralda – Lord of the Element of Air
King Djinn – Lord of the Element of Fire
King Nixsa – Lord of the Element of Water
King Ghob – Lord of the Element of Earth

Esoteric Titles

The Golden Dawn gave each card its own title, sometimes long, sometimes short, but always representing the essence of the card.

The Esoteric Titles here were compiled in part through these wonderful books:

The Golden Dawn: The Original Account of the Teachings, Rites & Ceremonies of the Hermetic Order by Israel Regardie and *The Book of Thoth (Egyptian Tarot)* by Aleister Crowley.

Fundamental Force

The four Fundamental Forces of the Universe are the means by which particles interact with each other, producing changes in either the size or shape of an object or body. The Four Forces are:

Electromagnetic Force, which is considered to have infinite range. We have assigned this force to **Air**.

Strong Force, which is considered to have limited range. We have assigned this force to **Fire**.

Weak Force, which is considered to have limited range. We have assigned this force to **Water**.

Gravity, which is considered to have infinite range. We have assigned this force to **Earth**.

Gematria Value

Gematria is a form of Numerology dealing specifically with the study of Hebrew letters and numbers, what their meanings are, and how they can be applied to our everyday lives. It works in concert with the Kabbalah. In the Hebrew language, each letter is assigned a numerical value, and then the significance of the words and phrases is calculated based on the values.

Gender

In all of Nature, everything has a duality, and the Tarot is no different. The suits are divided into either masculine or feminine, and then further divided into the nature, or Quality of the Suit:

Swords – Masculine and Active
Wands – Masculine and Immediate
Cups – Feminine and Receptive
Pentacles – Feminine and Passive

Hebrew Letter

Each of the 22 Paths on the Tree of Life has a Hebrew letter assigned to it. The Hebrew alphabet is divided into three main groups: the three Mother letters, the seven Double letters, and the twelve Simple letters.

The three Mother letters correspond to the elements of Air, Fire, and Water, while the Double letters correspond to the seven planets of ancient Astrology – the Sun, Mercury, Venus, the Moon, Mars, Jupiter, and Saturn. The twelve Simple letters align to the twelve signs of the Zodiac. We have listed the Hebrew letter, the English translation of the letter, and which group the letter belongs to:

Aleph, The Ox
(Mother Letter)   א

Beth, The House
(Double letter)   ב

Gimel, The Camel
(Double letter)   ג

Daleth, The Door
(Double letter)   ד

Heh, The Window
(Single letter)   ה

Vau, The Nail
(Single letter)

Zain, The Sword
(Single letter)

Cheth, The Fence
(Single letter)

Teth, The Serpent
(Single letter)

Yod, The Hand
(Single letter)

Kaph, The Palm of the Hand
(Double letter)

Lamed, The Ox Goad
(Single letter)

Mem, Water
(Mother letter)

Nun, The Fish
(Single letter)

Samech, The Staff
(Single letter)

Ayin, The Eye
(Single letter)

Peh, The Mouth
(Double letter)

Tzaddi, The Fishhook
(Single letter)

Qoph, The Back of the Head
(Single letter)

Resh, The Head
(Double letter)

Shin, The Tooth
(Mother letter)

Tau, The T Shaped Cross
(Double letter)

Herb

The use of herbs has been a staple of healing for centuries, but their wonderful properties extend past the boundaries of the medicinal. They have been used in religious ceremonies to invoke or banish spirits, as a calming influence in the form of potpourri or aromatherapy, or in spellwork or visualization as a trigger to produce imagery. We have assigned an herb to each of the Major Arcana, based on the properties of the herb compared to the qualities of the card.

For more in depth workings, there is a chapter devoted specifically to Stones and Herbs and their magickal uses.

Holy Creatures

On the Wheel of Fortune X in the Smith-Waite deck, there are four entities surrounding the Wheel itself. Sometimes referred to as the Four Holy Creatures, they are mentioned in the Bible, specifically Revelation 4:7 (King James Version):

"And the first beast was like a lion, and the second beast like a calf, and the third beast had a face as a man, and the fourth beast was like a flying eagle."

They are also very similar to the four creatures seen in a vision by Ezekiel (Ezekiel 1:10):

"As for the likeness of their faces, they four had the face of a man, and the face of a lion, on the right side: and they four had the face of an ox on the left side; they four also had the face of an eagle."

The four Holy Creatures have been described as representing the four divisions of animate creation:

The Winged Man, a symbol of rational thought, represents humankind. Sometimes referred to an Angel or the personification of Aquarius, the Man is the Holy Creature of **Air**.

The Winged Lion, a symbol of strength, represents all wild animals. This is the Holy Creature of **Fire**.

The Eagle, a symbol of swiftness, represents the birds and flying creatures. Although it would initially be thought that the Eagle would represent Air, this is the Holy Creature of Water. Looking closely at the legs of the Eagle, they are scaled as that of a fish, indicating that thought which leads to action has root in emotion, the **Attribute** of **Water**.

The Winged Bull, a symbol of humility, represents domesticated animals. This is the Holy Creature of **Earth**.

I-Ching - Book of Changes

This Oracle is among the most ancient in existence, estimated to be over 5,000 years old. Legend states that the first Emperor of China, Fu Hsi, discovered the eight Trigrams:

1. Heaven or Sky -
Aggressive

2. Earth -
Passive

3. Thunder -
Excitement

4. Water -
Danger

5. Mountain -
Stability

6. Wind -
Flexibility

7. Fire -
Brightness

8. Lake or Valley -
Serenity

Centuries later, the wise King Wen Wang divided the Trigrams in groups of two, representing the Chinese concept of Yin/Yang. There is a light and dark side to each aspect, the Yin (receptive, feminine, passive) being the dark side, and the Yang (creative, masculine, active) the light. He then further arranged them to form the 64 Hexagrams. The Hexagram is the six lined figures composed of various combinations of divided and undivided lines. Later, short descriptions for each of the six lines of each Hexagram were added by the Duke of Chou.

"Ching" in Chinese means "book," and "I" means "change," so literally, this is the *Book of Changes*. It has only one law: The one and only thing that never changes is change itself. The I-Ching sees the world around us as a constantly evolving and changing entity, so this is a very dynamic form of divination which stresses that we and Nature are one being. However, "I" also can mean "that which does not change" which in turn goes back to the Yin/Yang principles. Ancient as it is, the meanings are still relevant today. Each card of the Major and Minor Arcanas have an I-Ching correspondence. In the majority of cases, you will find that the meanings of the two are very, very similar.

Key Phrase

The Key Phrases used here are the ones that we felt best embodied the spirit of the **Element**:

Air – "I Think"
Air is the element associated with Thoughts and Ideas, the beginning of any undertaking.

Wands – "I Desire"
Fire is about Action and Intention, bringing the Thought into action.

Water – "I Feel"
Water is the element of Emotion and the Subconscious, tempering the Thought with sentiment.

Earth – "I Have"
Earth is the element association with Manifestation and Formation, bringing the Thought into Reality.

Keyword

Each card carries with it a multitude of meanings, but the one word Keyword was assigned by keeping the most basic meaning in mind, and is meant to be used as a springboard or trigger for learning card meanings.

Lunar Phase

There are four primary lunar phases, which correspond to the Tarot suits:

First Quarter – Air
Full Moon – Fire
Third Quarter – Water
New Moon – Earth

In ritual or in spellwork, timing is critical, and the Moon phase is often the first thing considered when planning a working. Different spells are most effective at different times of the month. The following is the customary schedule:

New Moon
When dealing with beginnings and new ideas or projects

First Quarter, or Waxing Moon
When encouraging growth, such as for financial gain or to encourage a romantic prospect

Full Moon
An all purpose time when all types of magick are worked

Last Quarter, or Waning Moon
When working with banishment, such as trying to rid oneself of a bad habit or unsettling influence

Magickal Organ

Magickal Organs were a relatively new concept for us, and one that added yet another facet to a reading. We were first introduced to this by a highly recommended audio course offered by Wald and Ruth Ann Amberstone of the Tarot School in New York, New York, entitled *Court Cards: Advanced Reading Techniques*:

Swords are represented by The **Brain**, and its Psychological Functions are Thoughts and Ideas. The Physical Property is symbolized by Motion. This is a Masculine, tangible organ.

Wands are represented by The **Spirit**, and its Psychological Functions are Energy and Desire. The Physical Property is symbolized by Intensity. This is a Masculine, intangible organ.

Cups are represented by The **Heart**, and its Psychological Functions are Emotions and Feelings. The Physical Property is symbolized by Fluidity. This is a Feminine, intangible organ.

Pentacles are represented by The **Body**, and its Psychological Functions are Manifestation and Formation. The Physical Property is symbolized by Solidity. This is a Feminine, tangible organ.

Magickal Phrase

Sometimes referred to as the Law of the Magus or the Witches Pyramid, the four sides of the pyramid reflect the four powers that a Magician must possess in order to be successful:

Noscere – To Know (Air)
Velle – To Will (Fire)
Audere – To Dare (Water)
Tacere – To Keep Silent (Earth)

To Know is to possess the knowledge, To Will is to possess the desire to manifest, To Dare is to consummate the spell or ritual, and to Keep Silent is just that, to not discuss what you are doing with anyone. To talk about a spell or ritual once cast is to disperse some of its energy, thus making it less effective.

Matter

Matter here is referred to as "state of being." It is usually defined as being the substance of which physical objects are composed of. For our purposes, we are using the four states of Matter: Gas, Solid, Liquid, and Energy, to correspond to the four Elements and Suits:

Swords – Gas
Wands – Energy
Water – Liquid
Earth – Solid

Meanings - Upright and Reversed

We have listed some keywords for each card, both upright and reversed, and allowed space to write in your own. Not every reader uses reversed, or upside down, cards, but we feel strongly that they should be taken into account in a reading. These keywords have been amassed over the years. You may find that occasionally the same word appears in the Upright or Reversed keywords,

seeming somewhat contradictory. For example, a temptation may be a good thing or a bad thing, depending on the situation. Don't assume that the Reversed meaning of the card is the opposite of the Upright meaning, as this is not always the case. We have tried to include as many keywords as possible; when trying to learn the cards, it may be helpful to read all of the keywords, and then put them all together to capture the essence of the true meaning of each one.

There are several good books on both combinations and reversals; to learn more, please check the references section of this book for recommended reading.

Musical Mood

There has always been a strong connection between music and learning, a perfect marriage between the left and right sides of the brain. We remember growing up during the 70s and watching cartoons on Saturday mornings. Nestled in between the cartoons were short three-minute songs, covering subjects such as multiplication, history, grammar, and science. We memorized our multiplication tables while humming such songs as "The Four Legged Zoo" and "Lucky Seven" and to this day – thirty+ years later – cannot recite the Preamble to the Constitution without singing it first.

We still remember well the Alphabet song, and the little tune that tells you how many days are in each month. Now we have little ones of our own. While on a drive

one afternoon, the elder of the two turned on the CD player and was listening to music. A song came on that we both knew, and as we were singing along, we commented that the lyrics reminded us of the 6 of Wands – the joyful homecoming. The younger one in the back piped up that he didn't know the words to this particular song, and started singing the Alphabet song instead. As one song faded into the other, the mental wheels started turning. What if the same principle could be applied to learning the Tarot?

We explored this topic briefly while creating the Legends of Rock Tarot, which matched an artist with each of the 78 cards. Cards such as the 7 of Swords became Angus Young of AC/DC, for the song "Dirty Deeds Done Dirt Cheap." We felt that this characterized the card well – dodging your responsibilities by having someone else do your dirty work. In the spirit of this, we have assigned a song to each card, the lyrics conveying what we consider to be the core meaning. Although our personal preferences run primarily with rock music, other genres from country to hip hop are represented as well.

Musical Note

This concept was an unusual one for us; although we both had spent time as musicians, we had not consciously considered that we were in fact beings of energy, and as such, vibrating at a set frequency or note. This is delving into the realms of Quantum Mechanics, Superconductivity and the unfamiliar territories of Einstein, Tesla, and the like, and ones that we don't profess to have much understanding of. Still, the thought of everything having its own musical note was very intriguing. We are not entirely certain who originated the thought of assigning musical notes to the Major Arcana, but they are included here as additional food for thought, in a manner of speaking.

Mythological Creatures

We have long been great lovers of mythology, so it would stand to reason that we would also assign mythological creatures to represent their native elements. These images may be used with the Tarot in spellwork or as a visualization tool.

Air: Gryphons and Pegasus

The **Gryphon** has the body of a lion, the head and wings of an eagle. The back is completely covered with feathers, and it builds nests such as a bird does. Gryphons are known for building large, hard-to-reach nests and for hoarding gold and other shiny trinkets. Its long talons are said to have been made into drinking horns by hunters lucky enough to have survived an encounter with one.

Pegasus is the beautiful winged horse from Greek and Roman Mythology. When Perseus defeated the Medusa and decapitated her, the blood that dripped from the head fell upon the ground, and from the drops Pegasus was born. The Roman Goddess Minerva (Athena to the Greek) caught and befriended the noble steed, and presented him as a gift to the Muses.

Fire: Dragons and Phoenix

Arguably one the best known mythological creatures, the reptilian **Dragon** has a long and illustrious history. Nearly every civilization has some form of dragon, ranging from the dancing dragons of China to the fearsome fire-breathing dragons of medieval times. Dragons come in nearly all colors, and breathe out numerous substances such as acid, ice, and fire.

The **Phoenix** has recently enjoyed a resurgence in popularity due to its inclusion into the best seller *Harry Potter and the Chamber of Secrets* by J.K. Rowling. Believed to have originated in Egypt, this glorious bird lives for 500 years, then spontaneously combusts, only to rise from its own ashes and live another 500 years. It is said that its tears can heal any wound.

Water: Merfolk and Hippocampus

It has been speculated that when sailors of old spied a beautiful half woman, half fish cavorting in the ocean, what they saw in actuality was a sea cow. Anyone who has ever seen a sea cow, or manatee, up close, knows this explanation doesn't hold water. It stands to reason that there would be both male and female **water spirits**, as well as **mer-babies**.

The **Hippocampus** is a combination of horse and fish, and originates from Greek mythology. They have the distinct honor of drawing the deep sea chariot of Poseidon. The name Hippocampus also applies to about 24 species of Sea Horse, which the ancient scientists believed were the youthful version of Hippocampoi. These monogamous creatures bond for life, are very affectionate towards each other, and share the parental responsibilities.

Earth: Giants and Elves

Nearly every civilization has legends and stories of huge men and women, possessing enormous strength (and occasionally appetites) but appearing human in all ways except size. Even the Bible has its own Giant story, that of Goliath, taken down by the diminutive David and one small, well placed stone. Depending on the purpose of the story, **Giants** range from people-eating monsters to gentle, intelligent beings.

Elves are another ancient race of supernatural beings, living in harmony with the Earth and staying out of sight of prying human eyes. Although generally believed to be Germanic in origin, tales of the wee folk are staples all over the world. Two notable examples are the Elves of Middle-Earth in J.R.R. Tolkien's *Lord of the Rings* trilogy, and the industrious toy builders in Santa's Workshop, North Pole.

Numerology

The science of numerology is believed to be over 10,000 years old, and can be found in many sacred texts throughout the world. There are several different types of numerology; however, the one used primarily today is the Pythagorean method, and this is the one we will be focusing on here.

Pythagoras (approximately 530 BC) was a Greek philosopher and widely considered the Father of Mathematics, as anyone who has ever taken

Algebra can attest. Not a great deal of information about Pythagoras is available; however, we do know that he also made great strides in the fields of mathematics, astronomy, and music theory. Pythagoras believed that numbers were inherently mystical in nature, and that everything could be explained by them. He also believed that numbers were divided by gender – male numbers were odd, and females were even. This corresponds to the Chinese concept of Yin/Yang. The I-Ching also assigns gender to even numbers as feminine (Yin) and odd numbers as masculine (Yang). There are several combinations that we will concern ourselves with here, and they are:

The Destiny, or Karmic Number (also called the Life Path)
The Personal Year Number
The Personal Month Number
The Birth Number

Using the table, we can quickly calculate the Karmic Number for the subject. This is one of the simplest and fastest to compute. For this number, take the date of month, day, and year of birth, and add them together like this:

Date of Birth - 09/19/1995 = 1995 (year of birth)
+ 09 (month of birth)
+ 19 (day of birth)
= 2023

Separate and add the four digit result:
2 + 0 + 2 + 3 = 7 (which is the Karmic Number)

1	2	3	4	5	6	7	8	9
A	B	C	D	E	F	G	H	I
J	K	L	M	N	O	P	Q	R
S	T	U	V	W	X	Y	Z	

Now we will calculate the Personal Year number. The Personal Year is calculated using the current year, the month, and day of birth.

Date of Birth – 08/29/2001 = 2006 (current year)
+ 08 (month of birth)
+ 29 (day of birth)
= 2043

Separate and add the four digit result:
2 + 0 + 4 + 3 = 9 (which is the Personal Year Number)

Using the same birthday, we will calculate the Personal Month. This is done by adding together the current month and the Personal Year Number. Choose a relevant date; we will be using for this example 11/15/2006. The Personal Year for the person listed above is 9. We will add the current month – 11 – to the Personal Year Number of 9. The answer is 20, which reduces to 2 (2+0=2).

You can also use the Pythagorean table above to calculate your Name Number. Many numerologists believe that some behaviors are influenced by the Name Number. There are several school of thought on this. Some feel that you should use each name to get a true reading (first, middle, last or maiden, married), while others feel that you should use the name you use most often, including nicknames.

The Birth Number is also easy to calculate, and is the first step to determining the Tarot card pair assigned to your particular number. Each number is broken down into three parts:

The **Soul Card**, which is what we aspire to become in this life.
The **Personality Card**, which is how we are seen by others.
The **Shadow Card**, which is that which we are afraid to face within ourselves

Using the birth date of 08/01/1958, we will total the following numbers:

8+1+1+9+5+8 = 32, which is 3+2 = 5.
The Birth Number for this person is a 5.
In the event that the numbers add up to a three digit number, such as 112, break that down into 1+1+2 = 4.

These are the 9 different pairings:

One
Soul Card – The Magician (1)
Personality Card – The Wheel of Fortune (10)
Shadow Card – The Sun (19)

Two
Soul Card – High Priestess (2)
Personality Card – Justice (11)
Shadow Card – Judgment (20)

Three
Soul Card – The Empress (3)
Personality Card – The Hanged Man (12)
Shadow Card – World (21)

Four
Soul Card – The Emperor (4)
Personality Card – The Emperor (4)
Shadow Card – Death (13)

Five
Soul Card – The High Priest (5)
Personality Card – The High Priest (5)
Shadow Card – Temperance (14)

Six
Soul Card – The Lovers (6)
Personality Card – The Lovers (6)
Shadow Card – The Devil (15)

Seven
Soul Card – The Chariot (7)
Personality Card – The Chariot (7)
Shadow Card – The Tower (16)

Eight
Soul Card – Strength (8)
Personality Card – Strength (8)
Shadow Card – The Star (17)

Nine
Soul Card – The Hermit (9)
Personality Card – The Hermit (9)
Shadow Card – The Moon (18)

The Meanings of Numbers

One

Ones generally indicate the beginning of a cycle. One people tend to take charge, take command and take over if they are allowed. They are original and creative, but can be driven to the point that they will stop at nothing to become successful. This is a time to take initiative and action, to prepare and plan. The color associated with this number is White.

Two

Two is a number of balance, partnership, and choices. Number Two people tend to chase two rabbits at once, catching neither, and this can cause frustration in their lives. They are born mediators, but can be insecure and not grounded in reality. This is a number of cooperation. The color associated with this number is Blue.

Three

Threes are the gifted children, the artists and musicians. They are dynamic and driven, witty and personable. This hides a truly competitive nature which can result in taking on more than they can comfortably handle. This is a happy number, one of joy and celebrations. The color associated with this number is Green.

Four

Fours are the salt of the Earth – reliable, practical, stable, and committed. Four people are methodical and have a strong attention to detail. Fours need to be needed above all else, and can sometimes take thing too seriously. This is a number of details and reading the fine print. The color associated with this number is Brown.

Five

Fives are all about change and challenge. Five people tend to be constantly in flux, looking for that next rush. Boredom is to be avoided at all costs. Fives are very active and restless, but can be moody and unpredictable. This is another number of action and preparation. The color associated with this number is Red.

Six

Six is a number of family and friends, of home and harmony. Six people are lovers of beauty and luxury, preferring to pamper and be pampered. They also can be artistic, but may also lean towards obsessive behaviors and perfectionism. Six is a number of receptiveness and harmony. The color associated with this number is Yellow.

Seven

Seven is a magickal number, full of spiritual and mystical influence. Seven people are psychic, intellectual and imaginative. Sevens are in tune with their surroundings, but the tendency is there to get lost inside themselves, isolating them from society. Seven is a number of introspection and reflection. The color associated with this number is Purple.

Eight

As another active number, Eight has a tendency towards the extreme. No holds barred, it is all or nothing with Eight people, as there is no in between. Eights can be overly dramatic at times, and arrogant about their accomplishments. Eight is a number of progress, accomplishment, and achievement. The color associated with this number is Orange.

Nine

Nine is the number of the humanitarian, working tirelessly towards saving the world, and fighting injustice wherever found. Nine people are naturally perceptive and psychic, but can also be volatile if provoked. Nine indicates the end of a cycle, and that it is time to plan for the future. The color associated with this number is Gray.

Master Numbers

Eleven and Twenty-Two are considered Master numbers, which do not reduce down. These indicate old souls who have reincarnated many times, and are visionary leaders. They feel a deeper sense of obligation to the World, and are in many cases teachers in humanitarian fields.

Eleven

Eleven is the number of independence and spiritual understanding. Elevens are very intuitive, and are natural counselors and leaders, open minded and without prejudice. Eleven can also exhibit characteristics of the number Two, 1+1. The color associated with this number is Silver.

Twenty-Two

The other master number, **Twenty-Two** is the number of perfection attained. Twenty-Twos lead by example, and make those around them strive to be better people as a result. They can also exhibit characteristics of the number Four, 2+2. The color associated with this number is Gold.

Having a basic working knowledge of Numerology can only enhance the amount of information you receive from your readings. For example, a spread showing a coming period of inactivity may be much more tolerable to a person with a Karmic number of Four than a person with a Karmic Number of Five. Conversely, a need for a cooperative effort will be better received by a Two than an Eight. Numerology itself is a fascinating study in synchronicity, and there are many resources available for further information.

Number Combinations in Readings

When the same number appears multiple times in a spread, there is a distinct possibility that this is not by chance. Here are some possible meanings of multiple numbers:

Aces – New beginnings and fresh starts
2 Aces – partnerships
3 Aces – good news is coming
4 Aces – profound change, Karmic activity

Twos – Relationships, decisions, balance
2 Twos – partnerships, usually emotional
3 Twos – rethinking the current status quo
4 Twos – collaborations

Threes – Growth and enterprise
2 Threes – clash of ideas
3 Threes – gossip, whispering and rumors
4 Threes – creativity

Fours – Rest, inactivity
2 Fours – down time needed
3 Fours – more work is needed to reach the goal
4 Fours – security, sound financial investments

Fives – Changes and disruptions
2 Fives – conflicting forces at work
3 Fives – stabilization needed
4 Fives – major changes

Sixes – Home life and harmony
2 Sixes – personality clashes
3 Sixes – compromise is needed
4 Sixes – happiness and contentment

Sevens – Spiritual matters
2 Sevens – conflicting beliefs, resolution is needed
3 Sevens – everything will work out in the end
4 Sevens – not grounded in reality

Eights – Material Progress
2 Eights – unexpected turn of events
3 Eights – important partnerships
4 Eights – much activity regarding employment

Nines – Material Satisfaction
2 Nines – messages are coming
3 Nines – goals are achieved
4 Nines – good luck smiles on you

Tens – Material, Emotional or Spiritual Completion
2 Tens – minor successes
3 Tens – everything comes full circle
4 Tens – complete success

Path on the Tree of Life

The Kabbalah is in itself worthy of a lifetime of study. It is a central text of Hassidic Judaism, believed to have been passed from directly from God to Moses on Mt. Sinai. There are some schools of thought, however, that place the origins with Adam and Eve. *The American Heritage Dictionary* defines it as "a body of mystical teachings of rabbinical origin, often based on an esoteric interpretation of the Hebrew Scriptures." It was referred to by Dion Fortune as "the Yoga of the West." Dolores Ashcroft-Nowicki defines it as a complete filing system for the hidden wisdom of the world, holding a vast wealth of knowledge in the 10 Sephiroth, or Spheres on the Tree of Life. Each of these Spheres is connected to each other by a Path – 22 in all, and each Path corresponds to a Trump in the Major Arcana. Each Path also has its own lesson to teach, and each card gives vision to the lesson. It is as hard to describe the Kabbalah as it is to give a short one sentence definition for "existentialism" and convey the full meaning. Our best advice is to seek out sources available to you, and determine for yourself if it is time for you to discover this truly amazing system.

Phase of Life

When discussing the cycles of life, we are immediately reminded of the riddle of the Great Sphinx of Egypt: "What walks on four legs in the morning, two legs in the afternoon, and three legs at night?" The answer is, of course, Man, who crawls as a child, walks as an adult, and uses a cane in the waning years. There are actually four phases of life, however. The phase of adult is actually two different parts – the fiery passion of youth, followed by the contemplative and nurturing adulthood. These four phases correspond to the suits of the Tarot, and take on their characteristics:

The Child – Air, or Communication and Learning
The Youth – Fire, or Passion and Energy
The Adult – Water, or Compassion and Understanding
The Elder – Earth, or Wisdom and Contemplation

Physical Property

The Physical Property of a Suit is that which most closely defines the energy of the Attributes:

The Physical Property of Swords is symbolized by Motion
The Physical Property of Wands is symbolized by Intensity.
The Physical Property of Cups is symbolized by Fluidity.
The Physical Property of Pentacles is symbolized by Solidity.

Plane

Everything that is falls under the categories of the four stages of Being, or Planes:

Mental – Air
Spiritual – Fire
Astral – Water
Physical – Earth

Plant

Aleister Crowley's *777 and other Qabalistic Writings of Aleister Crowley* was the inspiration for the attributions of plants associated with the Major Arcana. (See Resources and Recommended Reading). For more in depth workings, there is a glossary devoted specifically to Stones and Herbs and their magickal uses.

Playing Card Suit

The general consensus is that playing cards originated in China during or perhaps before the 9th century, predating the Tarot by thousands of years. The Tarot expanded on the original 52 cards, adding another 22 card suit of the Major Arcana, and the Page to the existing family of Court Cards. The French suits for playing cards (Spades, Clubs, Hearts and Diamonds) have come to be the standard known as the Anglo-American pattern deck. However, some other countries have different suits as their national preference, such as the German suits of Leaves, Acorns, Hearts, and Bells, the Swiss suits of Acorns, Flowers, Shields and Bells, or the Italian suits of Swords, Batons, Cups and Coins. The Tarot suits correspond neatly with the Italian suits.

Swords – Spades
Wands – Clubs
Cups – Hearts
Pentacles – Diamonds

Possibility

The Possibilities for each card are exactly that – something to keep in mind as a potential influence when this card comes up in a reading. These can also be found on our website in the One Card reading section at http://www.shadowfoxtarot.com.

Possible Influencing Cards

We have included a partial list of the potential meanings of card combinations, which tend to strengthen the impact or meanings of both cards; for example, the Empress appearing in a spread with the Page of Cups is a good sign that there is the distinct possibility of hearing the pitter patter of little feet in the near future. There are several very good books currently in print that deal specifically with card combinations; you can find these in the Resources and Recommended Reading section.

Psychological Function

This function is that of the intangible quality of the **Suit**:

The Psychological Functions of the **Swords** are **Thoughts and Ideas.**
The Psychological Functions of the **Wands** are **Energy and Desire.**
The Psychological Functions of the **Cups** are **Emotions and Feelings.**
The Psychological Functions of the **Pentacles** are **Manifestation and Formation.**

Quality

The Quality of the Suit is defined by its inherent nature:

Wands – Masculine and Immediate
Cups – Feminine and Receptive
Pentacles – Feminine and Passive
Swords – Masculine and Active

Regent

Often referred to as the Lords of Light, the Archangels or the Guardians of the Watchtowers, the Regents are:

Raphael, The Great Healer, Regent of Air, Guardian of the **East**.

Michael, Commander of the Celestial Armies, Regent of Fire, Guardian of the **South**.

Gabriel, The Great Communicator, Regent of Water, Guardian of the **West**.

Uriel, Lord of Peace and Ministration, Regent of Earth, Guardian of the **North**.

Royal Stars

The Royal Stars, also referred to as the Guardians of the Sky or World, were first utilized by Persian Astrologers around 3000 BC serving as a seasonal calendar. Each star appears brighter than the others at certain times of the year, thus taking its turn heralding the arrival of each new solstice or equinox. These fixed stars were later given angelic status by the Hebrews, associating them with the Archangels. They are also the four points on the compass.

We have found some conflicting information as to which season each Star is assigned to. Here, we are using the original ancient alignments. Although the term "fixed" implies that the Star does not move, they actually do move slightly – one degree every seventy-two years. The wobble of the Earth's orbit is the cause, and is also the reason for Precession, the movement of the equinoxes along the ecliptic, or plane of Earth's orbit. The Greek astronomer Hipparchus of Nicea is credited with the discovery that the world's orbit shifts gradually, but very, very slowly. By comparing his charts with those from a hundred years before, he realized that the intersections that mark the equinoxes and solstices were moving slowly forward. Modern science tells us that the entire cycle of Precession takes 26,000 years.

The four Royal Stars are:

Regulus – Referred to as the Star of Kings or the heart of the lion, this is the alpha, or brightest, star in the constellation Leo. This Star is the Watcher of the South. The Ancient Persian name is Venant. It is believed to represent the Nemean Lion, slain by Hercules as one of his 12 labors in Greek mythology. It is a large blue-white star that is approximately 100 times brighter than the Sun, and over 77 light years away. Its diameter is 4.2 times the size of the Sun.

Fomalhaut – The mouth of the fish in the constellation Pisces, this Star is the Watcher of the North. The Ancient Persian name is Haftorang. In the ancient Syrian culture, this star was the symbol for the sea God Dagon. In Greece, it was the symbol for the mythological monster Typhon. This is a white star, with a diameter twice that of our Sun and 14 times brighter. It is 23 light years from Earth. Fomalhaut is the alpha, or brightest, star in the constellation Pisces.

Alderbaran – The left eye of the Bull in the constellation Taurus, this Star is the Watcher of the East. The Ancient Persian name is Tascheter. This Star was called the Messenger of Light by the ancient Mesopotamians, for seeing the constellation Taurus meant the arrival of Spring, the beginning of their year. Alderbaran is an orange-red giant star roughly 68 light years from Earth, 125 times brighter and possessing a diameter 40 times greater than that of the Sun. Alderbaran is the alpha, or brightest, star in the constellation Taurus.

Antares – The heart of the Scorpion in the constellation Scorpio, this Star is the Watcher of the West. The Ancient Persian name is Satevis. Its red color inspired the name Antares, coming from the Greek Anti-Ares, or Rival of Mars. To the Ancient Egyptians, this star represented Selkit, the Scorpion Goddess, one of the many forms of Isis. This is a very large supergiant star, 700 times larger than the Sun, and 50 times brighter. Antares is the alpha, or brightest, star in the constellation Scorpio.

Runes

The word Rune itself means mystery or secret, and it is unknown where the Runes actually originated. The legend says that Odin Allfather invented the Runes, and hung for nine days and nine nights impaled on his own spear, high on the branches of the sacred tree Yggdrasl, to obtain this knowledge. This self-sacrifice was necessary to bring the gifts of knowledge and learning to humankind. Runes were used as early as the first century BC, but their origins may date back even further.

The name "futhark," like the word "alphabet," comes from the first six letters in the runic sequence (as opposed to Alpha-Beta). The futhark at first was made up of twenty-four letters, beginning with F and ending with O. It was used primarily by the Northern Germanic tribes of Denmark, Norway, Northern Germany, and Sweden. These are known as the Elder Futhark, which is the version we are working with here. The Blank Rune was added in the mid-1980s, and is therefore not included in a traditional rune cast.

The twenty-four letters are divided into groups of eight, call the Aett or Aettir (plural):

The First Aett – Freya – That Which Has Become

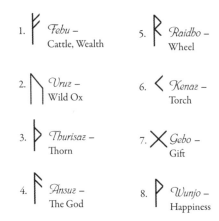

1. Fehu – Cattle, Wealth
2. Uruz – Wild Ox
3. Thurisaz – Thorn
4. Ansuz – The God
5. Raidho – Wheel
6. Kenaz – Torch
7. Gebo – Gift
8. Wunjo – Happiness

The Second Aett – Heimdall – That Which Is Becoming

1. Hagalaz – Hail
2. Nauthiz – Need
3. Isa – Ice
4. Jera – Harvest

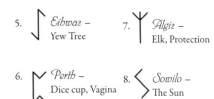

5. Eihwaz – Yew Tree
6. Perth – Dice cup, Vagina
7. Algiz – Elk, Protection
8. Sowilo – The Sun

The Third Aett – Tyr – That Which Will Be

1. Tiwaz – The Warrior God
2. Berkano – Birch Goddess
3. Ehwaz – Horse
4. Mannaz – Man
5. Laguz – Water
6. Ingwaz – The Earth God
7. Dagaz – Daybreak
8. Othila – Ancestral Property

Runes are traditionally made of wood or stones, since to the Pagans, Nature is a living, sacred entity. They are read as upright or reversed (merkstave); however, there is controversy on this, much like the Tarot. We have assigned each rune to a card in the Major Arcana, the one we feel best embodies the spirit of the card. Runes can be read in the same way the cards are, in various spreads or alone. One suggestion would be to use the Tarot cards, then pull a Rune as a Clarifier, or vice versa. Remember, however, that when doing a spread with Runes, it is very similar to doing a spread using only the Major Arcana.

Sabbat

The word "Sabbat" comes from Old French, but is believed to have originally derived from the Hebrew word "Shabbat," which means to cease or rest. The Sabbats, or Pagan/Neopagan festivals, associated with the four Suits of the Minor Arcana are:

(*NH – Northern Hemisphere, SH – Southern Hemisphere)

Swords: Ostara, the Spring Equinox (March 21st NH, Sept. 21st SH)

Wands: Litha, the Summer Solstice (June 21st NH, Dec. 21st SH)

Cups: Mabon, the Autumn Equinox (Sept. 21st NH, March 21st SH)

Pentacles: Yule, the Winter Solstice (Dec. 21st NH, June 21st SH)

These are also known as the "Quarter Days." The other four festival days (Imbolc, Beltane, Lughnasadh or Lammas, and Samhain) are the Fire Festivals, or Cross-Quarter Days.

Season

The Seasons associated with the four Suits are:

(*NH – Northern Hemisphere, SH – Southern Hemisphere)

Swords: Spring (March 21st NH, Sept. 21st SH)

Wands: Summer (June 21st NH, Dec. 21st SH)

Cups: Autumn (Sept. 21st NH, March 21st SH)

Pentacles: Winter (Dec. 21st NH, June 21st SH)

Stone

Since time immemorial, men have attached mystical, magickal, and curative properties to all types of stones, precious, semi-precious and garden variety alike. They have worn them as jewelry or amulets, carried them in mojo or gris-gris bags, or merely pocketed them as a protective talisman against whatever would cause harm or havoc.

The attributions of the Area of the Body, the Associated Illnesses, Stones, and Plants are inspired by *777 and other Qabalistic Writings of Aleister Crowley* by Aleister Crowley (see Resources and Recommended Reading). For more in depth workings, there is a glossary devoted specifically to Stones and Herbs and their magickal uses.

Suit

The Minor Arcana are divided into 4 main Suits:

Swords: Intellectual, Communication, Conflict, Study, Knowledge, Higher Learning, Thought
Swords may also appear as any of the following: Blades, Arrows, Bats, Air, Swords of Truth, Tomes, Eagles, Birds. Crystals, Cones.

Wands: Strength, Growth, Creativity, Imagination, Ideas, Passion, Courage, Energy, Power
Wands may also appear as any of the following: Rods, Staves, Spears, Scepters, Imps, Fire, Batons, Artifacts, Pipes, Wolves, Trees, Cylinders

Cups: Emotions, Subconscious, Instincts, Love, Intuition, Psychic Ability, Dreams, Visions
Cups may also appear as any of the following: Bowls, Vessels, Cauldrons, Chalices, Ghosts, Water, Hearts, Man, Bears, Rivers, Spheres

Pentacles: Financial and Material Matters, Prosperity, Fertility, Stability, Security, Employment

Pentacles may also appear as any of the following: Disks, Coins, Stones, Pumpkins, Earth, Earth Crystals, Shields, Sites, Buffaloes, Rings.

Temperament

The ancient Greek philosopher Hippocrates (460 - 370 BC) is credited with the concept of the Four Temperaments, or basic personality types or dispositions. Hippocrates believed that the Temperaments, or Humors, were caused by an abundance of one of the four types of bodily fluid. This theory was in later years completely discounted, but it is interesting to note how the Temperaments as stated by Hippocrates correspond to the four personality types as outlined by the Tarot. It is important to remember, however, that no person is only one type of personality, as we are all combinations of the four.

The Four Temperaments, or Personality Types are:

Sanguine, the Performer, corresponds to the element of Air and the body fluid Blood. The Sanguine temperament is outgoing and energetic, a natural entertainer, but also has tendencies of exaggeration and impatience while dealing with others.

Choleric, the Adventurer, corresponds to the element of Fire and the body fluid Yellow Bile. The Choleric personality is a born leader and independent to a fault, but can also be brash, opinionated, and judgmental.

Phlegmatic, the Intuitive, corresponds to the element of Water and the body fluid Phlegm. The Phlegmatic temperament is empathetic and compassionate, but can also be emotionally distant and stubborn to a fault.

Melancholic, the Thinker, corresponds to the element of Earth and the body fluid Black Bile. The Melancholic temperament is analytical, logical, and deliberate, but can also be suspicious and argumentative.

The Tetragrammaton

The Tetragrammaton is the four-lettered Divine Name, and too sacred to be spoken aloud. The word Tetragrammaton itself is a Greek word meaning literally "Word of Four Letters." The actual pronunciation is a mystery, as the Hebrew language does not contain any vowels, but it is said that whoever pronounces it correctly will receive all the wisdom of all the ages.

The four letters of the Name correspond with the four suits. Aleister Crowley among others believed that the letters reflect the order in which the world was created:

Yod: Fire, the first world to come into existence. This is considered to represent the Father, or in Tarot the King. This letter denotes the Primal Emergence, or Beginnings.

He: Water, the second world to come into existence. This is considered to represent the Mother, the Queen. This letter denotes the Transmission of Energy.

Vau: Air, the third world to come into existence. This is considered to represent the Son, or Knight. This letter denotes the Stabilization of Energy.

He: Earth, the fourth world to come into existence. This is considered to represent the Daughter, or Page. This letter denotes the Consolidation of Energy, and thusly, the cycle begins again.

Time of Day

There are specific times of day associated with the four elements, and can be beneficial when trying to determine timing in a reading:

Swords, being aligned with the East and the rising of the Sun, represent **Dawn**.

Wands, being aligned with the South and Fire, represent **Noon**, or the time when the Sun is at its peak.

Cups, being aligned with the West and the setting Sun, represent **Dusk**.

Pentacles, being aligned with the North and the Earth, represent **Midnight**.

Fool

O
The Fool

Alchemical Quality: Hot and Wet

Alchemical Symbol: △

Animal Energy: Coyote
(Wisdom and Folly)
Area of the Body Respiratory Tract
Associated Illness: Fluxes (Diarrhea)

Astrological Correspondence: ♅
Uranus

Astrological Quadruplicity:
   Cardinal Zodiac (Aggressive) – Libra ♎

   Fixed Zodiac (Rigid) – Aquarius ♒

   Mutable Zodiac (Passive) – Gemini ♊

Attribute: Intellectual
Blood Type: Type O
Celtic Tree Month: Mar 18 - April 14 – Alder
(Fearn)
Character Trait: Restlessness
Colors: Yellow, Red
Direction: East

Element: Air
Elemental: Slyphs, The Spirits of Air
Elemental King: Paralda
Esoteric Title: The Spirit of the Aethyr
Fundamental Force: Electromagnetic
Gematria Value: 1; 1,000; Numberless
Gender: Masculine

Hebrew Letter: Aleph, The Ox
(Mother letter)

Herb: Ginseng
Holy Creature: The Winged Man

I-Ching: 4: ䷃
Innocence, Immaturity and Learning

Keyword: Beginnings
Key Phrase: "I Think"
Lunar Phase: 1st Quarter Moon (waxing)
Magickal Organ: The Brain
Magickal Phrase: Noscere, To Know
Matter: Gas

Meanings:
  Upright:
  Adventure, change, childlike naivety,
  decisions, delusion, enchanting, energy,

enthusiasm, extravagance, fearless, fresh start, happiness, inexperience, innocence, inspiration, leap of faith, leaping into the unknown, movement, mystical, new beginnings, optimism, originality, possessing the tools and talent to move forward, possible travel, risk, spontaneity, starting the journey, the inner child, trial by fire, trusting your instincts, trusting, unconventional, unexpected, whimsical.

Reversed:

Ambiguity, carelessness, conventionality, cynicism, delirium, delusions, detriment, distraction, eccentricity, failure to follow through to completion, fear of the unknown, foolishness, frivolity, gambling, gullibility, instability, lack of experience, lack of motivation, liability and exposure, listen to your conscience, making assumptions, mania, mistakes, mistrust, not ready to take the next step, obsessive behavior, recklessness, unwilling to accept responsibility for actions, unwise move, wasted energy.

Musical Mood: "Ease On Down The Road" by Michael Jackson

Musical Note: E
Mythological Creatures: Gryphons and Pegasus
Numerology: Since the Fool is the number 0, He is everything and nothing, a blank slate on which to write.
Path on the Tree of Life: 11th Path, from Chokmah (Wisdom) to Kether (the Crown, First Manifestation)
Phase of Life: The Child
Physical Property: Motion
Plane: Mental
Plant: Aspen
Playing Card Suit: Spade

Possibility:

A new beginning is on the horizon. It could be a completely new start or perhaps another opportunity at a previous one. Either way a part of your life won't be the same anymore. You could start a new romance, or rediscover an old one. Get a new job, or perhaps a promotion at your current one. Now is a good time to allow yourself to be spontaneous and take a chance. Travel might show up in your plans.

Possible Influencing Cards:

    Chariot – surprises, unexpected events
    Hierophant – rigid thinking
    Devil – right road, wrong reason
    Sun – unexpected success
    Wheel of Fortune – materialism
    Psychological Function: Thoughts and Ideas
Quality: Active
Regent: Raphael
Royal Star: Aldebaran
Runes: The Fool does not have a specific Rune assigned, as all the Major Arcana are different aspects of the Journey of the Fool.
Sabbat: Ostara
Season: Spring
Stone: Topaz, Chalcedony
Suit: Swords
Temperament: Sanguine

Tetragrammaton: Vau

Time of Day: Dawn

1
The Magician

Alchemical Quality: Hot and Dry

Alchemical Symbol:

Animal Energy: Panther (Personal Power)
Area of the Body Cerebral and Nervous Systems
Associated Illness: Loss of Muscular Control

Astrological Correspondence: Mercury

Astrological Quadruplicity:

    Cardinal Zodiac (Aggressive) – Aries

    Fixed Zodiac (Rigid) – Leo

    Mutable Zodiac (Passive) – Sagittarius

Attribute: Spiritual, Creativity
Blood Type: Type B
Celtic Tree Month: May 13 - June 9 - Hawthorn (Uath)
Character Trait: Passion

Colors: Red, White
Direction: South
Element: Fire
Elemental: Salamanders, The Spirits of Fire
Elemental King: Djinn
Esoteric Title: The Magus of Power
Fundamental Force: Strong
Gematria Value: 2
Gender: Masculine

Hebrew Letter: Beth, The House (Double letter)

Herb: Frankincense
Holy Creature: The Winged Lion

I-Ching: 35: Success or Progress, Power, Creativity

Keyword: Manifestation
Key Phrase: "I Will"
Lunar Phase: Full Moon
Magickal Organ: Spirit
Magical Phrase: Velle, To Will
Matter: Energy

Meanings:

Upright:

Ability to manipulate your surroundings, action, adaptability, As above, so below, carpe diem – seize the day, catalyst, concentration, courage to succeed, creativity, dexterity, diplomacy, divination, great promise, ingenuity, initiative, innovations, intense level of focus, learning through practical application, manifestation of will into reality, mastery, movers and shakers, new life cycle, new skills, prioritizing, self awareness, self discipline, self-determination, skill with words, utilization of talents, versatility, willpower.

Reversed:

Abuse of power, agitator, arrested development, arrogance, blocked creativity, charlatan, con man, confusion, destructive behavior, dog and pony show, difficulties and delays, discontent, facades, hesitation, hindrance, illusions, imposters and posers, indecision, indirectness, lack of inspiration, manipulations, mis**Direction**, missed opportunity, mixed messages, overconfidence, scattered energies, sleight of hand, smoke screens, stagnation, trickster, ulterior motives, unrealistic expectations, weak willed.

Musical Mood: "King of Dreams" by Deep Purple
Musical Note: E
Mythological Creatures: Dragons and Phoenix
Numerology: 1 - New beginnings, confidence, creativity, possibility, potential
Path on the Tree of Life: 12th Path, from Binah (Understanding) to Kether (The Crown, First Manifestation)
Phase of Life: The Youth
Physical Property: Intensity
Plane: Spiritual
Plant: Vervain, Palm
Playing Card Suit: Club

Possibility:

It's time to focus the knowledge you have acquired and devote yourself to the achievement of your goal. Success cannot be achieved by giving half of your effort, any more than you can reach your destination by traveling halfway to it. You have consumed a vast amount of information, and tapped endless resources to get to this point, but it's not complete until you successfully apply it to the obstacle you face.

Possible Influencing Cards:
  5 of Wands - office politics
  7 of Wands - power struggles
  Chariot - overly aggressive
  Moon - manipulations
  Hanged Man - not taking necessary action
  High Priestess - misuse of power

Psychological Function: Energy and Desire
Quality: Immediate
Regent: Michael
Royal Star: Regulus

Runes: Ingwaz, The Earth God

Sabbat: Litha
Season: Summer
Stone: Opal, Agate
Suit: Wands
Temperament: Choleric

Tetragrammaton: Yod

Time of Day: Noon

2
The High Priestess

High Priestess

Alchemical Quality: Cold and Wet

Alchemical Symbol: ▽

Animal Energy: Lynx (Keeper of Secrets)
Area of the Body Lymphatic System
Associated Illness: Menstrual Disorders

Astrological Correspondence:
The Moon

Astrological Quadruplicity:

    Cardinal Zodiac (Aggressive) –
    Cancer

    Fixed Zodiac (Rigid) – Scorpio

    Mutable Zodiac (Passive) – Pisces

Attribute: Emotional
Blood Type: Type AB
Celtic Tree Month: Oct 28 - Nov 24 –
Reed (Ngetal)
Character Trait: Healing
Colors: Blue-Green, Gray
Direction: West
Element: Water

Elemental: Undines, The Spirits of Water
Elemental King: Nixsa
Esoteric Title: The Priestess of the Silver Star
Fundamental Force: Weak
Gematria Value: 3
Gender: Feminine

Hebrew Letter: Gimel,
The Camel (Double letter)

Herb: Lavender
Holy Creature: The Eagle

I-Ching: 29: Danger or Water,
Crisis, Abyss
Keyword: Secrets
Key Phrase: "I Feel"
Lunar Phase: 3rd Quarter (Waning)
Magical Organ: Heart
Magical Phrase: Audere, To Dare
Matter: Liquid

Meanings:
    Upright:
    Ancient wisdom, artistic and creative
    ability, enlightenment, fey, harmony,

illumination, inner wisdom, instinctual, intuition, keeping your thoughts to yourself, knowing and seeing, logical, meditation, mysteries, need for independence, occult, passive, past lives, peace, perceptive, psychic knowledge, secrets, silent counsel, subconscious, subtle, teacher, that which is hidden, thinking outside the box, untapped potential.

Reversed:
Conceit, failing to acknowledge the spiritual in life, failure to listen to your inner voice, false knowledge, fear of commitment, hypocrisy, ignorance, loss of self worth, manipulation, naivety, overly sensitive, prejudice, preoccupation, psychological disorders, reclusive, repression, secrets revealed, shallowness, superficiality, undeveloped talent, unstable, vagueness, untrustworthy, weakness of character.

Musical Mood: "Rhiannon" by Fleetwood Mac
Musical Note: G#
Mythological Creatures: Merfolk and Hippocampus
Numerology: 2 – Relationships, decisions, balance, cooperation, emotions

Path on the Tree of Life: 13th Path, from Tiphereth (Beauty) through Daath (Knowledge of Difference) to Kether (The Crown, First Manifestation)
Phase of Life: The Adult
Physical Property: Fluidity
Plane: Astral
Plant: Almond, Mugwort, Hazel
Playing Card Suit: Hearts

Possibility:
You have missed something, and although you are consciously aware of it in substance, you have yet to see its significance to your situation. You must look within yourself to find the correct path, or clear the path before you. Don't be afraid to admit to yourself who you are. The principles that control, or perhaps impede your progress, may very well not be the principles that you truly believe in.

Possible Influencing Cards:

7 of Swords – deceptions
Devil – hidden enemy
Emperor – misuse of information
Lovers – a secret affair
Moon – deceptions, hidden agendas

Hermit – answers are found within
Wheel of Fortune – legal proceedings

Psychological Function: Feelings and Emotions
Quality: Receptive
Regent: Gabriel
Royal Star: Antares

Runes: Perth, The Hidden

Sabbat: Mabon
Season: Autumn
Stone: Moonstone, Pearl, Crystal
Suit: Cups
Temperament: Phlegmatic

Tetragrammaton: Heh

Time of Day: Dusk

3
The Empress

Alchemical Quality: Cold and Dry

Alchemical Symbol:

Animal Energy: Rabbit (Fertility)
Area of the Body Genitals
Associated Illness: Venereal Diseases

Astrological Correspondence: Venus ♀

Astrological Quadruplicity:

    Cardinal Zodiac (Aggressive) – ♑
    Capricorn

    Fixed Zodiac (Rigid) – Taurus ♂

    Mutable Zodiac (Passive) – Virgo ♍

Attribute: Physical
Blood Type: Type A
Celtic Tree Month: Dec. 24 - Jan 20 – Birch Moon (Beth)
Character Trait: Hibernation
Colors: White, Black
Direction: North
Element: Earth
Elemental: Gnomes, The Spirits of Earth

Elemental King: Ghob
Esoteric Title: The Daughter of the Mighty Ones
Fundamental Force: Gravity
Gematria Value: 4
Gender: Feminine

Hebrew Letter: Daleth, The Door
(Double letter)

Herb: Acorn
Holy Creature: Winged Bull

I-Ching: 2 - Natural Response or Receptive, Responsive, Relaxing

Keyword: Fertility
Key Phrase: "I Have"
Lunar Phase: New Moon
Magical Organ: The Body and Senses
Magical Phrase: Tacere, To Keep Silent
Matter: Solid

Meanings:
  Upright:
  Abundance, birth, comfortable, creativity, encouragement, fertility, fruitfulness, good fortune, good luck, growth, hard work is

paying off, harmony, healing reassurance, material wealth, maternal love, nurturing, open to new ideas, parental guidance, passion, planning for the future, pregnancy, productive, prosperity, sensuality, the good life, The Great Mother, unconditional love, vitality.

Reversed:
Barrenness, creativity is blocked, demanding, depressing situation, destruction, discrimination, dissatisfaction, financial problems, frigidity, impatience, infidelity, material or emotional needs are unmet, materialism, mother complex, narrow minded, need for good counsel, poverty, problem or unwanted pregnancy, promiscuity, self inflicted pain, selfish, sexually manipulative, smothering, sterility, struggling to thrive, vanity.

Musical Mood: "She's Every Woman" by Garth Brooks
Musical Note: F#
Mythological Creatures: Giants and Elves
Numerology: 3 - Growth, enterprise, manifestation, unity, intuition

Path on the Tree of Life: 14th Path, from Binah (Understanding) to Chokmah (Wisdom)
Phase of Life: The Elder
Physical Property: Solidity
Plane: Physical
Plant: Rose, Clover, Myrtle
Playing Card Suit: Diamond

Possibility:

The path you have chosen will inspire growth and accomplishment in you, or if you are in a nurturing situation, someone that you care about. The seed you have planted, provided for, and nurtured is nearing fruition, and you will be pleased with the results. If you, or someone that you know, is pregnant, or perhaps hoping to be, the news will be good. It's time to get back to nature.

Possible Influencing Cards:
Chariot - improvement in finances
Lovers - sexual fulfillment
Magician - need for tact
Page of Cups - pregnancy
Star - abundance and pleasure
Sun - pregnancy

Psychological Function: Manifestation and Formation
Quality: Passive
Regent: Uriel
Royal Star: Fomalhaut

Runes: Berkano, The Birch Goddess

Sabbat: Yule
Season: Winter
Stone: Emerald, Turquoise
Suit: Pentacles
Temperament: Melancholic

Tetragrammaton: Heh

Time of Day: Midnight

4
The Emperor

Alchemical Quality: Hot and Dry

Alchemical Symbol:

Animal Energy: Elk (Strength and Nobility)
Area of the Body Head
Associated Illness: Apoplexy (Stroke)

Astrological Correspondence: Aries

Astrological Quadruplicity:

    Cardinal Zodiac (Aggressive) – Aries

    Fixed Zodiac (Rigid) – Leo

    Mutable Zodiac (Passive) Sagittarius

Attribute: Spiritual, Creativity
Blood Type: Type B
Celtic Tree Month: July 8 - Aug 4 – Holly (Tinne)
Character Trait: Passion
Colors: Red, White
Direction: South
Element: Fire

Elemental: Salamanders, The Spirits of Fire
Elemental King: Djinn
Esoteric Title: Sun of the Morning, Chief Among the Mighty
Fundamental Force: Strong
Gematria Value: 90
Gender: Masculine

Hebrew Letter: Heh, The Window (Single letter)

Herb: Sandalwood
Holy Creature: The Winged Lion

I-Ching: 28 – Excess, Pressure, Tension

Keyword: Power
Key Phrase: "I Will"
Lunar Phase: Full Moon
Magical Organ: The Spirit
Magical Phrase: Velle, To Will
Matter: Energy

Meanings:
    Upright:
    Action, assertiveness, authority, benevolence, civilization, clarity of vision,

competitive, controlled passion, forcefulness, healthy ambition, law, leadership, legacy, logic, long term achievement, manifestation, mind over matter, order and structure, organization, paternal love, powerful ally, protection, rational thought, reasonable, regulation, responsibility, ruling power, security, stability, The Great Father, the high king, wisdom from experience, worldly power.

Reversed:

Being manipulated for someone else's gain, bully, chauvinism, cowardice, egocentric, failure, father complex, immaturity, impatience, indecision, irresponsibility, juvenile, lack of progress, lack of self control, loss of control, loss or abuse of power, megalomaniac, overcompensation, prejudice, preoccupied with sex, problems with authority, rebellion, rigidity, subservience, tyranny, unwise decisions, vacillation, weakness.

Musical Mood: "Broadsword" by Jethro Tull
Musical Note: C
Mythological Creatures: Dragons and Phoenix

Numerology: 4 - Rest, inactivity, patience, stability, legal matters
Path on the Tree of Life: 28th Path, from Yesod (Dreams) to Netzach (Will)
Phase of Life: The Youth
Physical Property: Intensity
Plane: Spiritual
Plant: Tiger Lily, Geranium
Playing Card Suit: Clubs

Possibility:

It is not good to be passively waiting right now, as the time for action has arrived. If you are not the one to assert control over the circumstances at hand, seek out the person you know that can. Allowing the situation to run its course, or stagnate in committee, will produce an undesired outcome. If you are a father, desire to be a father, or know of someone that is or does, good news is coming.

Possible Influencing Cards:

5 of Pentacles – dictatorship
Fool – struggle for control
High Priest – egomaniac
King of Pentacles – resistance to change
World – peace will prevail

Psychological Function: Energy and Desire
Quality: Immediate
Regent: Michael
Royal Star: Regulus

Runes: Mannaz, A Man

Sabbat: Litha
Season: Summer
Stone: Ruby
Suit: Wands
Temperament: Choleric

Tetragrammaton: Yod

Time of Day: Noon

5
The Hierophant

Hierophant

Alchemical Quality: Hot and Wet

Alchemical Symbol:

Animal Energy: Rhino (Ancient Wisdom)
Area of the Body Shoulders and Arms
Associated Illness: Indigestion

Astrological Correspondence:
Aquarius

Astrological Quadruplicity:

    Cardinal Zodiac (Aggressive) –
    Libra

    Fixed Zodiac (Rigid) – Aquarius

    Mutable Zodiac (Passive) – Gemini

Attribute: Intellectual
Blood Type: Type O
Celtic Tree Month: Sept 2 - Sept 29 – Vine (Muin)
Character Trait: Restlessness
Colors: Yellow, Red
Direction: East
Element: Air

Elemental: Sylphs, The Spirits of Air
Elemental King: Paralda
Esoteric Title: The Magus of the Eternal
Fundamental Force: Electromagnetic
Gematria Value: 6
Gender: Masculine

Hebrew Letter: Vau, The Nail
(Single letter)

Herb: Thistle
Holy Creature: The Winged Man

I-Ching: 18 – Decay or Repair,
Responsibility

Keyword: Knowledge
Key Phrase: "I Think"
Lunar Phase: 1st Quarter Moon
Magical Organ: The Brain
Magical Phrase: Noscere, To Know
Matter: Gas

Meanings:
  Upright:
  Advice, alliances, blind faith, celibacy, commitment, conformity, conservative, conventional, counselor, educa-

tion, exposition, inspiration, loyalty, morality, old school, possible marriage, practical, sincere and truthful, social mores, spiritual authority, status quo, stubbornness, teacher, the "powers that be," too much emphasis on appearances, traditional, well thought out arguments.

Reversed:
Arrogance, ascetical, disloyal, dishonest, distorting the truth, dogmatic, extremism, false prophet, fanaticism, free thinking, fundamentalism, hidden agendas, inflexibility, intolerance, irreverent, lack of imagination, nonconformist, nontraditional, outspoken, perverse, plagiarism, question authority, rebelling for no reason, self indulgent, speaking of things of which you have no knowledge, unconventional, unethical, unorthodox.

Musical Mood: "Free Will" by Rush
Musical Note: C#
Mythological Creatures: Gryphons and Pegasus
Numerology: 5 - Changes, disruptions, instability, conflict, uncertainty
Path on the Tree of Life: 16th Path, from

Chesed (Mercy) to Chokmah (Wisdom)
Phase of Life: The Child
Physical Property: Motion
Plane: Mental
Plant: Mallow
Playing Card Suit: Spades

Possibility:

Someone, or something, of an orthodox nature, is going to have an effect on your current path. Conformity to traditional beliefs or dogmatic principles of a religious nature is a matter of issue with you, or someone that you know. It is not necessary to abandon ones morality or social conscious to change ones belief, as they are the reason for having a belief. You might be invited to a church wedding or event.

Possible Influencing Cards:
4 of Cups – spiritual disillusionment
Death – unavoidable change
Emperor – refusal to accept change
High Priestess – inner conflicts
Lovers – possible marriage
Sun – possible religious event

Psychological Function: Thoughts and Ideas
Quality: Active
Regent: Raphael
Royal Star: Aldebaran

Runes: Othila, The Ancestral

Sabbat: Ostara
Season: Spring
Stone: Topaz
Suit: Swords
Temperament: Sanguine

Tetragrammaton: Vau

Time of Day: Dawn

6
The Lovers
(This card is a duality)

Lovers

Alchemical Quality: Hot and Wet, Cold and Wet

Alchemical Symbol: △ ▽

Animal Energy: Otter (Joy and Discovery)
Area of the Body Lungs
Associated Illness: Pneumonia

Astrological Correspondence: ♊
Gemini
Cancer ♋

Astrological Quadruplicity:

    Cardinal Zodiac (Aggressive) – ♎
    Libra –
    Cancer ♋

    Fixed Zodiac (Rigid) – ♒
    Aquarius –
    Scorpio ♏

    Mutable Zodiac (Passive) – ♊
    Gemini –
    Pisces ♓

Attributes: Intellectual and Emotional

Blood Type: Type O and Type AB
Character Trait: Restlessness and Healing
Colors: Yellow, Red, Blue-Green, and Gray
Direction: East and West
Element: Air and Water
Elemental: Sylphs and Undines, The Spirits of Air and Water
Elemental King: Paralda and Nixsa
Esoteric Title: The Children of the Voice, The Oracle of the Mighty Gods
Fundamental Force: Electromagnetic and Weak
Gematria Value: 7
Gender: Masculine and Feminine

Hebrew Letter: Zain, The Sword
(Single letter)

Herb: Thyme
Holy Creatures: The Winged Man and The Eagle

I-Ching: 8 – Unity or Teamwork, ䷇ Agreement, Friendship

Keyword: Commitment
Key Phrase: "I Think" and "I Feel"
Lunar Phase: 1st and 3rd Quarter Moon

Magical Organ: The Brain and The Heart
Magical Phrase: Noscere, To Know and Audere, To Dare
Matter: Gas and Liquid

Meanings:

Upright:

Choices, commitment, communication, decisions, dilemma, engagement, evolving relationship, fidelity, harmony, inspirations, integrity, love affairs, making responsible choices, marriage, moral stability, need for balance, negotiations, personal relationships, personal values, possible short term travel, responsibilities, stick to your resolve, temptations, trust, union.

Reversed:

Bad choices, being used, conflicting advice, contradictions, difficulties, disillusionment, divorce, envy, fear of commitment, fickle, hedonism, hurt feelings, immaturity, indiscretions, infidelity, interference, irresponsibility, jealousy, lack of tact, love triangles, lust, not following your heart, pettiness, physical cruelty, promiscuity, seduction, strong opposition, temptations, vacilation

Musical Mood: "Lips of an Angel" by Hinder
Musical Note: D
Mythological Creatures: Gryphons and Pegasus, Merfolk and Hippocampus
Numerology: 6 – Home life, harmony, nostalgia, responsibility, reconciliation
Path on the Tree of Life: 17th Path, from Tiphereth (Beauty) to Binah (Understanding)
Phase of Life: The Child and The Adult
Physical Property: Motion and Fluidity
Plane: Mental and Astral
Plant: Hybrids, Orchids
Playing Card Suit: Spades and Hearts

Possibility:

Giving a commitment to someone or something can at times seem a difficult choice to make. However, if after thought the doubt remains then your choice is clear. A commitment with harbored doubts is not a commitment at all, but a façade of devotion that will inevitably be exposed, leaving behind feelings of rancorousness. A commitment either is or it isn't; there aren't any trial versions.

Possible Influencing Cards:

3 of Cups – wedding party
Chariot – possible separation, end to relationship
Devil – physical attraction
Empress – sexual fulfillment
Hermit – detachment, distance
Magician – indecision, imbalance of power

Psychological Function: Thoughts and Ideas, Feelings and Emotions
Quality: Active and Receptive
Regent: Raphael and Gabriel
Royal Star: Aldebaran and Antares

Runes: Gebo, The Gift

Sabbat: Ostara and Mabon
Season: Spring and Autumn
Stone: Alexandrite, Tourmaline
Suit: Air and Water
Temperament: Sanguine and Phlegmatic

Tetragrammaton: Vau and Heh

Time of Day: Dawn and Dusk

Chariot

Alchemical Quality: Cold and Wet

Alchemical Symbol:

Animal Energy: Horse (Travel and Power)
Area of the Body: Stomach
Associated Illness: Rheumatism

Astrological Correspondence:
Cancer

Astrological Quadruplicity:

　Cardinal Zodiac (Aggressive) –
　Cancer

　Fixed Zodiac (Rigid) – Scorpio

　Mutable Zodiac (Passive) – Pisces ♓

Attribute: Emotional
Blood Type: Type AB
Celtic Tree Month: Jan 21 - Feb 17 – Rowan Moon (Luis)
Character Trait: Healing
Colors: Blue-Green, Gray
Direction: West
Element: Water

Elemental: Undines, The Spirits of Water
Elemental King: Nixsa
Esoteric Title: The Child of the Powers of the Waters, The Lord of the Triumph of Light
Fundamental Force: Weak
Gematria Value: 8, Infinity
Gender: Feminine

Hebrew Letter: Cheth, The Fence
(Single letter)

Herb: Mint
Holy Creature: The Eagle

I-Ching: 32 – Duration or
Endurance, Purposeful, Persistent

Keyword: Progress
Key Phrase: "I Feel"
Lunar Phase: 3rd Quarter Moon
Magical Organ: The Heart
Magical Phrase: Audere, To Dare
Matter: Liquid

Meanings:
　Upright:
　Action, ambition, centered, conquest, control, decision, decisiveness, determination,

focused, graceful winner, grounded, heavy handed control, journey, making progress, mental control and strength, perseverance, pioneering spirit, prestige, resisting temptation, resolutions, responsible, self discipline, self reliance, sticking to the game plan, taking matters into your own hands, triumph over adversity, victory, warrior spirit, well balanced.

Reversed:

Arrogance, avarice, blind or unhealthy ambition, chaos, complete disregard for others, conquered, destruction, difficulty completing tasks, egotistical, envy, failure, forced compromise or cooperation, imbalance, lack of direction, legal problems, outdated ideas, overly high expectations, overwhelmed, plans fall through, pride, quarrels, resentment, ruthlessness, sore loser, stagnation, substance abuse, superstitious, suspicion, unfair, unhealthy addictions, wrong use of energy or talent.

Musical Mood: "Highway Star" by Deep Purple
Musical Note: D#
Mythological Creatures: Merfolk and

Hippocampus
Numerology: 7 – Mystical, spiritual, dreams, discipline, struggles
Path on the Tree of Life: 18th Path, from Geburah (Justice) to Binah (Understanding)
Phase of Life: The Adult
Physical Property: Fluidity
Plane: Astral
Plant: Lotus
Playing Card Suit: Hearts

Possibility:

Look to yourself to achieve your objective. Your self-discipline and determination brought you this far, and will take you as far as you need to go. Don't let impatience derail your efforts, stay the course that you have already defined. Action for the sake of action may adversely affect the outcome. If you are waiting on action or response from someone go to them. An opportunity for travel may be near at hand.

Possible Influencing Cards:

High Priest – strong willed, focused
Knight of Swords – transportation problems

Magician – focus and concentration
Tower – perseverance is needed for success
World – success will be yours

Psychological Function: Feelings and Emotions
Quality: Receptive
Regent: Gabriel
Royal Star: Antares

Runes: Raidho, The Journey

Sabbat: Mabon
Season: Autumn
Stone: Amber
Suit: Cups
Temperament: Phlegmatic

Tetragrammaton: Heh

Time of Day: Dusk

Alchemical Quality: Hot and Dry

Alchemical Symbol:

Animal Energy: Elephant (Power and Gentle Strength)
Area of the Body Heart
Associated Illness: Heart Attack

Astrological Correspondence: Leo

Astrological Quadruplicity:

    Cardinal Zodiac (Aggressive) – Aries

    Fixed Zodiac (Rigid) – Leo

    Mutable Zodiac (Passive) – Sagittarius

Attribute: Spiritual, Creativity
Blood Type: Type B
Celtic Tree Month: Sept 30 - Oct 27 – Ivy (Gort)
Character Trait: Passion
Colors: Red, White
Direction: South
Element: Fire

Elemental: Salamanders, The Spirits of Fire
Elemental King: Djinn
Esoteric Title: The Daughter of the Flaming Sword, Leader of the Lion
Fundamental Force: Strong
Gematria Value: 9
Gender: Masculine

Hebrew Letter: Teth, The Serpent
(Single letter)

Herb: Borage
Holy Creature: The Winged Lion

I-Ching: 11 – Prosperity or Peace, Harmony, Benevolence

Keyword: Strength
Key Phrase: "I Will"
Lunar Phase: Full Moon
Magical Organ: The Spirit
Magical Phrase: Velle, To Will
Matter: Energy

Meanings:
    Upright:
    Catching more flies with honey than with vinegar, charisma, conviction,

courage, desire, diplomacy, empowerment, fortitude, generosity, gentle control, harmonious balance, harnessing destructive forces, inner strength, opportunities will present themselves, optimism, overcoming obstacles, patience, quiet authority, self confidence, self control, self esteem, self worth, selfless love, sheer will, tact, taming the wilder nature of yourself, virility, warranted pride, will, wisdom.

Reversed:
Abuse of power, anger, argumentative, base urges, brute strength is ineffective, concession, controlling, cowardice, deception, defeatist attitude, dependency, depression, destructive behavior, envy, failure to act, helplessness, illness, inertia, insecurity, jealousy, lack of determination, lack of integrity, misdirected aggression, self abuse, self doubt, self fear, self pity, tyranny, vanity, vulnerability, weakness.

Musical Mood: "I Will Survive" by Gloria Gaynor
Musical Note: E
Mythological Creatures: Dragons and Phoenix

Numerology: 8 – Material progress, security, expansion, priorities, advancement
Path on the Tree of Life: 19th Path, from Geburah (Justice) to Chesed (Mercy)
Phase of Life: The Youth
Physical Property: Intensity
Plane: Spiritual
Plant: Sunflower
Playing Card Suit: Clubs

Possibility:
There is no greater strength than the mastery of restraint. Now is not the time to assert your will upon someone in an attempt to achieve your objective. The more you act as the irresistible force the greater the resolve of the immovable object that is blocking your path. Apply patience and diplomacy to the situation, and allow the obstacle the opportunity to move on its own. Quiet confidence and composure is the best course.

Possible Influencing Cards:
Chariot – hard work brings success
Death – stay calm in the face of change
Hanged Man – patience is needed
Temperance – long road ahead to reach the goal

Psychological Function: Energy and Desire
Quality: Immediate
Regent: Michael
Royal Star: Regulus

Runes: Uruz, The Wild Ox

Sabbat: Litha
Season: Summer
Stone: Cat's Eye
Suit: Wands
Temperament: Choleric

Tetragrammaton: Yod

Time of Day: Noon

9
The Hermit

Hermit

Alchemical Quality: Cold and Dry

Alchemical Symbol:

Animal Energy: Snow Leopard (Seeker of Clarity and Insight)
Area of the Body: The Back
Associated Illness: Paralysis, Spinal Injury

Astrological Correspondence: Virgo ♍

Astrological Quadruplicity:

    Cardinal Zodiac (Aggressive) – ♑ Capricorn

    Fixed Zodiac (Rigid) – Taurus ♂

    Mutable Zodiac (Passive) – Virgo ♍

Attribute: Physical
Blood Type: Type A
Celtic Tree Month: Aug 5 – Sept – Hazel (Coll)
Character Trait: Hibernation
Colors: White, Black

Direction: North
Element: Earth
Elemental: Gnomes, The Spirits of Earth
Elemental King: Ghob
Esoteric Title: The Prophet of the Eternal, The Magus of the Voice of Power
Fundamental Force: Gravity
Gematria Value: 10
Gender: Feminine

Hebrew Letter: Yod, The Hand ✏ (Single letter)

Herb: Asafoetida
Holy Creature: The Winged Bull

I-Ching: 26 – Grounding or The Power that Restrains, Harnessing Power, Control

Keyword: Introspection
Key Phrase: "I Have"
Lunar Phase: New Moon
Magical Organ: The Body and Senses
Magical Phrase: Tacere, To Keep Silent
Matter: Solid

Meanings:

Upright:

Assimilation, atonement, attunement, caution, contemplations, discretion, disguise, enlightenment, evolved, guidance, in depth analysis, introspection, intuition, isolation, loneliness, need to let go of old grudges, open minded, personal space, prudence, rest, solitary, soul searching, spiritual pursuits, spiritual sabbatical, time to re-examine priorities, vigilance, withdrawal.

Reversed:

Anti-social, bereavement, boredom, conceited, confusion, deception, depression, excitability, fear, groundless suspicions, hypersensitive, hypochondria, immaturity, imprudent, irresponsibility, isolation, lack of communication, loneliness, making excuses for your behavior, obstinacy, paranoia, perfectionist, personal façades, reclusive, self deception, spiritually vacant, victimization.

Musical Mood: "Kashmir" by Led Zeppelin
Musical Note: F

Mythological Creatures: Giants and Elves
Numerology: 9 – Satisfaction, fulfillment, luck, complacency, just desserts
Path on the Tree of Life: 20th Path, from Tiphereth (Beauty) to Chesed (Mercy)
Phase of Life: The Elder
Physical Property: Solidity
Plane: Physical
Plant: Snowdrop, Lily, Narcissus
Playing Card Suit: diamonds

Possibility:

Right now is your opportunity to seek out solitude and take some time for reflection. Find a place where you can leave the world behind and eliminate all your constraints of time and presence for a while. Rest and contemplation will give you new eyes to see your situation with, and in time the answers will come. Participate in something that you no longer have the time to do, or have always wished that you had time to do.

Possible Influencing Cards:

Devil – secret enemies will be exposed
High Priestess – secrets, sacred knowledge

Star – the answer to your question is within
World – turning your back on society

Psychological Function: Manifestation and Formation
Quality: Passive
Regent: Uriel
Royal Star: Fomalhaut

Runes: Kenaz, The Torch

Sabbat: Yule
Season: Winter
Stone: Peridot
Suit: Pentacles
Temperament: Melancholic

Tetragrammaton: Heh

Time of Day: Midnight

Alchemical Quality: All
Alchemical Symbol: All
Animal Energy: Purple Martin (Luck)
Area of the Body Digestive System
Associated Illness: Gout (Joint Inflammation)

Astrological Correspondence: Jupiter

Astrological Quadruplicity: All
    Note: The Wheel of Fortune has in its symbology four divine creatures, each guarding a corner of the Wheel. The four creatures correspond with the four fixed signs of the Zodiac; the Winged Bull for Taurus (Earth/Pentacles); the Winged Lion for Leo (Fire/Wands); The Eagle for Scorpio (Water/Cups); and the Winged Human for Aquarius (Air/Swords). This is the embodiment of Fate, or forces that are beyond our immediate control. As a note, the Eagle may at first seem an incorrect choice to represent Water, but was selected due to the fish scale-like texture of the great raptor's legs.

Attribute: All
Blood Type: All

Character Trait: All
Colors: All
Direction: All
Element: All
Elemental: All
Elemental King: All
Esoteric Title: The Lord of the Forces of Life
Fundamental Force: All
Gematria Value: 20
Gender: Both

Hebrew Letter: Kaph, The Palm of the Hand (Double letter)

Herb: Clover
Holy Creature: All

I-Ching: 24 - Repeating or Return, Renewal, Rebirth

Keyword: Cycles
Key Phrase: All
Lunar Phase: All
Magical Organ: All
Magical Phrase: All
Matter: All

Meanings:

Upright:

Abundance, activity and excitement, advancements, catching a break, cause and effect, coincidences, cycles, destiny, expansion, fortune smiles on you, getting caught up in the moment, good luck, improvements, laws of Karma, movement, positive changes, prosperity, rapid changes, roll of the dice, seize the moment, turning point, unexpected success, what goes around comes around, winds of change.

Reversed:

Adversity, bad call, bad luck, blaming others for your mistakes, can't break free, carelessness, changes are difficult, disappointment, disillusionment, failure, inconsistency, insecurity, instability, limited vision, luck of the draw, materialistic, missed opportunities, negligence, not seeing the big picture, poor judgment, retribution, resisting necessary changes, setbacks, shallow, stagnation, stuck in the same old routines, timing is off, victim of misfortune.

Musical Mood: "Turn, Turn, Turn" by The

Byrds
Musical Note: All
Mythological Creatures: All
Numerology: 10 – Completions, resolutions, beginning and/or ending of a cycle
Path on the Tree of Life: 21st Path, from Netzach (Will) to Chesed (Mercy)
Phase of Life: All
Physical Property: All
Plane: All
Plant: Hyssop, Oak, Poplar, Fig
Playing Card Suit: All

Possibility:

If it seems that progress has been slow, or nonexistent, that is about to change. A chance to improve your situation and move dramatically closer to your goal is imminent. A fortuitous event may signal a more advantageous chapter in your life. You may be focusing on what is wrong so intently that an opportunity for a reversal of fortune is going unnoticed. Now is the time to meet opportunity with preparation.

Possible Influencing Cards:

2 of Pentacles – luck in gambling

8 of Wands – caught up in a whirlwind of activity
Chariot – great success after a rapid turn of events
Fool – right place, right time
Star – time is right to take a gamble
Tower – brace for bad luck ahead

Psychological Function: All
Quality: All
Regent: All
Royal Star: All

Runes: Jera, The Good Harvest

Sabbat: All
Season: All
Stone: Amethyst, Lapis Lazuli
Suit: All
Temperament: All
Tetragrammaton: All four letters
Time of Day: All

11
Justice

Justice

Alchemical Quality: Hot and Wet

Alchemical Symbol:

Animal Energy: Camel (Balance and Equality)
Area of the Body Liver
Associated Illness: Kidney Disease

Astrological Correspondence:
Libra

Astrological Quadruplicity:

    Cardinal Zodiac (Aggressive) –
    Libra

    Fixed Zodiac (Rigid) – Aquarius

    Mutable Zodiac (Passive) – Gemini

Attribute: Intellectual
Blood Type: Type O
Character Trait: Restlessness
Colors: Yellow, Red
Direction: East
Element: Air
Elemental: Sylphs, The Spirits of Air

Elemental King: Paralda
Esoteric Title: The Daughter of the Lords of Truth; The Ruler of the Balance
Fundamental Force: Electromagnetic
Gematria Value: 30
Gender: Masculine

Hebrew Letter: Lamed,
The Ox Goad (Single letter)

Herb: Sage
Holy Creature: The Winged Man

I-Ching: 55 – Zenith or
Abundance, Plenty, Harvest

Keyword: Responsibility
Key Phrase: "I Think"
Lunar Phase: New Moon
Magical Organ: The Brain
Magical Phrase: Noscere, To Know
Matter: Gas

Meanings:
    Upright:
    Agreements, arbitration, balance, being judged, cause and effect, clarity, decision, emotional housecleaning, equilibrium,

fairness, harmony, impartiality, just desserts, Karma resolved, laws of Karma, legal matters, logic, long arm of the law, marriage/divorce documents, neutrality, rationality, reason, rectification is necessary, resolution of conflict, responsibility, righteousness, seek legal advice, stability, subrogation, vindication, what goes around comes around

Reversed:
Being judged unfairly, being taken advantage of, bias, bigotry, complications, delays, discrimination, disharmony, dishonesty, extremes, getting railroaded, imbalance, indecisive, inequality, intemperate, intolerance, illogical, jumping to conclusions, lack of integrity, legal proceedings not in your favor, manipulation, negativity, prejudice, red tape, separations, unable to make a commitment, underhanded dealings, vigilante justice.

Musical Mood: "Deserve" by Marillion
Musical Note: F#
Mythological Creatures: Gryphons and Pegasus

Numerology: 2 – Relationships, decisions, balance, cooperation, emotions
Path on the Tree of Life: 22nd Path, from Tiphereth (Beauty) to Geburah (Justice)
Phase of Life: The Child
Physical Property: Motion
Plane: Mental
Plant: Aloe
Playing Card Suit: Spades

Possibility:

Which side of the scale have you been living on? It's time for the counterweight to fall for those that are beholden, and then the scales will come to rest with all things being equal? Karmic equilibrium is forthcoming and reparation is due. It's time to pay the piper. Legal matters are soon to be at issue, or should be initiated if you are the one is owed. Any pending matters of adjudication will be ruled upon in short time.

Possible Influencing Cards:
　7 of Wands – legal struggles
　10 of Swords – legal losses
　Emperor – legal issues for the better
　Hanged Man – understanding and

tolerance needed
　High Priestess – legal issues for the worse
　Judgment – time to take responsibility for your actions
　Star – legal wins

Psychological Function: Thoughts and Ideas
Quality: Active
Regent: Raphael
Royal Star: Aldebaran

Runes: Tiwaz, Justice

Sabbat: Ostara
Season: Spring
Stone: Emerald
Suit: Swords
Temperament: Sanguine

Tetragrammaton: Vau

Time of Day: Dawn

12
The Hanged Man

Alchemical Quality: Cold and Wet

Alchemical Symbol:

Animal Energy: Opossum (Appearances and Facades)
Area of the Body: Organs of Nutrition
Associated Illness: Chill

Astrological Correspondence: Ψ
Neptune

Astrological Quadruplicity:

Cardinal Zodiac (Aggressive) – Cancer

Fixed Zodiac (Rigid) – Scorpio

Mutable Zodiac (Passive) – Pisces

Attribute: Emotional
Blood Type: Type AB
Celtic Tree Month: Feb 18 - Mar 17 – Ash (Nuin)
Character Trait: Healing
Colors: Blue-Green, Gray
Direction: West

Element: Water
Elemental: Undines, The Spirits of Water
Elemental King: Nixsa
Esoteric Title: The Spirit of the Mighty Waters
Fundamental Force: Weak
Gematria Value: 40
Gender: Feminine

Hebrew Letter: Mem, Water (Mother letter)

Herb: Coriander
Holy Creature: The Eagle

I-Ching: 49 – Changing or Revolution, Reform

Keyword: Decisions

Key Phrase: "I Feel"
Lunar Phase: 3rd Quarter
Magical Organ: The Heart
Magical Phrase: Audere, To Keep Silent
Matter: Liquid

Meanings:
  Upright:

Choices, cleaning out the emotional closet, commitment to a cause, complete turnaround, devotion, dilemma, enlightenment, foresight, freedom from limitations, humility, impasse, initiation, inspiration, isolation, letting go, limbo, rebirth, repentance, self contemplation, self sacrifice, separation, spiritual growth, standstill, stasis, stuck in a rut, submission, surrender, suspension, transformation, turning point, withstanding temptations.

Reversed:
Apathy, arrogance, emotional imprisonment, envy, false imprisonment, false promises, fear of commitment, futility, hidden agendas, indecision, irresponsibility, lack of commitment, loss of faith, materialism, misdirection, mixed emotions, negativity, poor decisions, preoccupation, ready to make a move, rigidity, self centered, selfishness, unnecessary martyrdom, unwilling to take good advice, uselessness, wallowing in self pity, wasted effort.

Musical Mood: "Self Esteem" by The Offsprings

Musical Note: G#
Mythological Creatures: Merfolk and Hippocampus
Numerology: 3 – Growth, enterprise, manifestation, unity, intuition
Path on the Tree of Life: 23rd Path, from Hod (Communication) to Geburah (Justice)
Phase of Life: The Adult
Physical Property: Fluidity
Plane: Astral
Plant: Lotus, All Water Plants
Playing Card Suit: Hearts

Possibility:
You must earn what it is that you wish to acquire with selflessness and generosity of spirit. Self-sacrifice is needed to best provide for the welfare of another, or to increase the value of the sum of the parts. Your path to success will require you to be the supportive understudy, waiting in the wings. Consider the value of paying your karma in advance, because all things will inevitably come in to balance.

Possible Influencing Cards:
    8 of Pentacles – being overworked
    Death – letting go of an old way of life
    Devil – sacrifices must be made to maintain the status quo
    Lovers – uneven relationship
    Magician – acting in your own best interests
    Strength – need for more patience
    Temperance – false promises

Psychological Function: Feelings and Emotions
Quality: Receptive
Regent: Gabriel
Royal Star: Antares

Runes: Isa, Ice

Sabbat: Mabon
Season: Autumn
Stone: Beryl, Aquamarine
Suit: Cups
Temperament: Phlegmatic

Tetragrammaton: Vau

Time of Day: Dusk

13

Death

Alchemical Quality: Cold and Wet

Alchemical Symbol:

Animal Energy: Snake (Rebirth)
Area of the Body Intestines
Associated Illness: Cancer

Astrological Correspondence:
Scorpio

Astrological Quadruplicity:

    Cardinal Zodiac (Aggressive) –
    Cancer

    Fixed Zodiac (Rigid) – Scorpio

    Mutable Zodiac (Passive) – Pisces ♓

Attribute: Emotional
Blood Type: Type AB
Character Trait: Healing
Colors: Blue-Green, Gray
Direction: West
Element: Water
Elemental: Undines, The Spirits of Water
Elemental King: Nixsa

Esoteric Title: The Child of the Great Transformers; The Lord of the Gate of Death
Fundamental Force: Weak
Gematria Value: 50
Gender: Feminine

Hebrew Letter: Nun, The Fish (Single letter)

Herb: Parsley
Holy Creature: The Eagle

I-Ching: 12 – Stagnation or Stopped, Powerless, Obstructed

Keyword: Transition
Key Phrase: "I Feel"
Lunar Phase: 3rd Quarter Moon
Magical Organ: The Heart
Magical Phrase: Audere, To Dare
Matter: Liquid

Meanings:
    The Death Card almost never refers to physical death. This is a card of Change.

Upright:

Alterations, consciousness, destruction, detachment, elimination, ending of a situation, facing the music, immortality, inheritance, intensity, lack of productivity, leaving the past behind, letting go, liberation, major changes, massive upheaval, out with the old and in with the new, possible birth of a child, purging, rebirth, reconstruction, rejuvenation, renewal, resignation, resourcefulness, transformation, transition.

Reversed:

Abusive behavior, changes for the worse, clinging to the past, cruelty, decay, depression, deterioration, dishonesty, envy, exhaustion, forced sacrifice, impulsiveness, inertia, involuntary reactions, jealousy, lethargy, outdated ideas, pessimism, promiscuity, rage, resisting or fear of change, revolution, rising from the ashes like a phoenix, ruin, secrets, self centered, stagnation, take advantage of downtime to prepare for the future.

Musical Mood: "Changes" by David Bowie
Musical Note: G

Mythological Creatures: Merfolk and Hippocampus
Numerology: 4 – Rest, inactivity, patience, stability, legal matters
Path on the Tree of Life: 24th Path, from Netzach (Will) to Tiphereth (Beauty)
Phase of Life: The Adult
Physical Property: Fluidity
Plane: Astral
Plant: Cactus
Playing Card Suit: Hearts

Possibility:

This represents a point of adjustment for you in that a significant change is on the horizon. Some of the possibilities are move to a new home, change jobs, reach the end of a relationship, or perhaps get a divorce. What is about to occur will change your life dramatically, but it may only appear to be for the worse. The only constant of existence that can be counted on is change, like it or not, change will still occur.

Possible Influencing Cards:

Chariot – caught in a crossfire of activity
Fool – forced new beginnings
Lovers – end of a relationship
Tower – personal loss or crisis

Psychological Function: Emotions and Feelings
Quality: Receptive
Regent: Gabriel
Royal Star: Antares

Runes: Ehwaz, The Horse

Sabbat: Mabon
Season: Autumn
Stone: Snakestone
Suit: Cups
Temperament: Phlegmatic

Tetragrammaton: Heh

Time of Day: Dusk

Temperance

Alchemical Quality: Hot and Dry

Alchemical Symbol:

Animal Energy: Manatee (Gentleness)
Area of the Body Hips and Thighs
Associated Illness: Apoplexy (Stroke)

Astrological Correspondence:
Sagittarius

Astrological Quadruplicity:

Cardinal Zodiac (Aggressive) – Aries

Fixed Zodiac (Rigid) – Leo

Mutable Zodiac (Passive) –
Sagittarius

Attribute: Spiritual, Creativity
Blood Type: Type B
Character Trait: Passion
Colors: Red, White
Direction: South
Element: Fire
Elemental: Salamanders, The Spirits of Fire
Elemental King: Djinn

Esoteric Title: The Daughter of the Reconcilers; The Bringer-Forth of Light
Fundamental Force: Strong
Gematria Value: 60
Gender: Masculine

Hebrew Letter: Samech,
The Staff (Single letter)

Herb: Pepper
Holy Creature: The Winged Lion

I-Ching: 15 - Moderation or
Modesty, Humility, Gentleness

Keyword: Moderation
Key Phrase: "I Will"
Lunar Phase: Full Moon
Magical Organ: The Spirit
Magical Phrase: Velle, To Will
Matter: Energy

Meanings:
Upright:
Adaption, adjustments, balance, blending of opposites, change, compassion, coordination, diplomacy, discretion, don't rush, easy does it, go with the flow, good

management, inspiration, moderation, negotiations, on the right path, one day at a time, open communication, patience, peace, placid, progress, restoration, self control, slow and steady wins the race, synergy, take your time, timing, tolerance, tranquility, unity, vitality.

Reversed:
Acting out, bluntness, conflict of interest, emotional instability, emotional stress, extremism, fanaticism, fear of change, foolhardy, frivolousness, illness, inappropriate actions or words, ineptitude, instability, intolerance, lack of cooperative effort, misguided, out of balance, overindulgence, overly impressionable, poor judgment, stalling, strife, suppressing emotions, unwillingness to compromise, volatility, wanderlust.

Musical Mood: "Fight the Good Fight" by Triumph
Musical Note: G#
Mythological Creatures: Dragons and Phoenix
Numerology: 5 – Changes, disruptions, instability, conflict, uncertainty

Path on the Tree of Life: 25th Path, from Yesod (Dreams) to Tiphereth (Beauty)
Phase of Life: The Youth
Physical Property: Intensity
Plane: Spiritual
Plant: Rush
Playing Card Suit: Clubs

Possibility:
You need to moderate your indulgences and strive for better balance between the material and spiritual in your life. There is a profound discordance in your priorities. Don't rush to judgment over the choices of another, as their actions reflect their perspective of circumstance, not yours. Patience is your only viable option right now. The shortcuts you see are illusions and will lead you to a place you have already been.

Possible Influencing Cards:
Devil – lifestyle change is needed
Fool – you are right where you are supposed to be
Justice – legal wins
Lovers – potential infidelity

Psychological Function: Energy and Desire
Quality: Immediate
Regent: Michael
Royal Star: Regulus

Runes: Nauthiz, Need

Sabbat: Litha
Season: Summer
Stone: Jacinth
Suit: Wands
Temperament: Choleric

Tetragrammaton: Yod

Time of Day: Noon

15
The Devil

15

Devil

Alchemical Quality: Cold and Dry

Alchemical Symbol:

Animal Energy: Crow (Intelligent Trickster)
Area of the Body Male Genitals
Associated Illness: Arthritis

Astrological Correspondence: Capricorn

Astrological Quadruplicity:

    Cardinal Zodiac (Aggressive) – Capricorn

    Fixed Zodiac (Rigid) – Taurus

    Mutable Zodiac (Passive) – Virgo

Attribute: Physical
Blood Type: Type A
Character Trait: Hibernation
Colors: White, Black
Direction: North
Element: Earth
Elemental: Gnomes, the Spirits of the Earth

Elemental King: Ghob
Esoteric Title: The Lord of the Gates of Matter; The Child of the Forces of Time
Fundamental Force: Gravity
Gematria Value: 70
Gender: Feminine

Hebrew Letter: Ayin, The Eye (Single letter)

Herb: Dill
Holy Creature: The Winged Bull

I-Ching: 44 - Temptation or Indulgence, Intrusions, Undermining

Keyword: Obsessions
Key Phrase: "I Have"
Lunar Phase: New Moon
Magical Organ: The Body and Senses
Magical Phrase: Tacere, To Keep Silent
Matter: Solid

Meanings:
    Upright:
    Abuse of authority, addictions, blasphemy, cruelty, emotional blackmail, Entertain-

ment Industry (Music), fear, frustration, fulfillment of desires at any cost, greed, hidden obstacles, hopelessness, hostility, ignorance, inhibitions, lust, materialism, misdirection, narrow minded, obsessions, oppression, overindulgence, perversions, physical urges, self imposed limitations, shallowness, socializing, spendthrift, temptations, trapped in a bad situation, tunnel vision, turpitude, unnecessary use of force, weakness.

Reversed:

12-step programs, avoid being timid, breaking free, careful planning needed, clear thinking, complications, cutting your losses, divorce, indecision, loving thoughts and actions, moving forward, need to lighten up, never too late to say I'm sorry, recovery, rehabilitation, release, removing the chains, resolutions, self love and forgiveness, taking the first step towards a better life, turning over a new leaf, undue influence, unwilling to face reality.

Musical Mood: "Rock and Roll All Night" by Kiss

Musical Note: A
Mythological Creatures: Giants and Elves
Numerology: 6 – Home life, harmony, nostalgia, responsibility, reconciliation
Path on the Tree of Life: 26th Path, from Hod (Communication) to Tiphereth (Beauty)
Phase of Life: The Elder
Physical Property: Solidity
Plane: Physical
Plant: Indian Hemp, Orchis Root, Thistle
Playing Card Suit: Diamonds

Possibility:

Your belief that you are trapped within a prison from which you cannot escape is quite real, but it is the weakness of your resolve that gives your belief the strength to contain you. You have given yourself to the material and are soon to discover that the fuller the coffers the emptier the soul. Temptation is sparked by interest; therefore, it won't help to fight the temptation as long as the interest remains.

Possible Influencing Cards:

8 of Cups – breaking an addiction
Hanged Man – hidden agendas

Justice – lies and slander
King of Pentacles – getting swindled
Lovers – lust and physical attraction
Magician – misuse of power

Psychological Function: Manifestation and Formation
Quality: Passive
Regent: Uriel
Royal Star: Fomalhaut

Runes: Fehu, Cattle

Sabbat: Yule
Season: Winter
Stone: Black Diamond
Suit: Pentacles
Temperament: Melancholic

Tetragrammaton: Heh

Time of Day: Midnight

16
The Tower

16

Tower

Alchemical Quality: Hot and Dry

Alchemical Symbol:

Animal Energy: Bat (Transitions)
Area of the Body Muscular System
Associated Illness: Inflammation

Astrological Correspondence: Mars

Astrological Quadruplicity:

Cardinal Zodiac (Aggressive) – Aries

Fixed Zodiac (Rigid) – Leo

Mutable Zodiac (Passive) – Sagittarius

Attribute: Spiritual, Creativity
Blood Type: Type B
Character Trait: Passion
Colors: Red, White
Direction: South
Element: Fire
Elemental: Salamanders, The Spirits of Fire
Elemental King: Djinn
Esoteric Title: The Lords of the Hosts of the Mighty

Fundamental Force: Strong
Gematria Value: 80
Gender: Masculine

Hebrew Letter: Peh, The Mouth
(Double letter)

Herb: Tobacco
Holy Creature: The Winged Lion

I-Ching: 23 – Deterioration or
Disintegration, Separation, Annihilation

Keyword: Pride
Key Phrase: "I Will"
Lunar Phase: Full Moon
Magical Organ: The Spirit
Magical Phrase: Velle, To Will
Matter: Energy

Meanings:

Upright:
All is lost, bankruptcy, calamity, chaos, cleansing, collapse of a situation, complete upheaval, crushed dreams, destitution, devastation, downfall, epiphany, growing up, ignorance, illness, loss of hope, loss of

self esteem, megalomania, misery, poverty, purging, reconstruction, re-evaluation, release, renovation, revelation, ruin, self defeat, selfish ambition, separation or divorce, shocking situation, the light at the end of the tunnel is a train, trauma, upheaval.

Reversed:
Aftermath of a catastrophe, arguments, bankruptcy, cruelty, dead end street, false accusations or slander, humility, impotence, impracticality, imprisonment, learning from your mistakes, liberation, light at the end of the tunnel, loss of ambition, oppression, persecution, picking up the pieces, problems are increasing, restrictions, self destruction, starting over, starting to rebuild, the party's over, the phoenix rising from the ashes, tyranny, violence, weakness.

Musical Mood: "It's the End of the World as We Know It" by R.E.M.
Musical Note: C
Mythological Creatures: Dragons and Phoenix
Numerology: 7 – Mystical, spiritual, dreams, discipline, struggles

Path on the Tree of Life: 27ᵗʰ Path, from Hod (Communications) to Netzach (Will)
Phase of Life: The Youth
Physical Property: Intensity
Plane: Spiritual
Plant: Absinthe, Rue
Playing Card Suit: Clubs

Possibility:
Your well-placed intentions have been squandered, and you are at the threshold of an event with catastrophic repercussions. That which should matter to you the most is about to be lost, and it behooves you to heed the warning that this event represents, because things can get worse. You are about to experience an epiphany of belief, but it won't affect what you believe, only the reason you believe it.

Possible Influencing Cards:
5 of Swords – violent arguments
Chariot – inner strength will see you through the current crisis
Death – chaos
Star – calmness and serenity needed
Sun – current situation is for the best
Wheel of Fortune – be careful what you wish for

Psychological Function: Energy and Desire
Quality: Immediate
Regent: Michael
Royal Star: Regulus

Runes: Hagalaz, The Hailstone

Sabbat: Litha
Season: Summer
Stone: Ruby
Suit: Wands
Temperament: Choleric

Tetragrammaton: Yod

Time of Day: Noon

17
The Star

Alchemical Quality: Hot and Wet

Alchemical Symbol:

Animal Energy: Dog (Faith and Love)
Area of the Body Kidneys and Bladder
Associated Illness: Cystitis

Astrological Correspondence:
Aquarius

Astrological Quadruplicity:

Cardinal Zodiac (Aggressive) – Libra

Fixed Zodiac (Rigid) – Aquarius

Mutable Zodiac (Passive) – Gemini

Attribute: Intellectual
Blood Type: Type O
Celtic Tree Month: Nov 25 – Dec 22 – Elder (Ruis)
Character Trait: Restlessness
Colors: Yellow, Red
Direction: East
Element: Air

Elemental: Sylphs, The Spirits of Air
Elemental King: Paralda
Esoteric Title: The Daughter of the Firmament; The Dweller Between the Waters
Fundamental Force: Electromagnetic
Gematria Value: 5
Gender: Masculine

Hebrew Letter: Tzaddi, The Fishhook (Single letter)

Herb: Cloves
Holy Creature: The Winged Man

I-Ching: 64 – Beginnings or Before Completion, Transition, Unfinished Business

Keyword: Hope
Key Phrase: "I Think"
Lunar Phase: 1st Quarter
Magical Organ: The Brain
Magical Phrase: Noscere, To Know
Matter: Gas

Meanings:

Upright:

A new sense of purpose, beauty, better times are coming, bright expectations, calmness, contemplation, Entertainment Industry (Artists), fertility, grace, harmony, healing, health is improving, idealism, illumination, insight, inspiration, new concepts, new energy, optimism, peace, positivity, promises, protection, renewed hope, satisfaction, serenity, unexpected gifts, wish fulfillment.

Reversed:

Arrogance, closed minded, conceit, depression, disappointment, dreams seem to be unattainable, emotional challenges or tests, friction, futility, ignoring the obvious, illness, intolerance, loss of faith, need for clarity, negativity, obstacles, out of balance, overconfidence, pessimism, procrastination, refusing a helping hand up, self depreciation, self doubt, delays and difficulties, separation, stubbornness.

Musical Mood: "Imagine" by John Lennon
Musical Note: A#
Mythological Creatures: Gryphons and

Pegasus
Numerology: 8 – Material progress, security, expansion, priorities, advancement
Path on the Tree of Life: 15th Path, from Tiphereth (Beauty) to Chokmah (Wisdom)
Phase of Life: The Child
Physical Property: Motion
Plane: Mental
Plant: Coconut, Olive
Playing Card Suit: Spades

Possibility:

It's time to leave what is over behind, as this is the onset of a period of renewed hope and optimism. You need to replenish your spirit in the serenity that follows the storm. Regain your equanimity before you refocus your energy, and allow yourself the time to relax with a pet, in a favorite place, or both. Be receptive to new alternatives, as inspiration might generate momentum on the wings of a new idea.

Possible Influencing Cards:

Empress – happy and fruitful life
Devil – loss of faith
Magician – beginning of a new project
Temperance – on the right path

Psychological Function: Thoughts and Ideas
Quality: Active
Regent: Raphael
Royal Star: Aldebaran

Runes: Ansuz, A God

Sabbat: Ostara
Season: Spring
Stone: Artificial glass
Suit: Swords
Temperament: Sanguine

Tetragrammaton: Vau

Time of Day: Dawn

18
The Moon

Moon

Alchemical Quality: Cold and Wet

Alchemical Symbol:

Animal Energy: Cat (Mystery and Magick)
Area of the Body Legs and Feet
Associated Illness: Gout (Joint Inflammation)

Astrological Correspondence:
Pisces

Astrological Quadruplicity:

Cardinal Zodiac (Aggressive) –
Cancer

Fixed Zodiac (Rigid) – Scorpio

Mutable Zodiac (Passive) – Pisces

Attribute: Emotional
Blood Type: Type AB
Celtic Tree Month: April 15 - May 12 – Willow (Saille)
Character Trait: Healing
Colors: Blue-Green, Gray
Direction: West
Element: Water
Elemental: Undines, The Spirits of Water

Elemental King: Nixsa
Esoteric Title: The Ruler and Flux and Reflux; The Child of the Sons of the Mighty
Fundamental Force: Weak Force
Gematria Value: 100
Gender: Feminine

Hebrew Letter: Qoph, The Back of the Head (Single letter)

Herb: Star Anise
Holy Creature: The Eagle

I-Ching: 63 – Completions or After Completions, Climax, Culmination, Achievement

Keyword: Illusions
Key Phrase: "I Feel"
Lunar Phase: 3rd Quarter Moon
Magical Organ: The Heart
Magical Phrase: Audere, To Dare
Matter: Liquid

Meanings:
  Upright:
  Acute awareness, bewilderment, confusion, cycles, deceptions, disguises,

emotional crisis, Entertainment Industry (Writers), exaggeration, false hopes, false promises, fear of loss or the unknown, fear, hidden agendas, hidden enemies, illusions, indecision, insight, intuition, laziness, lies, losing control, magick, magnetism, mixed emotions, mood swings, mystery, need for more independence, overactive imagination, psychic, secrets, subconscious, substance abuse, taking unfair advantage, treachery, unconscious, vacillation, wild and untamed.

Reversed:

Clarity, clear thinking, coming into the light, desperate measures needed, don't take any risks, emotional problems, fraud is revealed, hidden addictions, inner reflections, instability, irrational change, listening to the inner voice, lunacy, moment of clarity, open to information from unconventional sources, rationality, secrets are exposed, self delusion, self fulfilling prophecies, sensitivity, sincerity, subterfuge, sudden realizations, trickery, trust your instincts, uncertainty, understanding, unmasking the stranger within, unsettling fears.

Musical Mood: "Black Masquerade" by Rainbow
Musical Note: B
Mythological Creatures: Merfolk and Hippocampus
Numerology: 9 – Satisfaction, fulfillment, luck, complacency, just desserts
Path on the Tree of Life: 29th Path, from Malkuth (Realization) to Netzach (Will)
Phase of Life: The Adult
Physical Property: Fluidity
Plane: Astral
Plant: Opium
Playing Card Suit: Hearts

Possibility:

The choices that you are making are based on something ulterior, and it could very well be you that is deceiving you. There is something hidden from you, and it is just barely out of site. The shadows, and who or what that may lurk in them, may seem frightening, but that is where you will find the answers you seek. If you are feeling an intuitive tug on your psyche, follow it, even if it contradicts the ideas of others.

Possible Influencing Cards:

   7 of Cups – not living in the real world
   Ace of Swords – disturbing news
   Hanged Man – hidden agenda
   Justice – lies and slander
   Lovers – deceit and infidelity
   Tower – rumors abound

Psychological Function: Feelings and Emotion
Quality: Receptive
Regent: Gabriel
Royal Star: Antares

Runes: Laguz, The Lake

Sabbat: Mabon
Season: Autumn
Stone: Pearl
Suit: Cups
Temperament: Phlegmatic

Tetragrammaton: Heh

Time of Day: Dusk

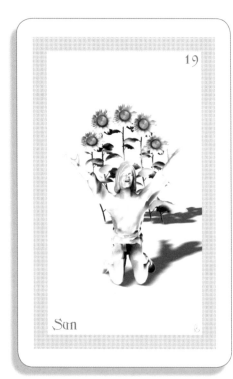

Alchemical Quality: Hot and Dry

Alchemical Symbol:

Animal Energy: Lion (New Power)
Area of the Body Circulatory Systems
Associated Illness: Repletion (Overeating or drinking)

Astrological Correspondence: Sun

Astrological Quadruplicity:

Cardinal Zodiac (Aggressive) – Aries

Fixed Zodiac (Rigid) – Leo

Mutable Zodiac (Passive) Sagittarius

Attribute: Spiritual
Blood Type: Type B
Celtic Tree Month: June 10 - July 7 – Oak (Duir)
Character Trait: Passion
Colors: Red, White
Direction: South
Element: Fire

Elemental: Salamanders, The Spirits of Fire
Elemental King: Djinn
Esoteric Title: The Lord of the Fire of the World
Fundamental Force: Strong
Gematria Value: 200
Gender: Masculine

Hebrew Letter: Resh, The Head (Double letter)

Herb: Chamomile
Holy Creature: The Winged Lion

I-Ching: 30 – Caressing Fire, Nurture, Reliance, Shining

Keyword: Happiness
Key Phrase: "I Will"
Lunar Phase: Full Moon
Magical Organ: The Spirit
Magical Phrase: Velle, To Will
Matter: Energy

Meanings:
   Upright:
   Acclaim, achievement, blessings, celebrations, conception, cooperation and teamwork, empowerment, enlightenment,

enrichment, Entertainment Industry (Actors, Directors, etc.), enthusiasm, free spirits, fulfillment, good health and vitality, good news, gratitude, happiness, liberation, lust for life, marriage, motivation, new inspirations, pleasant surprises, positive energy, pride, purity, regeneration, rewards seize the current opportunity, success, triumph.

Reversed:
Arrogance, being dominated by others, burnout, delays, egotism, facades, failure, false pride, fear of loss, future is cloudy, hidden obstacles, ill health, investigate before committing, keeping secrets, misjudgment, misuse of power, need to be more realistic, not seeing the big picture, overindulgence, psychic vampires, sadness, stagnation, superiority complex, too much emphasis on appearances, too much of a good thing, unclear future, vanity.

Musical Mood: "Three Little Birds" by Bob Marley
Musical Note: D
Mythological Creatures: Dragons and Phoenix

Numerology: 10 – Completions, resolutions, beginning and/or ending of a cycle
Path on the Tree of Life: 30th Path, from Yesod (Dreams) to Hod (Communication)
Phase of Life: The Youth
Physical Property: Intensity
Plane: Spiritual
Plant: Sunflower, Laurel, Heliotrope
Playing Card Suit: Clubs

Possibility:

It's a great time to be you. Any obstacles that you now face will capitulate before you, and you will bask in the warmth of your triumphs. All that is positive about you has now swelled up inside, as you find yourself unable to contain your exuberance. A great effort brings great feelings of accomplishment. Resplendent upon your mountain, you have found fulfillment in life. You are warm, comfortable, and happy.

Possible Influencing Cards:

Chariot – seize the day
Death – happy endings
High Priestess – confident knowledge
Tower – current troubles with pass

Psychological Function: Energy and Desire
Quality: Immediate
Regent: Michael
Royal Star: Regulus

Runes: Sowilo, The Sun

Sabbat: Litha
Season: Summer
Stone: Crysoleth
Suit: Wands
Temperament: Choleric

Tetragrammaton: Yod

Time of Day: Noon

Judgment

Alchemical Quality: Cold and Wet

Alchemical Symbol:

Animal Energy: Bison (Manifesting Abundance through Right Action)
Area of the Body: Organs of Circulation and Intelligence
Associated Illness: Fever and Death

Astrological Correspondence: Pluto

Astrological Quadruplicity:

  Cardinal Zodiac (Aggressive) – Cancer

  Fixed Zodiac (Rigid) – Scorpio

  Mutable Zodiac (Passive) – Pisces

Attribute: Emotional
Blood Type: Type AB
Character Trait: Healing
Colors: Blue-Green, Gray
Direction: West
Element: Water
Elemental: Undines, The Spirits of Water

Elemental King: Nixsa
Esoteric Title: The Spirit of Primal Fire
Fundamental Force: Weak
Gematria Value: 300
Gender: Feminine

Hebrew Letter: Shin, The Tooth (Mother letter)

Herb: Bay
Holy Creature: The Eagle

I-Ching: 7 - Collective Force, Honor, Loyalty, Integrity

Keyword: Karma
Key Phrase: "I Feel"
Lunar Phase: 3rd Quarter
Magical Organ: The Heart
Magical Phrase: Audere, To Dare
Matter: Liquid

Meanings:
  Upright:
  Absolution, atonement, breaking old habits, change, day of reckoning, decisions, destiny, end of a situation, Entertainment Industry (Dancers), freedom,

good judgment, humility, improvement of health, integrity, justified pride in accomplishments, Karma, life changing decisions, making amends, milestones reached, new cycles emerging, paying dues, rebirth, reincarnation, release, renewal, repentance, resolution, resurrection, rites of passage, self appraisal, spiritual awakening, transformation.

Reversed:

Alienation, being caught off guard, bitterness, decisions not in your favor, delays, disappointment, extreme attitudes, fear of change or death, forced change, guilt, holding a grudge, indecision, legal problems, limited successes, loss, miscommunications, narrow minded, negative criticism, out of control inner critic, revenge, restitution, separation, stagnation, stubbornness, terminations, unrealistic, unwillingness to accept needed change, wasted opportunities, weakness of character.

Musical Mood: "What It's Like" by Everlast
Musical Note: C
Mythological Creatures: Merfolk and Hippocampus

Numerology: 2 – Relationships, decisions, balance, cooperation, emotions
Path on the Tree of Life: 31ˢᵗ Path, from Malkuth (Realization) to Hod (Communication)
Phase of Life: The Adult
Physical Property: Fluidity
Plane: Astral
Plant: Hibiscus, Nettle, Almond in Flower
Playing Card Suit: Hearts

Possibility:

"Compared to a plume your heart will one day be, and if it is heavier than the feather Anubis will surely see. A life of truth and fairness, not perfidy, will grant you further passage, as virtue is the key." Now is the time to evaluate what you have left in your wake, and improve yourself from any lessons to be found there. A point in time where assessments are made has arrived. An end is just the step that comes before a beginning.

Possible Influencing Cards:

7 of Swords – getting caught in the act
Chariot – success is yours

Hanged Man – long reaching decisions to be made
Hermit – minor successes
High Priestess – a secret is exposed
Justice – legal proceedings are imminent

Psychological Function: Emotions and Feelings
Quality: Receptive
Regent: Gabriel
Royal Star: Antares

Runes: Dagaz, Day

Sabbat: Mabon
Season: Autumn
Stone: Fire Opal
Suit: Cups
Temperament: Phlegmatic

Tetragrammaton: Heh

Time of Day: Dusk

21
The World

Alchemical Quality: Cold and Dry

Alchemical Symbol:

Animal Energy: Ram (New Beginnings)
Area of the Body: Excretory System
Associated Illness: Arterio Sclerosis, Sluggishness

Astrological Correspondence:
Saturn

Astrological Quadruplicity:

Cardinal Zodiac (Aggressive) –
Capricorn

Fixed Zodiac (Rigid) – Taurus

Mutable Zodiac (Passive) – Virgo

Attribute: Physical
Blood Type: Type A
Character Trait: Hibernation
Colors: White, Black
Direction: North
Element: Earth
Elemental: Gnomes, The Spirits of Earth

Elemental King: Ghob
Esoteric Title: The Great One of the Night of Time
Fundamental Force: Gravity
Gematria Value: 400
Gender: Feminine

Hebrew Letter: Tau, The T
Shaped Cross (Double letter)

Herb: Pomegranate
Holy Creature: The Winged Bull

I-Ching: 37 – Family, Home,
Belonging, Inclusion

Keyword: Achievement
Key Phrase: "I Have"
Lunar Phase: New Moon
Magical Organ: The Body
Magical Phrase: Tacere, To Keep Silent
Matter: Solid

Meanings:
  Upright:
  Accomplishment, change of residence, completion, contentment, earned respect, elation, environmental and ecological

issues, fulfillment, goals are reached, happiness, happy ending, humanitarian issues, inner peace, liberation, life is good, moving on to the next phase in life, peace, perfect harmony, perfection, possible travel, recognition, self realization, spirituality, success, triumph, victory, wholeness

Reversed:

Always chasing rainbows, delays, despondency, distractions, failure, fear of change, giving up too soon, health problems, lack of vision, lack of closure, lessons not learned, need to re-examine priorities, not accepting Karmic lessons, not ready for the next step, obstacles and delays, repression, resistance to change, self sabotage, spendthrift, stuck in a rut, too many loose ends, unfinished business.

Musical Mood: "What a Wonderful World" by Louis Armstrong
Musical Note: A
Mythological Creatures: Giants and Elves
Numerology: 3 – Growth, enterprise, manifestation, unity, intuition
Path on the Tree of Life: 32nd Path, from Malkuth (Realization) to Yesod (Dreams)

Phase of Life: The Elder
Physical Property: Solidity
Plane: Physical
Plant: Ash, Cypress, Yew, Nightshade, Oak, Ivy
Playing Card Suit: Diamonds

Possibility:

Your quest is complete, and you have found your own personal Holy Grail. There are no more tests to take, no more obstacles to overcome, there is simply nothing left for you to do but enjoy the moment. Something you have dreamed about is now a reality, as your wish has come true. Although this is a wonderful time for you, and you enjoy great rewards, we live in perpetual cycles, and a new journey will soon begin.

Possible Influencing Cards:

Chariot – victory is yours

Magician – complete control

Hanged man – sacrifice needed to bring happiness

Sun – happy endings all around

Psychological Function: Manifestation and Formation
Quality: Passive
Regent: Uriel, Guardian of the North
Royal Star: Fomalhaut

Runes: Wunjo, Joy

Sabbat: Yule
Season: Winter
Stone: Onyx, Salt
Suit: Pentacles
Temperament: Melancholic

Tetragrammaton: Heh

Time of Day: Midnight

The Swords

Ace of Swords

Alchemical Quality: Hot and Wet

Alchemical Symbol: △

Animal Energy: Hawk
(Observation and Clarity)

Astrological Correspondence: Root of Air

Astrological Quadruplicity:
  Cardinal Zodiac (Aggressive) – ♎
  Libra

  Fixed Zodiac (Rigid) – Aquarius ♒

  Mutable Zodiac (Passive) – Gemini ♊

Attribute: Intellectual
Blood Type: Type O
Character Trait: Restlessness
Colors: Yellow, Red
Direction: East
Element: Air
Elemental: Sylphs, The Spirits of Air
Elemental King: Paralda
Esoteric Title: Root of the Powers of Air
Fundamental Force: Electromagnetic
Gender: Masculine
Holy Creature: The Winged Man

I-Ching: 1 – Creative, Power, Strength, Decisive
Keyword: Analysis
Key Phrase: "I Think"
Lunar Phase: 1st Quarter Moon
Magical Organ: The Brain
Magical Phrase: Noscere, To Know
Matter: Gas

Meanings:

Upright:

Authority, beginnings of activity associated with the suit, changes for the good, clarity, conquest, courage, determination, individuality, journey by air, legal issues, logic, make long term goals, mental energy, opening lines of communication, order, rebirth, right of force, righteous battle, spiritual strength, strength in adversity, success, sudden changes, timing is right, triumph, truth, victory, willpower.

Reversed:

Abuse, bitterness, confusion, controlling behavior, delays, destructive force, doubt, empty use of force, failure to think things completely through, illness requiring surgery, illusions, injustice, intellectual road-blocks, limitations, loss of power, misdirected energy, obstacles, poking a sleeping dragon, prejudice, punishment, sarcasm, slander, threats, tyranny, uncertainty, unnecessary harshness, violence.

Musical Mood: "Agreement" by Kitaro
Mythological Creatures: Gryphons and Pegasus
Numerology: 1 – New beginnings, confidence, creativity, possibility, potential
Phase of Life: The Child
Physical Property: Motion
Plane: Mental
Playing Card Suit: Spades

Possibility:

Grip your truths tightly, as they are about to come into question in the turbulent time ahead. It is from adversity that those that are on the path to righteous achievement emerge as the Phoenix, renewed of strength and resolve, and much wiser than before. Those that have challenged you, and those that have doubted you will not be able to hold their ground any longer if you remain steadfast in your beliefs.

Possible Influencing Cards:

7 of Swords – too many shortcuts, ill gotten gains
High Priest – lack of focus, scattered energy
Justice – situation is for the highest good of all concerned
Wheel of Fortune – bad luck, can't catch a break
World – refusal to accept advice or help

Psychological Function: Thoughts and Ideas
Quality: Active
Regent: Raphael
Royal Star: Alderbaran
Sabbat: Ostara
Season: Spring
Suit: Swords
Temperament: Sanguine

Tetragrammaton: Vau
Time of Day: Dawn

Two of Swords

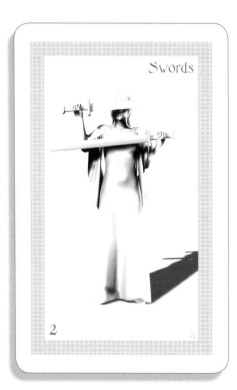

Alchemical Quality: Hot and Wet

Alchemical Symbol: △
Animal Energy: Hawk
(Observation and Clarity)

Astrological Correspondence:
Moon ☽ in Libra ♎

Astrological Quadruplicity:
    Cardinal Zodiac (Aggressive) –
    Libra ♎

    Fixed Zodiac (Rigid) – Aquarius ♒

    Mutable Zodiac (Passive) – Gemini ♊

Attribute: Intellectual
Blood Type: Type O
Character Trait: Restlessness
Colors: Yellow, Red
Direction: East
Element: Air
Elemental: Sylphs, The Spirits of Air
Elemental King: Paralda
Esoteric Title: Lord of Peace
Fundamental Force: Electromagnetic
Gender: Masculine

Holy Creature: The Winged Man

I-Ching: 57 – Willing
Submission or Gentleness, Flexibility

Keyword: Indecision
Key Phrase: "I Think"
Lunar Phase: 1st Quarter Moon
Magical Organ: The Brain
Magical Phrase: Noscere, To Know
Matter: Gas

Meanings:

Upright:

Avoidance, balance, blind vigilance, denial, dilemma, discipline, fear, ignoring a problem doesn't make it go away, impasse, inner conflict, inner strength, inner turmoil, need for guidance, noncommittal, passivity, personal crisis, procrastination, refusing to take sides, repressing emotions, stalemate, standstill, sticking your head in the sand, tension, truce, uncertainty, unwilling to make a decision.

Reversed:

Accepting the challenge, action begins anew, betrayal, change, cheating, facing reality, false friends, false information, forward progress, good decisions, impotence, lies, movement, peace is restored, relief from stress, removing the blindfold, running away from responsibilities, seeing the consequences of your actions, superficiality, taking needed action, treachery exposed, truce, truth shall be revealed.

Musical Mood: "Wake Up" by Alanis Morissette
Mythological Creatures: Gryphons and Pegasus
Numerology: 2 – Relationships, decisions, balance, cooperation, emotions
Phase of Life: The Child
Physical Property: Motion
Plane: Mental
Playing Card Suit: Spades

Possibility:

You are refusing to see the reality of your situation. The power of your desire to hold onto a love that you have lost, or to escape the emptiness of unrequited love, has you believing in something that does not really exist. You must lower your guard, open your eyes, and face what it is that is actually before you. An unwillingness to consider possible alternatives to your situation has left you at an impasse.

Possible Influencing Cards:

4 of Pentacles – stagnation
5 of Cups – overly stressed
6 of Cups – poor choices
7 of Pentacles – plagued by indecision
7 of Swords – self deception
9 of Wands – overly defensive
Ace of Swords – money concerns
Moon – possible ill health

Psychological Function: Thoughts and Ideas
Quality: Active
Regent: Raphael
Royal Star: Alderbaran
Sabbat: Ostara
Season: Spring
Suit: Swords
Temperament: Sanguine

Tetragrammaton: Vau
Time of Day: Dawn

Three of Swords

Swords

3

Alchemical Quality: Hot and Wet

Alchemical Symbol:
Animal Energy: Hawk (Observation and Clarity)

Astrological Correspondence:
Saturn ♄ in Libra ♎

Astrological Quadruplicity:
    Cardinal Zodiac (Aggressive) – ♎
    Libra

    Fixed Zodiac (Rigid) – Aquarius ♒

    Mutable Zodiac (Passive) – Gemini ♊

Attribute: Intellectual
Blood Type: Type O
Character Trait: Restlessness
Colors: Yellow, Red
Direction: East
Element: Air
Elemental: Sylphs, The Spirits of Air
Elemental King: Paralda
Esoteric Title: Lord of Sorrow
Fundamental Force: Electromagnetic
Gender: Masculine

Holy Creature: The Winged Man

I-Ching: 42 – Benefit or Increase, Expansion, Growth
Keyword: Betrayal
Key Phrase: "I Think"
Lunar Phase: 1st Quarter Moon
Magical Organ: The Brain
Magical Phrase: Noscere, To Know
Matter: Gas

Meanings:

Upright:
Absence, betrayal, conflict, death (rare), departures, disappointment, disillusionment, disruption, divorce, forlorn, grief, heartache, illness, loneliness, loss, misunderstandings, mourning, negative thinking, problem pregnancy, psychological blocks, quarrels, remorse, separation, sorrow, stormy weather ahead, truce is broken, unrequited love, upheaval.

Reversed:
Alienation, backstabbing, burying the hatchet, change of heart, confusion, denial, disorder, dwelling on past hurts, emotionally distant, getting on with your life, haven't got time for the pain, illness, loss, mental breakdown, new perspectives, overly emotional, petty arguments, seclusion, slow recovery, social blunders, uneasy truce, violence.

Musical Mood: "You'll Think of Me" by Keith Urban
Mythological Creatures: Gryphons and Pegasus
Numerology: 3 – Growth, enterprise, manifestation, unity, intuition
Phase of Life: The Child
Physical Property: Motion
Plane: Mental
Playing Card Suit: Spades

Possibility:
The pain of infidelity is about to be inflicted upon you by an unfaithful lover, disloyal friend, or backstabbing coworker. It is important to realize that when you are betrayed by someone it is actually a reflection of their character, not yours. Someone who claims to have been weakened by temptation was in fact interested beforehand because you cannot be tempted by something that holds no interest to you.

Possible Influencing Cards:
6 of Wands – work related stress
8 of Cups – holding a grudge
9 of Swords – depression, ill health
Emperor – slander
Lovers – end of a relationship
World – cleansing energy needed for a fresh star

Psychological Function: Thoughts and Ideas
Quality: Active
Regent: Raphael
Royal Star: Alderbaran
Sabbat: Ostara
Season: Spring
Suit: Swords
Temperament: Sanguine

Tetragrammaton: Vau
Time of Day: Dawn

Four of Swords

Alchemical Quality: Hot and Wet

Alchemical Symbol: △
Animal Energy: Hawk (Observation and Clarity)

Astrological Correspondence: Jupiter ♃ in Libra ♎

Astrological Quadruplicity:
    Cardinal Zodiac (Aggressive) – ♎ Libra

    Fixed Zodiac (Rigid) – Aquarius ♒

    Mutable Zodiac (Passive) ♊ Gemini

Attribute: Intellectual
Blood Type: Type O
Character Trait: Restlessness
Colors: Yellow, Red
Direction: East
Element: Air
Elemental: Sylphs, The Spirits of Air
Elemental King: Paralda
Esoteric Title: Lord of Rest from Strife
Fundamental Force: Electromagnetic

Gender: Masculine
Holy Creature: The Winged Man

I-Ching: 33 – Withdrawal, Retreat, Retire, Rest
Keyword: Inert
Key Phrase: "I Think"
Lunar Phase: 1st Quarter Moon
Magical Organ: The Brain
Magical Phrase: Noscere, To Know
Matter: Gas

Meanings:

 Upright:

Abstinence, banishment, break from the fighting, contemplations, exile, forced convalescence, illness, inactivity, introspection, patience, postponements, preparation for the future, putting everything on hold, recovery, recuperation, religious experiences, rest, retirement, retreat, situations involving hospitals, stagnation, stasis, time to relax and rejuvenate, vigilance, withdrawal.

 Reversed:

Awakening, back in the swing of things, becoming more visible, break time is over, call to arms, caution needed, energizing, foresight, isolation, outcast, precautions, recovery, rejoining society, rekindling desires, renewed activity, resentment, rising up, thriftiness, time for action, use discretion, work related difficulties.

Musical Mood: "Wake Me Up Inside" by Evanescence
Mythological Creatures: Gryphons and Pegasus
Numerology: 4 – Rest, inactivity, patience, stability, legal matters
Phase of Life: The Child
Physical Property: Motion
Plane: Mental
Playing Card Suit: Spades

Possibility:

Your goal is unobtainable at this point, but it is not lost to you forever, only temporarily out of reach. Step back from any conflict and allow those that challenge you to believe that you have given your best and lost. You still hold one advantage, but you must first prepare yourself thoroughly and impatience is your one true adversary. It is time to recharge your spirit and replenish your energy before continuing your quest.

Possible Influencing Cards:

 10 of Wands – overworked and underappreciated
 Devil – possible ill heath
 Hermit – isolation
 Judgment – need to learn from past mistakes
 King of Pentacles – necessary delays in business matters
 Wheel – caught up in a swirl of activity

Psychological Function: Thoughts and Ideas
Quality: Active
Regent: Raphael
Royal Star: Alderbaran
Sabbat: Ostara
Season: Spring
Suit: Swords
Temperament: Sanguine

Tetragrammaton: Vau
Time of Day: Dawn

Five of Swords

Alchemical Quality: Hot and Wet

Alchemical Symbol: △

Animal Energy: Hawk (Observation and Clarity)

Astrological Correspondence: Venus ♀ in Aquarius ♒

Astrological Quadruplicity:
    Cardinal Zodiac (Aggressive) – ♎ Libra

      Fixed Zodiac (Rigid) – Aquarius ♒

      Mutable Zodiac (Passive) – Gemini ♊

Attribute: Intellectual
Blood Type: Type O
Character Trait: Restlessness
Colors: Yellow, Red
Direction: East
Element: Air
Elemental: Sylphs, The Spirits of Air
Elemental King: Paralda
Esoteric Title: Lord of Defeat
Fundamental Force: Electromagnetic
Gender: Masculine

Holy Creature: The Winged Man

I-Ching: 36 – Censorship or Night, Rejection, Invalidation
Keyword: Humiliation
Key Phrase: "I Think"
Lunar Phase: 1st Quarter Moon
Magical Organ: The Brain
Magical Phrase: Noscere, To Know
Matter: Gas

Meanings:

Upright:
Cowardliness, defeat, destructive behavior, discord, dishonor, embarrassment, hollow victory, humiliation, indecision, insensitive, malice, manipulation, misfortune, not accepting your share of the blame, open hostility, paranoia, rash behavior, revenge, sabotage, selfishness, slander, sore loser, spite, spy in your midst, struggles, theft, treachery, turbulence, winning by unfair means

Reversed:
Acquittal, apologies, bad news, clearing the air, end of slander and gossip, evening up the playing field, fair victory, false pride, instigating a fight, intimidation, intrigue, loss, low self esteem, misfortune, need to prioritize, possible illness, slyness, the righteous will prevail, treachery exposed, unsympathetic, vengeance, vindication, weakness

Musical Mood: "Scream" by Michael and Janet Jackson
Mythological Creatures: Gryphons and Pegasus
Numerology: 5 – Changes, disruptions, instability, conflict, uncertainty
Phase of Life: The Child
Physical Property: Motion
Plane: Mental
Playing Card Suit: Spades

Possibility:

You have begun to believe that you are impotent, a paper tiger that can be vanquished with nary a fight, and your feelings of self worth have become virtually nonexistent. Downtrodden and humiliated, you are unable to accept that the loss of your pride is only a change in the way you think other people perceive you. The noblest of all actions is to turn from the fight that represents nothing but pride itself.

Possible Influencing Cards:

3 of Cups – fighting amongst friends
Devil – person involved that is totally bad news, watch finances
Emperor – rigidly following rules and regulations
Hanged Man – hidden agenda
Magician – misdirection of energies
Temperance – need for more patience

Psychological Function: Thoughts and Ideas
Quality: Active
Regent: Raphael
Royal Star: Alderbaran
Sabbat: Ostara
Season: Spring
Suit: Swords
Temperament: Sanguine

Tetragrammaton: Vau
Time of Day: Dawn

Six of Swords

Alchemical Quality: Hot and Wet

Alchemical Symbol:
Animal Energy: Hawk
(Observation and Clarity)

Astrological Correspondence:
Mercury ☿ in Aquarius ♒

Astrological Quadruplicity:
   Cardinal Zodiac (Aggressive) –
   Libra ♎

   Fixed Zodiac (Rigid) – Aquarius ♒

   Mutable Zodiac (Passive) – Gemini ♊

Attribute: Intellectual
Blood Type: Type O
Character Trait: Restlessness
Colors: Yellow, Red
Direction: East
Element: Air
Elemental: Sylphs, The Spirits of Air
Elemental King: Paralda
Esoteric Title: Lord of Earned Success
Fundamental Force: Electromagnetic
Gender: Masculine

Holy Creature: The Winged Man

I-Ching: 44 – Temptation or
Indulgence, Intrusions, Undermining
Keyword: Peace
Key Phrase: "I Think"
Lunar Phase: 1st Quarter Moon
Magical Organ: The Brain
Magical Phrase: Noscere, To Know
Matter: Gas

Meanings:

Upright:

Covert activity, earned success, end to suffering, healing energy, long journey ending, making forward progress, mind is open to new ideas, moving out of a stressful situation, objectivity, overly dependent on others, peaceful interludes, protection, release of destructive behavior, time to rest is near, transitions, travel by water, travel, turning point, visitors coming.

Reversed:

Confessions, depression, hard times coming, heading into rough waters, ignoring your problems won't make them go away, illness, no resolution in sight, oppression, stagnation, stormy weather ahead, surprises, swimming against the current, taking shortcuts, trials and tribulations, trouble, unwanted developments, unwanted public attention, unwelcome change of events.

Musical Mood: "Bridge Over Troubled Water" by Simon and Garfunkel
Mythological Creatures: Gryphons and Pegasus
Numerology: 6 – Home life, harmony, nostalgia, responsibility, reconciliation
Phase of Life: The Child
Physical Property: Motion
Plane: Mental
Playing Card Suit: Spades

Possibility:

The numbness you feel is transitional as you pass from the sorrow and mournfulness of loss through the acceptance of change in your life. It may still be difficult for you to look beyond what has happened, however there is someone near you that is guiding you through it with a selfless attitude and unwavering commitment. You will one day soon feel better, but to do that you must first face the change that is before you.

Possible Influencing Cards:

4 of Wands – end to hard times
Chariot – trip over ground
High Priestess – gather all facts before acting
Moon – trip by water, information is being concealed
Strength – unshakeable resolve
Sun – celebrations
Tower – abrupt change in plans
Wheel – possible financial gain
World – trip by air

Psychological Function: Thoughts and Ideas
Quality: Active
Regent: Raphael
Royal Star: Alderbaran
Sabbat: Ostara
Season: Spring
Suit: Swords
Temperament: Sanguine

Tetragrammaton: Vau
Time of Day: Dawn

Seven of Swords

Swords

7

Alchemical Quality: Hot and Wet

Alchemical Symbol:
Animal Energy: Hawk
(Observation and Clarity)

Astrological Correspondence:
Moon ☽ in Aquarius ♒

Astrological Quadruplicity:
  Cardinal Zodiac (Aggressive) – ♎
  Libra

  Fixed Zodiac (Rigid) – Aquarius ♒

  Mutable Zodiac (Passive) – Gemini ♊
Attribute: Intellectual
Blood Type: Type O
Character Trait: Restlessness
Colors: Yellow, Red
Direction: East
Element: Air
Elemental: Sylphs, The Spirits of Air
Elemental King: Paralda
Esoteric Title: Lord of Unstable Effort
Fundamental Force: Electromagnetic
Gender: Masculine
Holy Creature: The Winged Man

I-Ching: 6 – Collective Force or ䷅ Conflict, Dissension, Confrontation
Keyword: Thievery
Key Phrase: "I Think"
Lunar Phase: 1st Quarter Moon
Magical Organ: The Brain
Magical Phrase: Noscere, To Know
Matter: Gas

Meanings:

Upright:

Bad luck, betrayal of confidences, cowardice, cozen, deception, dirty little secrets, dishonesty, dodging responsibility, futility, greed, guilt, ill intentions, impulsive actions, insecurity, lack of conscience, legal concerns, new plans, no scruples, possible travel, preoccupations, refusing to take good advice, sabotage, sneaky, sudden impulses, thievery, trickery, undeserving effort, unprincipled actions.

Reversed:

Apology, arguments, condescending attitude, deserved criticism, full disclosure, giving up without a fight, inability to finish projects, incomplete facts, indecision, it's not as bad as you think, manipulation, missing the boat, payback, prudence, return of stolen property, slander, timidness, truth comes to light, warnings of deceptions.

Musical Mood: "Dirty Deeds Done Dirt Cheap" by AC/DC
Mythological Creatures: Gryphons and Pegasus
Numerology: 7 – Mystical, spiritual, dreams, discipline, struggles
Phase of Life: The Child
Physical Property: Motion
Plane: Mental
Playing Card Suit: Spades

Possibility:

Living the opportunistic life of attempting to parlay the success of one partially clever, mostly lucky, furtive plan into another and another will eventually collapse and fall apart. That you can choose the rules that you wish to abide by, while those that hinder you are intended only for other people, is a false perception on your part. Don't fool yourself into believing that you are serving the end, and can thusly justify the means.

Possible Influencing Cards:
   2 of Swords – reality challenged
   9 of Pentacles – refusal to accept outside help
   Fool – need to focus energy more positively
   High Priestess – covert operations
   Judgment – a secret is exposed
   Justice – need to accept responsibility for your actions

Psychological Function: Thoughts and Ideas
Quality: Active
Regent: Raphael
Royal Star: Alderbaran
Sabbat: Ostara
Season: Spring
Suit: Swords
Temperament: Sanguine

Tetragrammaton: Vau
Time of Day: Dawn

Eight of Swords

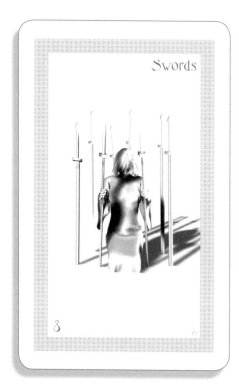

Swords

8

Alchemical Quality: Hot and Wet

Alchemical Symbol: △

Animal Energy: Hawk (Observation and Clarity)

Astrological Correspondence: Jupiter ♃ in Gemini ♊

Astrological Quadruplicity:
  Cardinal Zodiac (Aggressive) – Libra ♎

  Fixed Zodiac (Rigid) – Aquarius ♒

  Mutable Zodiac (Passive) – Gemini ♊

Attribute: Intellectual
Blood Type: Type O
Character Trait: Restlessness
Colors: Yellow, Red
Direction: East
Element: Air
Elemental: Sylphs, The Spirits of Air
Elemental King: Paralda
Esoteric Title: Lord of Shortened Force
Fundamental Force: Electromagnetic
Gender: Masculine
Holy Creature: The Winged Man

114

I-Ching: 47 – Weariness or Exhaustion, Depleted, Drained
Keyword: Repression
Key Phrase: "I Think"
Lunar Phase: 1st Quarter Moon
Magical Organ: The Brain
Magical Phrase: Noscere, To Know
Matter: Gas

Meanings:

Upright:

Adversity, blindness, censure, confusion, depression, despair, doubt, duplicity, emotional crisis, fear of confrontation, fear, feeling trapped, frustration, illness, indecision, insults, isolation, jealousy, legal problems, limitations, limited options, major difficulties, mental fatigue, miscommunications, prison of your own making, restrictions, unable to think clearly, victimization, waiting around to be rescued.

Reversed:

Accidents, breaking free, change, clarity of vision, depression, destiny, healing, improved feelings of worth, liberation, misapplied effort, moving on to a better situation, new beginnings, objectivity, obstacles are removed, passing the test, pressure is easing off, re-evaluation of present circumstances, relaxation after stress, self confidence returns, taking responsibility for yourself, trial by fire.

Musical Mood: "I Can't Leave" by Don Gibson
Mythological Creatures: Gryphons and Pegasus
Numerology: 8 – Material progress, security, expansion, priorities, advancement
Phase of Life: The Child
Physical Property: Motion
Plane: Mental
Playing Card Suit: Spades

Possibility:

The despair you feel is not from being trapped. It is your despair that confines you. When someone tells you that you can't do something, it is nothing more than an attempt to disable you. If you choose to believe them, then at that point in time you are in fact disabled. When you allow someone you love and trust to define you, you cease to be anything other than an idealistic fantasy within the mind of that person.

Possible Influencing Cards:

4 of Pentacles – financial limitations
10 of Swords – playing the role of victim unnecessarily
Ace of Wands – looking for an escape route
Hanged Man – use caution when asking for advice from others
Justice – legal limitations
Magician – the power is within your grasp
Moon – unable or unwilling to see clearly
Sun – change for the better is coming

Psychological Function: Thoughts and Ideas
Quality: Active
Regent: Raphael
Royal Star: Alderbaran
Sabbat: Ostara
Season: Spring
Suit: Swords
Temperament: Sanguine

Tetragrammaton: Vau
Time of Day: Dawn

Nine of Swords

Alchemical Quality: Hot and Wet

Alchemical Symbol: △
Animal Energy: Hawk (Observation and Clarity)

Astrological Correspondence: Mars ♂ in Gemini ♊

Astrological Quadruplicity:
    Cardinal Zodiac (Aggressive) – Libra ♎

    Fixed Zodiac (Rigid) – Aquarius ♒

    Mutable Zodiac (Passive) – Gemini ♊

Attribute: Intellectual
Blood Type: Type O
Character Trait: Restlessness
Colors: Yellow, Red
Direction: East
Element: Air
Elemental: Sylphs, The Spirits of Air
Elemental King: Paralda
Esoteric Title: Lord of Despair and Cruelty
Fundamental Force: Electromagnetic
Gender: Masculine
Holy Creature: The Winged Man

I-Ching: 9 – Restrained or Force of the Weak, Interference, Intuition
Keyword: Anxiety
Key Phrase: "I Think"
Lunar Phase: 1st Quarter Moon
Magical Organ: The Brain
Magical Phrase: Noscere, To Know
Matter: Gas

Meanings:

Upright:

Accusations, anguish, anxiety, broken promises, cruelty, depression, desolation, despair, doubt, failure, fear, feelings of impending doom, gloom, guilty conscience, harsh self criticism, hopelessness, illness, injustice, insomnia, isolation, lamentation, malice, nightmares, paralyzed into inactivity, pessimism, premonitions, runaway imagination, scandal, shame and disgrace, stress, suspicion, uncertainty, worry.

Reversed:

Clear conscience, clearing the ghosts out of the attic, darkness before the dawn, exaggerated overreaction, facing your fears, groundless fears, healing energy, improving health, liberation, light at the end of the tunnel, mercy, nightmare is ending, peace, pulling yourself together, rehabilitation, release, relief, renewed faith, resolution, rest, setting your mind at ease, time to begin recovery, vivid dreams.

Musical Mood: "Where Were You Last Night" by Nightwish
Mythological Creatures: Gryphons and Pegasus
Numerology: 9 – Satisfaction, fulfillment, luck, complacency, just desserts
Phase of Life: The Child
Physical Property: Motion
Plane: Mental
Playing Card Suit: Spades

Possibility:

Only the darkest part of the night brings with it the worst imaginable feelings of regret and trepidation. Perhaps you have feelings of guilt or regret. You may be experiencing the anguish of potential suffering, or of great loss. Things are never as troubling in the light of day, and are seldom as bad as what we imagine in our waking nightmares. Don't dwell on what is done or fear what has yet to come, worry changes nothing.

Possible Influencing Cards:
10 of Cups – better times are coming
10 of Wands – stress overload
Ace of Cups – bad news on the way
Devil – complete desolation
Empress – possible miscarriage or problems with pregnancy
High Priestess – be prepared to face the consequences
Star – don't lose faith

Psychological Function: Thoughts and Ideas
Quality: Active
Regent: Raphael
Royal Star: Alderbaran
Sabbat: Ostara
Season: Spring
Suit: Swords
Temperament: Sanguine

Tetragrammaton: Vau
Time of Day: Dawn

Ten of Swords

Alchemical Quality: Hot and Wet

Alchemical Symbol: △
Animal Energy: Hawk
(Observation and Clarity)

Astrological Correspondence:
Sun ☉ in Gemini ♊

Astrological Quadruplicity:
   Cardinal Zodiac (Aggressive) –
   Libra ♎

   Fixed Zodiac (Rigid) – Aquarius ♒

   Mutable Zodiac (Passive) – Gemini ♊

Attribute: Intellectual
Blood Type: Type O
Character Trait: Restlessness
Colors: Yellow, Red
Direction: East
Element: Air
Elemental: Sylphs, The Spirits of Air
Elemental King: Paralda
Esoteric Title: Lord of Ruin
Fundamental Force: Electromagnetic
Gender: Masculine

Holy Creature: The Winged Man

I-Ching: 59 – Dispersion or Dissolution, Scatter, Break Apart
Keyword: Inevitability
Key Phrase: "I Think"
Lunar Phase: 1st Quarter Moon
Magical Organ: The Brain
Magical Phrase: Noscere, To Know
Matter: Gas

Meanings:

Upright:

Bad advice, bankruptcy, desolation, devastation, disappointment, disruption, emotional isolation, enemies abound, exhaustion, forced change, forced martyrdom, hitting rock bottom, hysteria, legal problems, overkill, personal defeat, possible travel, ruin, salvage what you can, self inflicted pain, shattered dreams, skid row, the battle is lost, there is nothing left.

Reversed:

Accepting a helping hand, benevolence, cleansing, forgiveness, heartfelt charity, low self-esteem, moving forward, pulling yourself up by your bootstraps, punishment for transgressions, redemption, resignation, second wind, self acceptance, starting over, the worst is over, time to start rebuilding, unexpected financial windfall.

Musical Mood: "Veteran of the Psychic Wars" by Blue Oyster Cult
Mythological Creatures: Gryphons and Pegasus
Numerology: 10 – Completions, resolutions, beginning and/or ending of a cycle
Phase of Life: The Child
Physical Property: Motion
Plane: Mental
Playing Card Suit: Spades

Possibility:

Your plans have failed and your objective is no longer within your reach. You have suffered a terrible setback, undoubtedly, but all is not lost, you can start again. Claiming that you have been unfairly thwarted, betrayed, or cheated won't serve you now. There is no place for seeking sympathy or wallowing in self-pity, the sun is coming up and new opportunity will soon follow. Learn from this and get ready to move on.

Possible Influencing Cards:

3 of Swords – complete emotional breakdown
5 of Wands – sudden changes
8 of Swords – self pity
Death – professional intervention may be necessary
Fool – major changes in priorities, may have to start over
Hermit – rethink your position

Psychological Function: Thoughts and Ideas
Quality: Active
Regent: Raphael
Royal Star: Alderbaran
Sabbat: Ostara
Season: Spring
Suit: Swords
Temperament: Sanguine

Tetragrammaton: Vau
Time of Day: Dawn

Ace of Wands

The Wands

Alchemical Quality: Hot and Dry

Alchemical Symbol:
Animal Energy: Lioness
(Courage and Initiative)

Astrological Correspondence: Root of Fire

Astrological Quadruplicity:
  Cardinal Zodiac (Aggressive) – ♈
  Aries

  Fixed Zodiac (Rigid) – Leo ♌

  Mutable Zodiac (Passive) – ♐
  Sagittarius

Attribute: Spiritual
Blood Type: Type B
Character Trait: Passion
Colors: Red, White
Direction: South
Element: Fire
Elemental: Salamanders, The Spirits of Fire
Elemental King: Djinn
Esoteric Title: Root of the Powers of Fire
Fundamental Force: Strong
Gender: Masculine

Holy Creature: The Winged Lion

I-Ching: 3 - Difficult Beginnings, ䷂ Planning, Organizing, Problem Solving
Key Phrase: "I Will"
Keyword: Creation
Lunar Phase: Full Moon
Magical Organ: The Spirit
Magical Phrase: Velle, To Will
Matter: Energy

Meanings:

Upright:
Accept invitations, ambition, beginning of activity associated with the suit, confidence, conception, courage, drive, energy, enthusiasm, fertility, good foundations, idealism, inspiration, intuition, invention, new business, new challenges, opportunities, passion, pregnancy, profit, spark of creativity, stimulation, taking the initiative, virility.

Reversed:
Abandonment, all talk and no action, avarice, barrenness, cancellations, delays in business, disinterest, false start, frustration, greed, impotence, inertia, lack of initiative and motivation, laziness, overconfidence, persecution, pessimism, problem pregnancy, restlessness, ruin, scams and pyramid schemes, selfishness, shell game, stagnation, sterility.

Musical Mood: "Unwritten" by Natasha Bedingfield
Mythological Creatures: Dragons and Phoenix
Numerology: 1 – New beginnings, confidence, creativity, possibility, potential
Phase of Life: The Youth
Physical Property: Intensity
Plane: Spiritual
Playing Card Suit: Clubs

Possibility:

If there is a restless passion stirring within you, and you have been waiting for just the right moment to release it, that moment has arrived. The project that has been living on the edge of opportunity, waiting for you to kindle it, should have your full attention now. You are confident and enthusiastic about a future business project, and it's time to get started. It's time to open your eyes to the opportunity that is in front of you.

Possible Influencing Cards:

2 of Pentacles – money from an unexpected source
10 of Pentacles – new projects in the works
10 of Wands – taking on too much responsibility
Chariot – heading in the right direction
Devil – relationships need closer examination
Tower – unable to manifest your desires

Psychological Function: Energy and Desire
Quality: Immediate
Regent: Michael
Royal Star: Regulus
Sabbat: Litha
Season: Summer
Suit: Wands
Temperament: Choleric

Tetragrammaton: Yod ♪
Time of Day: Noon

Two of Wands

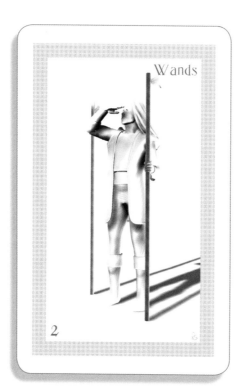

Wands

2

Alchemical Quality: Hot and Dry

Alchemical Symbol: △
Animal Energy: Lioness
(Courage and Initiative)

Astrological Correspondence:
Mars ♂ in Aries ♈

Astrological Quadruplicity:
  Cardinal Zodiac (Aggressive) – ♈
  Aries

  Fixed Zodiac (Rigid) – Leo ♌

  Mutable Zodiac (Passive) – ♐
  Sagittarius

Attribute: Spiritual
Blood Type: Type B
Character Trait: Passion
Colors: Red, White
Direction: South
Element: Fire
Elemental: Salamanders, The Spirits of Fire
Elemental King: Djinn
Esoteric Title: Lord of Dominion
Fundamental Force: Strong
Gender: Masculine

Holy Creature: The Winged Lion

I-Ching: 13 – Community or ☰☰ Fellowship, Companionship, Sharing
Key Phrase: "I Will"
Keyword: Planning
Lunar Phase: Full Moon
Magical Organ: The Spirit
Magical Phrase: Velle, To Will
Matter: Energy

Meanings:

Upright:
Alternatives, anxiety about the future, change is coming, creative ability, collaboration, disappointment, facing reality, grief, jealousy, melancholy, negotiations, originality, patience, planning, possible travel, preparation, quarrels, relocation, resentment, responsibility, study past successes, thinking outside the box, waiting for news, wakeup call.

Reversed:
Anxiety, ask for more clarification before acting, being let down, blind ambition, boredom, disagreements, disinterest, deception, dishonesty, disillusionment, domination, frustration, losing patience, loss, miracles out of nowhere, obstinacy, restrictions, reservation, self doubt, sense of entitlement, sorrow, surprise, unrealistic expectations.

Musical Mood: "Patience" by Guns N' Roses
Mythological Creatures: Dragons and Phoenix
Numerology: 2 – Relationships, decisions, balance, cooperation, emotions
Phase of Life: The Youth
Physical Property: Intensity
Plane: Spiritual
Playing Card Suit: Clubs

Possibility:
You have had significant success so far, and it appears that you have the world in your hand, but you must continue to exercise patience. The foundation for your success is your passion, and your devotion to aptly applying the knowledge of your expertise. Amidst that knowledge is the realization that sometimes the best course of action is waiting for results. If you have thoughts of travel, it would be appropriate at this time.

Possible Influencing Cards:
7 of Swords – overreacting
8 of Swords – inability to act
10 of Swords – self pity
Emperor – opportunity is at hand
Hermit – need for more information
High Priestess – keeping a low profile
Sun – possible travel

Psychological Function: Energy and Desire
Quality: Immediate
Regent: Michael
Royal Star: Regulus
Sabbat: Litha
Season: Summer
Suit: Wands
Temperament: Choleric

Tetragrammaton: Yod ׳
Time of Day: Noon

Three of Wands

Alchemical Quality: Hot and Dry

Alchemical Symbol: △

Animal Energy: Lioness
(Courage and Initiative)

Astrological Correspondence:
Sun ☉ in Aries ♈

Astrological Quadruplicity:
    Cardinal Zodiac (Aggressive) – ♈
    Aries

    Fixed Zodiac (Rigid) – Leo ♌

    Mutable Zodiac (Passive) – ♐
    Sagittarius

Attribute: Spiritual
Blood Type: Type B
Character Trait: Passion
Colors: Red, White
Direction: South
Element: Fire
Elemental: Salamanders, The Spirits of Fire
Elemental King: Djinn
Esoteric Title: Lord of Established
Strength

Fundamental Force: Strong
Gender: Masculine
Holy Creature: The Winged Lion

I-Ching: 35 - Progress, Success, 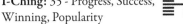 Winning, Popularity
Key Phrase: "I Will"
Keyword: Assumptions
Lunar Phase: Full Moon
Magical Organ: The Spirit
Magical Phrase: Velle, To Will
Matter: Energy

Meanings:

Upright:

Business sense, boldness, compromise, cooperation, courage, efforts are paying off, effort, enterprise, explorations, first stages are complete, foresight, good advice, honesty, initiative, integrity, kick starting things into motion, limited success, new opportunities, setting goals, ship is coming in, strength of conviction, time to ask for assistance, trade, travel.

Reversed:

Arrogance, carelessness, deceit, distrust, false pride, looking a gift horse in the mouth, missed opportunities, miscommunications, more work to be done, new direction needed, overconfidence, peer pressure, poor communication, right place/wrong time, scattered energy, slipping through your fingers, stubbornness, ulterior motives, unattainable goals.

Musical Mood: "My Ship is Coming In" by The Walker Brothers
Mythological Creatures: Dragons and Phoenix
Numerology: 3 – Growth, enterprise, manifestation, unity, intuition
Phase of Life: The Youth
Physical Property: Intensity
Plane: Spiritual
Playing Card Suit: Clubs

Possibility:

Expectations, and the actions to meet those expectations, are driven by focus and perspective. If your focus is narrow, or your perspective is unrealistic, influenced by the prestige of past accomplishments, then your future success will be dictated by chance. Step back from your current view and observe the situation from a broader perspective. You can't determine the destination of a ship by looking only at the rudder.

Possible Influencing Cards:

2 of Swords – answer is right in front of you
3 of Pentacles – planning for the future
7 of Cups – uncertain about business direction
Justice – you get what is coming to you
Strength – stay focused
Tower – unexpected change in business or employment
Wheel of Fortune – keep a positive attitude

Psychological Function: Energy and Desire
Quality: Immediate
Regent: Michael
Royal Star: Regulus
Sabbat: Litha
Season: Summer
Suit: Wands
Temperament: Choleric

Tetragrammaton: Yod ♪
Time of Day: Noon

Four of Wands

Alchemical Quality: Hot and Dry

Alchemical Symbol: △
Animal Energy: Lioness
(Courage and Initiative)

Astrological Correspondence:
Venus ♀ in Aries ♈

Astrological Quadruplicity: ♈
   Cardinal Zodiac (Aggressive) –
   Aries

   Fixed Zodiac (Rigid) – Leo ♌

   Mutable Zodiac (Passive) – ♐
   Sagittarius

Attribute: Spiritual
Blood Type: Type B
Character Trait: Passion
Colors: Red, White
Direction: South
Element: Fire
Elemental: Salamanders, The Spirits of Fire
Elemental King: Djinn
Esoteric Title: Lord of Perfected Work
Fundamental Force: Strong

Gender: Masculine
Holy Creature: The Winged Lion

I-Ching: 51– Awakening or Shock, Surprise, Excitement
Key Phrase: "I Will"
Keyword: Revelry
Lunar Phase: Full Moon
Magical Organ: The Spirit
Magical Phrase: Velle, To Will
Matter: Energy

Meanings:

Upright:
Attainment, celebration, culture and refinement, excitement, freedom, fun, goodness, marriage, merriment, joy, happiness, moving to or buying a new house, party, productivity, recreation, relationships are committed, rest and relaxation, rites of passage, satisfaction, taking a well deserved break, taking charge of your life, tranquility, vacation.

Reversed:
Disappointment, disapproval, ending a long term relationship, ingratitude for blessings, inhibitions, insecurity, lackluster, not speaking up when necessary, overdoing it, possible delays, shirking responsibilities, snobbishness, superiority complex, social anxiety, the morning after, unforeseen obstacles, unwanted relationships.

Musical Mood: "Celebration" by Kool and the Gang
Mythological Creatures: Dragons and Phoenix
Numerology: 4 – Rest, inactivity, patience, stability, legal matters
Phase of Life: The Youth
Physical Property: Intensity
Plane: Spiritual
Playing Card Suit: Clubs

Possibility:
Too much to be done to be wasting time with the frivolity of a celebration, is there? That kind of sentiment is sure to cause one to lose their grip on why they work hard in the first place. Congratulations are in order and there is a need to celebrate with those that have helped in this grand success. If you tip your glass and wave to the revelers in the distance, whilst working still, will they feel adequate to your efforts?

Possible Influencing Cards:
2 of Wands – shopping for a new home
10 of Wands – holding yourself back
Ace of Pentacles – real estate investments
Devil – guard against overindulgence
Hermit – loosen your creativity
Magician – new projects on the horizon
World – new ideas are possible

Psychological Function: Energy and Desire
Quality: Immediate
Regent: Michael
Royal Star: Regulus
Sabbat: Litha
Season: Summer
Suit: Wands
Temperament: Choleric

Tetragrammaton: Yod ◗
Time of Day: Noon

Five of Wands

Alchemical Quality: Hot and Dry

Alchemical Symbol: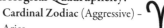
Animal Energy: Lioness
(Courage and Initiative)

Astrological Correspondence:
Saturn ♄ in Leo ♌

Astrological Quadruplicity:
  Cardinal Zodiac (Aggressive) - ♈
  Aries

  Fixed Zodiac (Rigid) – Leo

  Mutable Zodiac (Passive) – ♐
  Sagittarius

Attribute: Spiritual
Blood Type: Type B
Character Trait: Passion
Colors: Red, White
Direction: South
Element: Fire
Elemental: Salamanders, The Spirits of Fire
Elemental King: Djinn
Esoteric Title: Lord of Strife
Fundamental Force: Strong
Gender: Masculine

Holy Creature: The Winged Lion

I-Ching: 21 – Reform or Reprimand, Effort, Determination
Key Phrase: "I Will"
Keyword: Conflict
Lunar Phase: Full Moon
Magical Organ: The Spirit
Magical Phrase: Velle, To Will
Matter: Energy

Meanings:

Upright:
Aggravations, aggression, agitation, anxiety, burning off energy, call it as you see it, challenges, competition, conceit, corporate raider mentality, cutthroat, frustration, hormonal flare-ups, inner conflict, legal matters, opposition, rivalry, stakes are high, taking the lions share, twice the pride – double the fall, willingness to fight, winning isn't everything – it's the only thing

Reversed:
Arguments, communication problems, conflicts, cruelty, curmudgeon, disputes, fraud, irritations and annoyances, getting the runaround, legal problems, malicious intent, meanness, minor health issues, overly defensive, pettiness, playing dirty, pettiness, practical jokes at the expense of others, red tape, setbacks, taking unfair advantages, taunting, wasted energy

Musical Mood: "You Got Another Thing Coming" by Judas Priest
Mythological Creatures: Dragons and Phoenix
Numerology: 5 – Changes, disruptions, instability, conflict, uncertainty
Phase of Life: The Youth
Physical Property: Intensity
Plane: Spiritual
Playing Card Suit: Clubs

Possibility:

Those that fear competition are usually woefully unprepared for it, or perhaps pride has taken them from their natural arena. The challenge of working to better your opposition defeats your complacency, and generates energy for you to use in the achievement of your goals. If you have come to suffer from frustration, or find yourself tilting at windmills, seek a productive outlet for the adverse energy in friendly competition.

Possible Influencing Cards:

2 of Cups – reconciliation
7 of Wands – power struggles
Devil – no one is interested in your excuses
Hermit – don't depend on others for help
Justice – legal concerns
Star – others do not have your best interests at heart
Sun – opinions of others do not matter

Psychological Function: Energy and Desire
Quality: Immediate
Regent: Michael
Royal Star: Regulus
Sabbat: Litha
Season: Summer
Suit: Wands
Temperament: Choleric

Tetragrammaton: Yod ♪
Time of Day: Noon

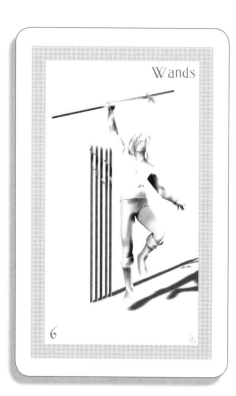

Six of Wands

Alchemical Quality: Hot and Dry

Alchemical Symbol:
Animal Energy: Lioness
(Courage and Initiative)

Astrological Correspondence:
Jupiter ♃ in Leo ♌

Astrological Quadruplicity:
  Cardinal Zodiac (Aggressive) –
  Aries

  Fixed Zodiac (Rigid) – Leo ♌

  Mutable Zodiac (Passive) –
  Sagittarius

Attribute: Spiritual
Blood Type: Type B
Character Trait: Passion
Colors: Red, White
Direction: South
Element: Fire
Elemental: Salamanders, The Spirits of Fire
Elemental King: Djinn
Esoteric Title: Lord of Victory
Fundamental Force: Strong

Gender: Masculine
Holy Creature: The Winged Lion

I-Ching: 14 – Sovereignty,
Possessions, Prosperity, Affluence
Key Phrase: "I Will"
Keyword: Limelight
Lunar Phase: Full Moon
Magical Organ: The Spirit
Magical Phrase: Velle, To Will
Matter: Energy

Meanings:

Upright:

Acclaim, accomplishment, advancement, diplomacy, fame and recognition, good news, hopefulness, inspiration, leadership, nobility, pride, progress, public recognition, reaching a goal or milestone, resolution of difficulties, return of the conquering hero, rewards, safe journey, satisfaction, self confidence, success, travel, victory, warm welcomes.

Reversed:

Anticipation, arrogance, betrayal, coldness, delays, disrespect, false pride, getting upstaged, indecision, infidelity, insolence, lack of foresight, misunderstandings, not up to the challenge, payoff is not as good as expected, rivalry, second best, snatching defeat from the jaws of victory, stress needs an outlet, unwelcoming atmosphere.

Musical Mood: "Home Again" by Blackmore's Night
Mythological Creatures: Dragons and Phoenix
Numerology: 6 – Home life, harmony, nostalgia, responsibility, reconciliation
Phase of Life: The Youth
Physical Property: Intensity
Plane: Spiritual
Playing Card Suit: Clubs

Possibility:

Arrogance grows from unrestrained pride, and twice the pride means double the fall. If you practice an attitude of superiority over others you will foster antipathy in them, which you will falsely perceive to be jealousy. This in turn will result in relationships that will be irrevocably lost. Manage your pride and be respectful of those you have bested. Victory is never an individual effort, so always share it with the deserving.

Possible Influencing Cards:

Fool – don't let your guard down
High Priest – need to be more tolerant and understanding
High Priestess – it is not all about you
Sun – major accomplishment
Tower – pride comes before a fall

Psychological Function: Energy and Desire
Quality: Immediate
Regent: Michael
Royal Star: Regulus
Sabbat: Litha
Season: Summer
Suit: Wands
Temperament: Choleric

Tetragrammaton: Yod ♪
Time of Day: Noon

Seven of Wands

Alchemical Quality: Hot and Dry

Alchemical Symbol: △
Animal Energy: Lioness
(Courage and Initiative)

Astrological Correspondence:
Mars ♂ in Leo ♌

Astrological Quadruplicity:
  Cardinal Zodiac (Aggressive) – ♈
  Aries

  Fixed Zodiac (Rigid) – Leo ♌

  Mutable Zodiac (Passive) – ♐
  Sagittarius

Attribute: Spiritual
Blood Type: Type B
Character Trait: Passion
Colors: Red, White
Direction: South
Element: Fire
Elemental: Salamanders, The Spirits of Fire
Elemental King: Djinn
Esoteric Title: Lord of Valor
Fundamental Force: Strong

Gender: Masculine
Holy Creature: The Winged Lion

I-Ching: 38 - Contradictions or
Oppositions, Solitary, Estrangement
Key Phrase: "I Will"
Keyword: Resolve
Lunar Phase: Full Moon
Magical Organ: The Spirit
Magical Phrase: Velle, To Will
Matter: Energy

Meanings:

Upright:

Advancement, challenges, change of employment, competition is fierce, courage of convictions, defiance, devotion, fortitude, gossip, having the advantage, high moral fiber, honor, inner strength, need for more self-confidence, observant, opportunity, productivity, stand your ground, taking a firm stand, taking responsibility for your actions, under pressure, upper hand.

Reversed:

Anxiety, arguments for arguments sake, competitive atmosphere, disadvantage, doubt, embarrassment, envy, failure, fear of rejection, fear, feeling threatened or challenged, health issues, hesitation, impatience, indecision, obsessive/compulsive, overcompensation, retreat, running away from problems, sitting on the fence, this too shall pass, victimization.

Musical Mood: "I Won't Back Down" by Tom Petty & The Heartbreakers
Mythological Creatures: Dragons and Phoenix
Numerology: 7 – Mystical, spiritual, dreams, discipline, struggles
Phase of Life: The Youth
Physical Property: Intensity
Plane: Spiritual
Playing Card Suit: Clubs

Possibility:

The principle difference between holding the higher ground and being on top relates directly to the purpose that drives you. Being combative because we feel threatened when we are on top is pridefulness, not purpose. It is easy to transpose the words fighting for a cause into cause for a fight, and the latter is always the result of vainglory thinking. Pride offers only the ascent to a height from which you will surely fall.

Possible Influencing Cards:

3 of Cups – peer pressure
5 of Swords – major clash of personality
Chariot – watch levels of aggression
Death – sort out your priorities
Emperor – misuse of power
Hanged Man – stubbornness will make things worse
Temperance – examine your motives

Psychological Function: Energy and Desire
Quality: Immediate
Regent: Michael
Royal Star: Regulus
Sabbat: Litha
Season: Summer
Suit: Wands
Temperament: Choleric

Tetragrammaton: Yod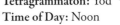
Time of Day: Noon

Eight of Wands

Alchemical Quality: Hot and Dry

Alchemical Symbol: △
Animal Energy: Lioness
(Courage and Initiative)

Astrological Correspondence:
Mercury ☿ in Sagittarius ♐

Astrological Quadruplicity:
    Cardinal Zodiac (Aggressive) – ♈
    Aries

    Fixed Zodiac (Rigid) – Leo ♌

    Mutable Zodiac (Passive) – ♐
    Sagittarius
Attribute: Spiritual
Blood Type: Type B
Character Trait: Passion
Colors: Red, White
Direction: South
Element: Fire
Elemental: Salamanders, The Spirits of Fire
Elemental King: Djinn
Esoteric Title: Lord of Swiftness
Fundamental Force: Strong
Gender: Masculine

Holy Creature: The Winged Lion

I-Ching: 56 - Traveling or Transition, Movement, Momentum
Key Phrase: "I Will"
Keyword: Arrival
Lunar Phase: Full Moon
Magical Organ: The Spirit
Magical Phrase: Velle, To Will
Matter: Energy

Meanings:

Upright:

Apology is due, caught up in a whirlwind of activity, communications, creative inspirations, events are now in motion, excitement, falling in love, goal is within reach, lighting strike, messages are coming, no more delays, possible travel, progress, sense of purpose, sense of urgency, sparks of creativity, swiftness, taking initiative, travel by air

Reversed:

Anxiety, apology owed, delays and unforeseen obstacles, disagreements, disputes, domestic disputes, futility, jealousy, marital interference, momentum is blocked, need for emotional control, overwhelmed by current activity, paddling upstream, personality clashes, quarrels, remorse, refusing to see the obvious, stagnation, standstill, wasted effort

Musical Mood: "Something's Coming" sung by character of Tony, *West Side Story*
Mythological Creatures: Dragons and Phoenix
Numerology: 8 – Material progress, security, expansion, priorities, advancement
Phase of Life: The Youth
Physical Property: Intensity
Plane: Spiritual
Playing Card Suit: Clubs

Possibility:

At this point what you have begun has left your control and will fall to Earth, as it will. If your preparation and planning were sound, and your efforts were focused, the results are sure to be favorable. The answers to the questions you seek will soon find you, but the question remains, will you recognize them when you see them? Anticipate with discretion, as worry, impatience, and rigid expectations, will likely block your view.

Possible Influencing Cards:

High Priestess – wait for the right moment
Devil – consider all angles before acting
Lovers – future plans are now being made
Sun – be more positive

Psychological Function: Energy and Desire
Quality: Immediate
Regent: Michael
Royal Star: Regulus
Sabbat: Litha
Season: Summer
Suit: Wands
Temperament: Choleric

Tetragrammaton: Yod
Time of Day: Noon

Nine of Wands

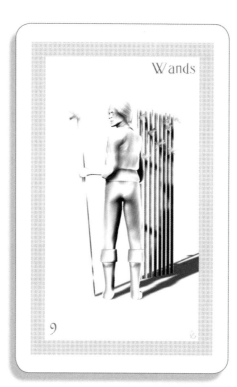

Alchemical Quality: Hot and Dry

Alchemical Symbol: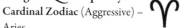
Animal Energy: Lioness
(Courage and Initiative)

Astrological Correspondence:
Moon ☽ in Sagittarius ♐

Astrological Quadruplicity:
   Cardinal Zodiac (Aggressive) –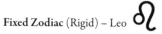
   Aries

   Fixed Zodiac (Rigid) – Leo

   Mutable Zodiac (Passive) – ♐
   Sagittarius

Attribute: Spiritual
Blood Type: Type B
Character Trait: Passion
Colors: Red, White
Direction: South
Element: Fire
Elemental: Salamanders, The Spirits of Fire
Elemental King: Djinn
Esoteric Title: Lord of Great Strength
Fundamental Force: Strong

Gender: Masculine
Holy Creature: The Winged Lion

I-Ching: 36 - Censorship,
Night, Damaged, Rejection
Key Phrase: "I Will"
Keyword: Suspicion
Lunar Phase: Full Moon
Magical Organ: The Spirit
Magical Phrase: Velle, To Will
Matter: Energy

Meanings:

Upright:

Calm before the storm, challenges, defensive, delays, diligence, estrangement, fortification, frustration, health problems, hidden obstacles, keep your own counsel, miscommunications, not a time to make decisions, obstinacy, on guard, perseverance, preparations, resilience, stability, stamina, strength, suspension, use discretion, watchful

Reversed:

Adversity, barriers, being taken advantage of, caught off guard, cheap shots, defenses are inadequate, delays, disarray, exhaustion, false faces, illness, importunate, impracticality, lacking initiative, misfortune, not paying attention, obstacles, rest needed, stubbornness, tension, unforeseen problems, unpreparedness, unwillingness to compromise

Musical Mood: "Battle We Have Won" by Eric Johnson
Mythological Creatures: Dragons and Phoenix
Numerology: 9 – Satisfaction, fulfillment, luck, complacency, just desserts
Phase of Life: The Youth
Physical Property: Intensity
Plane: Spiritual
Playing Card Suit: Clubs

Possibility:

Does the up and down, up and down of life have you looking over your shoulder? Then just when you think you have it pretty good, it knocks you down, and keeps you down until it breaks your spirit? Once you let it in and give it control of your thoughts, you become petty and paranoid, scornful and bellicose. Happiness is a state of mind that you create within yourself, and what affects others have on it is entirely up to you.

Possible Influencing Cards:

6 of Pentacles – unscrupulous financial advice
10 of Swords – fighting a losing battle
Lovers – possible infidelity
Magician – attention needed in business matters
Strength – perseverance is key
Sun – attention needed in financial matters
Psychological Function: Energy and Desire

Quality: Immediate
Regent: Michael
Royal Star: Regulus
Sabbat: Litha
Season: Summer
Suit: Wands
Temperament: Choleric

Tetragrammaton: Yod
Time of Day: Noon

Ten of Wands

Wands

1o

Alchemical Quality: Hot and Dry

Alchemical Symbol: △
Animal Energy: Lioness (Courage and Initiative)

Astrological Correspondence: Saturn ♄ in Sagittarius ♐

Astrological Quadruplicity:
  Cardinal Zodiac (Aggressive) – Aries

  Fixed Zodiac (Rigid) – Leo

  Mutable Zodiac (Passive) – Sagittarius

Attribute: Spiritual
Blood Type: Type B
Character Trait: Passion
Colors: Red, White
Direction: South
Element: Fire
Elemental: Salamanders, The Spirits of Fire
Elemental King: Djinn
Esoteric Title: Lord of Oppression
Fundamental Force: Strong

138

Gender: Masculine
Holy Creature: The Winged Lion

I-Ching: 47 - Weariness or Exhaustion, Depleted, Drained
Key Phrase: "I Will"
Keyword: Burdens
Lunar Phase: Full Moon
Magical Organ: The Spirit
Magical Phrase: Velle, To Will
Matter: Energy

Meanings:

Upright:

Ambition out of control, anger, burdens, cruelty, disruption, failure, falsehoods, feelings of indispensability, guilt, heavy workload, jealousy, no end in sight, no social life, oppression, over extension, overestimation, overwhelming, playing the martyr, struggles, success at any cost, suffering, taking on too much, treachery, under pressure, work related stress, workaholic.

Reversed:

Accepting help, anxiety, catching a break, getting left holding the bag, guile, intrigue, lightening the load, manipulation, misuse of ability, obstacles, overcoming limitations, plots, prioritizing, realizing your limitations, release, relief from stress, rewards are less than expected, traps, trying to shirk responsibility, wolf in sheep's clothing, unexpected assistance, worry.

Musical Mood: "Hollow Years" by Dream Theater
Mythological Creatures: Dragons and Phoenix
Numerology: 10 – Completions, resolutions, beginning and/or ending of a cycle
Phase of Life: The Youth
Physical Property: Intensity
Plane: Spiritual
Playing Card Suit: Clubs

Possibility:

Consumed with work, or a hobby perhaps, you are taking refuge from something that you don't want to face. Although you are successfully escaping your demons for now you will eventually have to face them. When you decided this singular purpose would be your only care, did you take into account the feelings of the people that care about you? If you are only seeing one aspect to your life, than you are not looking.

Possible Influencing Cards:

8 of Pentacles – picking up everyone else's slack

Psychological Function: Energy and Desire
Quality: Immediate
Regent: Michael
Royal Star: Regulus
Sabbat: Litha
Season: Summer
Suit: Wands
Temperament: Choleric

Tetragrammaton: Yod
Time of Day: Noon

The Cups

Cups

Ace

Alchemical Quality: Cold and Wet

Alchemical Symbol:

Animal Energy: Dolphin (Joy and Love)

Astrological Correspondence:
Root of Water

Astrological Quadruplicity:
  Cardinal Zodiac (Aggressive) –
  Cancer

  Fixed Zodiac (Rigid) – Scorpio

  Mutable Zodiac (Passive) – Pisces ♓

Attribute: Emotional
Blood Type: Type AB
Character Trait: Healing
Colors: Blue-Green, Gray
Direction: West
Element: Water
Elemental: Undines, The Spirits of Water
Elemental King: Nixsa
Esoteric Title: Lord of the Powers of Water
Fundamental Force: Weak
Gender: Feminine
Holy Creature: The Eagle

I-Ching: 58 – Joy or Serenity, Self Confidence, Encouragement
Key Phrase: "I Feel"
Keyword: Abundance
Lunar Phase: 3rd Quarter
Magical Organ: The Heart
Magical Phrase: Audere, To Dare
Matter: Liquid

Meanings:

Upright:

Abundance, beginning of activity associated with the suit, blessings, breakthroughs, closeness, compassion, faithfulness, fertility, friendship, good news, happiness, intimacy, invitations, joy, kindness, new emotional beginnings, new love, nourishment, opening of psychic awareness, opening up to the possibilities, peace, pregnancy, sharing, sparks of love, stability.

Reversed:

Abandonment, apathy, barrenness, broken heart, change, depression, despair, detachment, egotism, emptiness, false love, false promises, hesitancy, inconsistency, insecurity, loneliness, loss of faith, loss of love, mental blocks, running away from love, sadness, stagnation, sterility, toying with another's emotions, unrequited love, using sex as a weapon, unfulfilling.

Musical Mood: "So Much In Love" by Timothy B. Schmidt
Mythological Creatures: Merfolk and Hippocampus
Numerology: 1 – New beginnings, confidence, creativity, possibility, potential
Phase of Life: The Adult
Physical Property: Fluidity
Plane: Astral
Playing Card Suit: Hearts

Possibility:

You have felt something stirring in your heart recently, or you are about to. Somebody, or quite possibly something, is about to get your full attention, and love will become your motivating force. There isn't any point in resisting, or challenging the feeling. If you try to talk yourself out of it, you won't listen anyway, so relax and be swept away. Now is the time for romance, so don't let them wonder how you feel.

Possible Influencing Cards:

6 of Cups – lover from the past reappears, surprise gifts
Devil – physical infatuation
Empress – possible pregnancy
Lovers – relationships improve
Page of Cups – possible wedding or pregnancy
Wheel of Fortune – finances improve

Psychological Function: Emotions and Feelings
Quality: Receptive
Regent: Gabriel
Royal Star: Antares
Sabbat: Mabon
Season: Autumn
Suit: Cups
Temperament: Phlegmatic

Tetragrammaton: Heh
Time of Day: Dusk

Two of Cups

Cups

2

Alchemical Quality: Cold and Wet

Alchemical Symbol:
Animal Energy: Dolphin (Joy and Love)

Astrological Correspondence:
Venus ♀ in Cancer ♋

Astrological Quadruplicity:
Cardinal Zodiac (Aggressive) –
Cancer ♋

Fixed Zodiac (Rigid) – Scorpio ♏

Mutable Zodiac (Passive) – Pisces ♓

Attribute: Emotional
Blood Type: Type AB
Character Trait: Healing
Colors: Blue-Green, Gray
Direction: West
Element: Water
Elemental: Undines, The Spirits of Water
Elemental King: Nixsa
Esoteric Title: Lord of Love
Fundamental Force: Weak
Gender: Feminine
Holy Creature: The Eagle

I-Ching: 31 – Attraction, ䷞ Interest, Influence, Sensitivity
Key Phrase: "I Feel"
Keyword: Partnership
Lunar Phase: 3rd Quarter
Magical Organ: The Heart
Magical Phrase: Audere, To Dare
Matter: Liquid

Meanings:

Upright:

Admiration, affection, attraction, balance, becoming lovers, burying the hatchet, choices, commitment, cooperation, devotion, emotional affinity, empathy, finding a common ground, harmony, ideas, love, marriage, mutual appreciation and trust, partnership, reconciliation, romance, peace offering, pleasant surprises, sharing, sincerity, truce, understanding both male/female sides of our personalities, union.

Reversed:

Bad influences, breakups, broken heart, deceit, destructive emotions, disillusionment, dissatisfaction, dissent, distrust, divorce or separation, ending of a relationship, envy, greed, incompatibility, infidelity, jealousy, obstacles, overly possessive and demanding, philandering, pride, quarrels, rejection, sadness, telling a secret, temptation, unhealthy relationships, unrequited love, violent passion.

Musical Mood: "We've Only Just Begun" by The Carpenters
Mythological Creatures: Merfolk and Hippocampus
Numerology: 2 – Relationships, decisions, balance, cooperation, emotions
Phase of Life: The Adult
Physical Property: Fluidity
Plane: Astral
Playing Card Suit: Hearts

Possibility:

The beginning of a partnership is at hand. A marriage or mutually exclusive relationship, or even a business partnership is favorable for you now. You are feeling the edges of a symbiotic relationship, and it is time to acquiesce, and let them know how you feel. If you have an existing relationship that has cooled or has seemed to come apart, and reconciliation is what you wish, then proceed forthwith.

Possible Influencing Cards:

4 of Cups – one partner more involved than the other
5 of Cups – possible breakup
7 of Pentacles – joint investments
7 of Swords – infidelity
Ace of Pentacles – business partnership
Devil – shallow relationship
Sun – possible soul mate

Psychological Function: Emotions and Feelings
Quality: Receptive
Regent: Gabriel
Royal Star: Antares
Sabbat: Mabon
Season: Autumn
Suit: Cups
Temperament: Phlegmatic

Tetragrammaton: Heh
Time of Day: Dusk

Three of Cups

Cups

3

Alchemical Quality: Cold and Wet

Alchemical Symbol:
Animal Energy: Dolphin (Joy and Love)

Astrological Correspondence:
Mercury ☿ in Cancer ♋

Astrological Quadruplicity:
    Cardinal Zodiac (Aggressive) – ♋
    Cancer

    Fixed Zodiac (Rigid) – Scorpio ♏

    Mutable Zodiac (Passive) – Pisces

Attribute: Emotional
Blood Type: Type AB
Character Trait: Healing
Colors: Blue-Green, Gray
Direction: West
Element: Water
Elemental: Undines, The Spirits of Water
Elemental King: Nixsa
Esoteric Title: Lord of Abundance
Fundamental Force: Weak
Gender: Feminine
Holy Creature: The Eagle

I-Ching: 54 – Living Together, The Bride, Passionate, Impulsive
Key Phrase: "I Feel"
Keyword: Celebration
Lunar Phase: 3rd Quarter
Magical Organ: The Heart
Magical Phrase: Audere, To Dare
Matter: Liquid

Meanings:

Upright:

Abundance, achievement, celebrations, closeness and bonding, completion, compromise, contentment, creativity engagements, exuberance, favorable outcomes, fertility, fulfillment, happiness, happy anticipation, health is improving, holidays, hospitality, joy, marriage, party, pregnancy, reunions, sense of community, success, time to relax and play.

Reversed:

Accidents, bad trips, change of plans, embarrassments, endings, feeling sorry for yourself, hangovers, idle gossip, infidelity, illness, inappropriate lust, living in the past, overdoing it, loss of reputation, overextension, personal addictions, pessimism, promiscuity, sarcasm, setbacks, social faux pas, substance abuse, unwanted or difficult pregnancy, terminations.

Musical Mood: "We are Family" by Sister Sledge
Mythological Creatures: Merfolk and Hippocampus
Numerology: 3 – Growth, enterprise, manifestation, unity, intuition
Phase of Life: The Adult
Physical Property: Fluidity
Plane: Astral
Playing Card Suit: Hearts

Possibility:

If you haven't been anticipating good news, you're about to be surprised. It's time to get together with the people that matter because this calls for a celebration. Perhaps a new member of the family will be welcomed, via marriage or birth. It could be the achievement of a graduation, or the milestone of an anniversary. Whatever the occasion – even if it's just friends getting together after work – it's time for merriment.

Possible Influencing Cards:
  3 of Swords – smiling on the outside, crying on the inside
  5 of Wands – manipulative friends
  9 of Wands – not trustworthy
  Death – complete and abrupt changes in relationship
  Devil – false friends
  Hermit – need for some alone time
  Temperance – make the effort to adjust

Psychological Function: Emotions and Feelings
Quality: Receptive
Regent: Gabriel
Royal Star: Antares
Sabbat: Mabon
Season: Autumn
Suit: Cups
Temperament: Phlegmatic

Tetragrammaton: Heh
Time of Day: Dusk

Four of Cups

Alchemical Quality: Cold and Wet

Alchemical Symbol: ▽
Animal Energy: Dolphin (Joy and Love)

Astrological Correspondence:
Moon ☽ in Cancer ♋

Astrological Quadruplicity:
  Cardinal Zodiac (Aggressive) – ♋
  Cancer

  Fixed Zodiac (Rigid) – Scorpio ♏

  Mutable Zodiac (Passive) – Pisces ♓

Attribute: Emotional
Blood Type: Type AB
Character Trait: Healing
Colors: Blue-Green, Gray
Direction: West
Element: Water
Elemental: Undines, The Spirits of Water
Elemental King: Nixsa
Esoteric Title: Lord of Blended Pleasure
Fundamental Force: Weak
Gender: Feminine
Holy Creature: The Eagle

I-Ching: 5 – Waiting,
Patience, Pausing, Anticipation
Key Phrase: "I Feel"
Keyword: Apathy
Lunar Phase: 3rd Quarter
Magical Organ: The Heart
Magical Phrase: Audere, To Dare
Matter: Liquid

Meanings:

Upright:

Apathy, aversion, bitterness, boredom with life, demoralized, depression, disgust, dissatisfaction, excesses, feeling empty inside, inner turmoil, lack of motivation, let downs, living in the past, monotony, need for re-evaluation, need for stimulation, self-absorbed, the Morning After card, timidity, too much of a good thing, unfulfilling relationships, way over it, weariness, withdrawing from society.

Reversed:

Change is coming, clarity, feeling better about yourself, fog is lifting, have more patience, momentum, motivation, need to stop worrying and use time more construc-tively, new accomplishments, new energy, new lease on life, new opportunities, premonitions, ready to get moving, reconsider your options, rejuvenation, renewal, revival, satisfaction, second wind, socializing.

Musical Mood: "Too Much Time on My Hands" by Styx
Mythological Creatures: Merfolk and Hippocampus
Numerology: 4 – Rest, inactivity, patience, stability, legal matters
Phase of Life: The Adult
Physical Property: Fluidity
Plane: Astral
Playing Card Suit: Hearts

Possibility:

You are feeling dissatisfied, bored, and uninterested in things that once captivated you. You are immersing yourself in the emptiness you feel inside, as you search yourself for the cause of your apathy. Take time for introspection, but don't overdo it and devalue what you once cherished. You will come to regret too much self-absorption. It's possible that the key to feeling better is right in front of you.

Possible Influencing Cards:
4 of Swords – feeling crowded
6 of Swords – depression
7 of Cups – escapism
7 of Swords – substance abuse
8 of Pentacles – putting forth a good effort
Hanged Man – wallowing in self pity
Wheel of Fortune – new project coming up

Psychological Function: Emotions and Feelings
Quality: Receptive
Regent: Gabriel
Royal Star: Antares
Sabbat: Mabon
Season: Autumn
Suit: Cups
Temperament: Phlegmatic

Tetragrammaton: Heh
Time of Day: Dusk

Five of Cups

Alchemical Quality: Cold and Wet

Alchemical Symbol: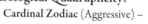
Animal Energy: Dolphin (Joy and Love)

Astrological Correspondence:
Mars ♂ in Scorpio ♏

Astrological Quadruplicity:
    Cardinal Zodiac (Aggressive) –
    Cancer ♋

    Fixed Zodiac (Rigid) – Scorpio ♏

    Mutable Zodiac (Passive) – Pisces ♓

Attribute: Emotional
Blood Type: Type AB
Character Trait: Healing
Colors: Blue-Green, Gray
Direction: West
Element: Water
Elemental: Undines, The Spirits of Water
Elemental King: Nixsa
Esoteric Title: Lord of Loss in Pleasure
Fundamental Force: Weak
Gender: Feminine
Holy Creature: The Eagle

I-Ching: 47 – Weariness or Exhaustion, Depleted, Burnt Out
Key Phrase: "I Feel"
Keyword: Regret
Lunar Phase: 3rd Quarter
Magical Organ: The Heart
Magical Phrase: Audere, To Dare
Matter: Liquid

Meanings:

Upright:
Abandonment, anxiety, betrayal, crying over loss but losing sight of what is left, defeatist attitude, despair, dishonor, divorce or separation, disappointment, drama king/queen, emotional letdowns, false starts, gloom, I tried positive thinking once but knew it wouldn't work, imperfection, loss of love, miscarriage, need to re-evaluate priorities, not seeing the obvious, picking up the pieces, regrets, self pity, sorrow.

Reversed:
Confronting your shortcomings, counting your blessings, facing reality, gratitude and appreciation, learning from past mistakes, moving on to a better situation, network-ing, new hope for love, on the road to recovery, outlook is improving, renewal, resolving emotional issues, return of happiness, reunions, someone from the past returns, sun will come out again, today is a new day, turning over a new leaf, waking up and smelling the coffee.

Musical Mood: "Since I Don't Have You" by the Skyliners
Mythological Creatures: Merfolk and Hippocampus
Numerology: 5 – Changes, disruptions, instability, conflict, uncertainty
Phase of Life: The Adult
Physical Property: Fluidity
Plane: Astral
Playing Card Suit: Hearts

Possibility:

Blinded by the despair that accompanies the loss of something dear, you can't manage to account for the blessings you still have. You are crossing over the line between mourning and self-pity, and those that remain by your side now, won't follow. Allow yourself the grief that comes when you have lost something, but do not hide in your despondency to avoid the inevitable change that loss brings. Let go of what is gone.

Possible Influencing Cards:

6 of Cups – loss of a friend
6 of Wands – success is imminent
10 of Pentacles – bankruptcy
Death – loss or grief
Devil – energy is being wasted
Judgment – self forgiveness

Psychological Function: Emotions and Feelings
Quality: Receptive
Regent: Gabriel
Royal Star: Antares
Sabbat: Mabon
Season: Autumn
Suit: Cups
Temperament: Phlegmatic

Tetragrammaton: Heh
Time of Day: Dusk

Six of Cups

Cups

6

Alchemical Quality: Cold and Wet

Alchemical Symbol: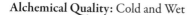
Animal Energy: Dolphin (Joy and Love)

Astrological Correspondence:
Sun ☉ in Scorpio ♏

Astrological Quadruplicity:
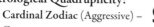
   Cardinal Zodiac (Aggressive) –
   Cancer ♋

   Fixed Zodiac (Rigid) – Scorpio ♏

   Mutable Zodiac (Passive) – Pisces ♓

Attribute: Emotional
Blood Type: Type AB
Character Trait: Healing
Colors: Blue-Green, Gray
Direction: West
Element: Water
Elemental: Undines, The Spirits of Water
Elemental King: Nixsa
Esoteric Title: Lord of Pleasure
Fundamental Force: Weak
Gender: Feminine
Holy Creature: The Eagle

I-Ching: 37 – Family, Home, Belonging, Indecision

Key Phrase: "I Feel"
Keyword: Memories
Lunar Phase: 3rd Quarter
Magical Organ: The Heart
Magical Phrase: Audere, To Dare
Matter: Liquid

Meanings:

Upright:

Back in the day, Blast from the past, childhood memories, experience, fond memories, former lovers, indecision, inheritance, innocence, Karmic lessons, matters dealing with children, nostalgia, old friends, old school, past love returning, pastime activities or hobbies, possible change of job, possible travel opportunities, reminiscing, reunions, selective memories, sharing.

Reversed:

Clinging to the past, delays, disappointments, emotional baggage, family secrets, living in the past, longings, new friends, not being realistic, outmoded ideas, past is coming back to haunt you, preoccupations, refusal to grow up, regeneration, resting on your laurels and not pursuing new ones, time to move into the future, trip may be postponed, wearing rose colored glasses.

Musical Mood: "Brown Eyed Girl" by Van Morrison
Mythological Creatures: Merfolk and Hippocampus
Numerology: 6 – Home life, harmony, nostalgia, responsibility, reconciliation
Phase of Life: The Adult
Physical Property: Fluidity
Plane: Astral
Playing Card Suit: Hearts

Possibility:

Nostalgia is about to stir within you, perhaps from the smell of honeysuckle in the spring, an old song on the radio, or maybe sitting on the floor sifting through an old box you found while cleaning out the closet. Memories of the innocence of your youth and the time when the world was new to you, will find their way to your conscience thoughts. Somebody special, a close friend, or perhaps a past lover will re-emerge in your life.

Possible Influencing Cards:

4 of Cups – living in the past, re-evaluating a relationship

5 of Swords – hypercritical

Ace of Pentacles – long term friendships

Emperor – miscommunications cause hurt feelings

Moon – time to drop the emotional baggage

Strength – goals are achievable

Psychological Function: Emotions and Feelings
Quality: Receptive
Regent: Gabriel
Royal Star: Antares
Sabbat: Mabon
Season: Autumn
Suit: Cups
Temperament: Phlegmatic

Tetragrammaton: Heh
Time of Day: Dusk

Alchemical Quality: Cold and Wet

Alchemical Symbol:  ▽

Animal Energy: Dolphin (Joy and Love)

Astrological Correspondence:
Venus ♀ in Scorpio ♏

Astrological Quadruplicity:
 Cardinal Zodiac (Aggressive) –
 Cancer

 Fixed Zodiac (Rigid) – Scorpio

 Mutable Zodiac (Passive) – Pisces

Attribute: Emotional
Blood Type: Type AB
Character Trait: Healing
Colors: Blue-Green, Gray
Direction: West
Element: Water
Elemental: Undines, The Spirits of Water
Elemental King: Nixsa
Esoteric Title: Lord of Illusionary Success
Fundamental Force: Weak
Gender: Feminine
Holy Creature: The Eagle

I-Ching: 60 – Limitations or restrictions, Rules, Regulations
Key Phrase: "I Feel"
Keyword: Daydreams
Lunar Phase: 3rd Quarter
Magical Organ: The Heart
Magical Phrase: Audere, To Dare
Matter: Liquid

Meanings:

Upright:

Castles in the air, change for the worse, confusion, daydreams, escapism, false hope, fear of success, get rich quick schemes, illusion of success, indecision, imagination, intuition, lack of focus, never thinking about where you are and what you are doing, options, scattered energy, self delusion, selfish indulgence, substance abuse, unrealistic expectations, wishful thinking.

Reversed:

Clarity, confidence and security, changes for the better, cutting to the chase, dedication, desires and goals are attainable, determination, focus, getting things in perspective, good choices, high aspirations, intentions, inspiration, perseverance, realism, resolve, seeing things as they really are, setting realistic goals, taking charge, taking responsibility, vision is clearing, will power.

Musical Mood: "Choose" by Santana
Mythological Creatures: Merfolk and Hippocampus
Numerology: 7 – Mystical, spiritual, dreams, discipline, struggles
Phase of Life: The Adult
Physical Property: Fluidity
Plane: Astral
Playing Card Suit: Hearts

Possibility:

You're taking mental short cuts. Presumptions are creating false perceptions in your life, and you think you have the answers but you haven't done your homework. Dreams don't come true because you want them to. They come true when the want in you motivates you to focus your efforts upon them. It's possible that you aren't sure what you want, or you have changed your mind, either one leaving you unmotivated.

Possible Influencing Cards:

2 of Cups – unrealistic expectations concerning a relationship
5 of Pentacles – misleading financial advice
Emperor – need for discipline
Lovers – consider the feelings of others before acting
Magician – keep focus strong to success
Wheel – look before you leap
World – assume responsibility for your actions

Psychological Function: Emotions and Feelings
Quality: Receptive
Regent: Gabriel
Royal Star: Antares
Sabbat: Mabon
Season: Autumn
Suit: Cups
Temperament: Phlegmatic

Tetragrammaton: Heh
Time of Day: Dusk

Eight of Cups

Cups

Alchemical Quality: Cold and Wet

Alchemical Symbol: ▽
Animal Energy: Dolphin (Joy and Love)

Astrological Correspondence:
Saturn ♄   in Pisces ♓

Astrological Quadruplicity:
   Cardinal Zodiac (Aggressive) – ♋
   Cancer

   Fixed Zodiac (Rigid) – Scorpio ♏

   Mutable Zodiac (Passive) – Pisces ♓

Attribute: Emotional
Blood Type: Type AB
Character Trait: Healing
Colors: Blue-Green, Gray
Direction: West
Element: Water
Elemental: Undines, The Spirits of Water
Elemental King: Nixsa
Esoteric Title: Lord of Abandoned Success
Fundamental Force: Weak
Gender: Feminine
Holy Creature: The Eagle

I-Ching: 17 - Adapting, ▤ Following, Pursuit, Ambition
Key Phrase: "I Feel"
Keyword: Abandonment
Lunar Phase: 3rd Quarter
Magical Organ: The Heart
Magical Phrase: Audere, To Dare
Matter: Liquid

Meanings:

Upright:
Abandonment, breaking emotional ties, change of heart, change of perspective, crusades, cutting your losses, disappointment, discontent, disillusionment, emotional distance, fear of emotional commitment, letting go, misery, moving on, partings, problems may resolve themselves within 28 days, quests, severing ties, travel, turning point, walking away from a situation, withdrawal.

Reversed:
Apology is past due, clinging to outdated ideas, contentment, cutting off your nose to spite your face, living in the past, mediocrity, satisfaction, stubbornness, refusing to let go of a losing situation, refusing to move on, unwillingness to accept change, refusal to think outside the box, recklessness, restlessness, same old same old, stagnation, some things just never change, stuck in a rut, wasted time and efforts.

Musical Mood: "Free Bird" by Lynyrd Skynyrd
Mythological Creatures: Merfolk and Hippocampus
Numerology: 8 – Material progress, security, expansion, priorities, advancement
Phase of Life: The Adult
Physical Property: Fluidity
Plane: Astral
Playing Card Suit: Hearts

Possibility:
Your emotional needs aren't being met. Your love is not being returned, or you are giving love to something that is incapable of returning it. You are turning your back on what you have. The love of material things always leaves an empty feeling, and your insatiableness just leads to the acquirement of more and more material objects in a futile attempt to fill the void. It is important to love, yet equally important to be loved.

Possible Influencing Cards:
3 of Wands – possible travel
5 of Swords – walk away from a fight
Chariot – don't be sidetracked
Death – current situation is ending
Hanged Man – refusal to commit
Hermit – answers will be found within
Magician – success is near

Psychological Function: Emotions and Feelings
Quality: Receptive
Regent: Gabriel
Royal Star: Antares
Sabbat: Mabon
Season: Autumn
Suit: Cups
Temperament: Phlegmatic

Tetragrammaton: Heh
Time of Day: Dusk

Nine of Cups

Alchemical Quality: Cold and Wet

Alchemical Symbol:  ▽
Animal Energy: Dolphin (Joy and Love)

Astrological Correspondence:
Jupiter ♃ in Pisces ♓

Astrological Quadruplicity:
Cardinal Zodiac (Aggressive) – Cancer ♋

Fixed Zodiac (Rigid) – Scorpio ♏

Mutable Zodiac (Passive) – Pisces ♓

Attribute: Emotional
Blood Type: Type AB
Character Trait: Healing
Colors: Blue-Green, Gray
Direction: West
Element: Water
Elemental: Undines, The Spirits of Water
Elemental King: Nixsa
Esoteric Title: Material Happiness
Fundamental Force: Weak
Gender: Feminine
Holy Creature: The Eagle

I-Ching: 48 – The Well, Source, Resources
Key Phrase: "I Feel"
Keyword: Satisfaction
Lunar Phase: 3rd Quarter
Magical Organ: The Heart
Magical Phrase: Audere, To Dare
Matter: Liquid

Meanings:

Upright:
Abundance, advantage, contentment, dreams are coming true, emotional stability, excess, fulfillment, generosity, good luck, gratification, gratitude, happiness, indulgence, it's all good, lacking for nothing, luxury, material gain, nearing the end of a cycle, pride, prosperity, satisfaction, security, sensual pleasure, smugness, The Wish Card, your wish will be fulfilled, victory.

Reversed:
Adrenaline junkie, aimlessness, complacency, debauchery, deprivation, imperfections, ingratitude, insincerity, laziness, lust, minor illnesses, mistakes, monetary problems, obstacles, opposition, over dependency on others, overindulgence, self absorption, self indulgence, shallowness, smugness, substance abuse, wish will not be fulfilled, or it will not be exactly as you wanted it to be, vanity.

Musical Mood: "I Could Not Ask for More" by Edwin McCain
Mythological Creatures: Merfolk and Hippocampus
Numerology: 9 – Satisfaction, fulfillment, luck, complacency, just desserts
Phase of Life: The Adult
Physical Property: Fluidity
Plane: Astral
Playing Card Suit: Hearts

Possibility:
You are in danger of becoming prideful of your overall good fortune and the material possessions that it has afforded you. You are not miserly, as you love that others are jealous of you, or so you believe. You are very content amongst your material trophies as they are prominently on display for others to covet. If you have a wish that you are holding on to, it is about to come true. Grasp the full weight of that wish being granted.

Possible Influencing Cards:
5 of Pentacles – watch spending
6 of Wands – self confidence
7 of Cups – overindulgence
Devil – overindulgence
Sun – happy endings
Tower – unexpected turn of events

Psychological Function: Emotions and Feelings
Quality: Receptive
Regent: Gabriel
Royal Star: Antares
Sabbat: Mabon
Season: Autumn
Suit: Cups
Temperament: Phlegmatic

Tetragrammaton: Heh
Time of Day: Dusk

Alchemical Quality: Cold and Wet

Alchemical Symbol:

Animal Energy: Dolphin (Joy and Love)

Astrological Correspondence:
Mars ♂ in Pisces ♓

Astrological Quadruplicity:
    Cardinal Zodiac (Aggressive) – Cancer ♋

    Fixed Zodiac (Rigid) – Scorpio ♏

    Mutable Zodiac (Passive) – Pisces ♓

Attribute: Emotional
Blood Type: Type AB
Character Trait: Healing
Colors: Blue-Green, Gray
Direction: West
Element: Water
Elemental: Undines, The Spirits of Water
Elemental King: Nixsa
Esoteric Title: Lord of Perfected Success
Fundamental Force: Weak
Gender: Feminine
Holy Creature: The Eagle

I-Ching: 40 – Liberation or Freedom, Escape, Relief
Key Phrase: "I Feel"
Keyword: Harmony
Lunar Phase: 3rd Quarter
Magical Organ: The Heart
Magical Phrase: Audere, To Dare
Matter: Liquid

Meanings:

Upright:

All is well that ends well, blood is thicker than water, brotherhood, compatibility, completion, contentment, don't look a gift horse in the mouth, end of a cycle, gifts, good reputation, gratitude, family matters, happiness, happy marriage, harmony, honor, inheritance, joy, love of home, peace, prosperity, quiet celebrations, satiety, sense of community, sincerity, virtue, wholeness.

Reversed:

Antisocial behavior, arguments, betrayal, callous and calculating, debauchery, depression, disrupted harmony, divorce, empty nest syndrome, family quarrels, infighting, insults, interruptions, irritation, misplaced loyalties, personality clashes, problem child, sorrow, strife, turning your back on the family unit, unchecked greed, unreasonable demands, violence, wantonness.

Musical Mood: "Our House" by Crosby, Stills, Nash & Young
Mythological Creatures: Merfolk and Hippocampus
Numerology: 10 – Completions, resolutions, beginning and/or ending of a cycle
Phase of Life: The Adult
Physical Property: Fluidity
Plane: Astral
Playing Card Suit: Hearts

Possibility:

In life there is like, and there is love. You will find yourself blessed with both, which often tends to be as allusive as a butterfly. You have discovered that sharing an appreciation of the beauty of the rainbow itself is the true treasure, not the metal trinkets one hopes to find at the end of it. If you want to experience true happiness and fulfillment try giving all the credit and taking all the blame, not the other way around.

Possible Influencing Cards:

Ace of Wands – buying a new home
Devil – dissatisfaction
Empress – time to make plans for the future
Hermit – change of residence
Star – hope for the future
Tower – dark shadows on the horizon
World – self fulfillment

Psychological Function: Emotions and Feelings
Quality: Receptive
Regent: Gabriel
Royal Star: Antares
Sabbat: Mabon
Season: Autumn
Suit: Cups
Temperament: Phlegmatic

Tetragrammaton: Heh
Time of Day: Dusk

The Pentacles

Ace of Pentacles

Alchemical Quality: Cold and Dry

Alchemical Symbol: ▽

Animal Energy: Bear (Introspection and Dreams)

Astrological Correspondence: Root of Earth

Astrological Quadruplicity:
    Cardinal Zodiac (Aggressive) – Capricorn

    Fixed Zodiac (Rigid) – Taurus

    Mutable Zodiac (Passive) – Virgo

Attribute: Physical
Blood Type: Type A
Character Trait: Hibernation
Colors: White, Black
Direction: North
Element: Earth
Elemental: Gnomes, The Spirits of Earth
Elemental King: Ghob
Esoteric Title: Root of the Powers of Earth
Fundamental Force: Gravity
Gender: Feminine
Holy Creature: The Winged Bull

I-Ching: 19 – Promotion or ▤ Approach, Involvement, Encounter, Action

Key Phrase: "I Have"

Keyword: Potential

Lunar Phase: New Moon

Magical Organ: The Body and Senses

Magical Phrase: Tacere, To Keep Silent

Matter: Solid

Meanings:

Upright:

Abundance, attainment, beginning of activity associated with the suit, beginning of potential prosperity, career changes, gifts, inheritance, luxury, manifestation of goals, material gain, new employment, new opportunities, physical well being, practicality, recognition, security, sensual pleasure, stoicism, success, successful projects, take a chance, trust.

Reversed:

Avarice, big plans fall through, carelessness, delayed payments, false promises, fear of change or death, gambles don't pay off, facades, get rich quick schemes, greed, hasty decisions, insecurity, materialism, miserliness, money doesn't buy happiness, overconfidence, overindulgence, overly possessive, standing on shaky ground, unimaginative, wealthy in appearance only.

Musical Mood: "Pennies from Heaven" by Louis Prima

Mythological Creatures: Giants and Elves

Numerology: 1 – New beginnings, confidence, creativity, possibility, potential

Phase of Life: The Elder

Physical Property: Solidity

Plane: Physical

Playing Card Suit: Diamonds

Possibility:

The time to begin a successful business endeavor is now. Currently you should have both feet on the ground and your focus on your goal. Now is not the time to be dramatizing or fictionalizing, unless of course that is your area of expertise. There is no better time to put your financial plan into action. A monetary gift or offering will make itself available if you are in need of capital to get the ball rolling.

Possible Influencing Cards:

3 of Pentacles – possible new job or business

3 of Wands – your efforts will see good results

6 of Pentacles – good financial advice

Lovers – possible marriage or other beneficial partnership

Magician – lucrative beginning to project

Sun – happiness abounds

Psychological Function: Manifestation and Formation

Quality: Passive

Regent: Uriel

Royal Star: Fomalhaut

Sabbat: Yule

Season: Winter

Suit: Pentacles

Temperament: Melancholic

Tetragrammaton: Heh

Time of Day: Midnight

Two of Pentacles

Pentacles

2

Alchemical Quality: Cold and Dry

Alchemical Symbol:
Animal Energy: Bear
(Introspection and Dreams)

Astrological Correspondence:
Jupiter ♃ in Capricorn ♑

Astrological Quadruplicity:
  Cardinal Zodiac (Aggressive) – ♑
  Capricorn

  Fixed Zodiac (Rigid) – Taurus ♂

  Mutable Zodiac (Passive) – Virgo ♍

Attribute: Physical
Blood Type: Type A
Character Trait: Hibernation
Colors: White, Black
Direction: North
Element: Earth
Elemental: Gnomes, The Spirits of Earth
Elemental King: Ghob
Esoteric Title: Lord of Harmonious
Change
Fundamental Force: Gravity

Gender: Feminine
Holy Creature: The Winged Bull

I-Ching: 60 – Limitations or Restrictions, Discipline, Rules, Regulations
Key Phrase: "I Have"
Keyword: Balancing
Lunar Phase: New Moon
Magical Organ: The Body and Senses
Magical Phrase: Tacere, To Keep Silent
Matter: Solid

Meanings:

Upright:
Balance, juggling, flexibility, decisions, trying to make ends meets, adaptability, equilibrium, social status and obligations, stamina, gifts, creative bookkeeping, spreading yourself thin, preoccupation with money, ineffective time management, stay focused, imminent change, possible, change of residence

Reversed:
Communication breakdown, decisions need to be made, debt, disorganization, envy, greed, ignorance, impracticality, impulsive spending, inattention to finan-cial matters, information overload, living only in the moment, not planning for the future, overindulgence, overwhelmed, paperwork piling up, poor foundation, recklessness, rigidity, unable to maintain finances, unrealistic attitude

Musical Mood: "Juggling Knives" by Enchant
Mythological Creatures: Giants and Elves
Numerology: 2 – Relationships, decisions, balance, cooperation, emotions
Phase of Life: The Elder
Physical Property: Solidity
Plane: Physical
Playing Card Suit: Diamonds

Possibility:
Caught in a seemingly eternal balancing act of resources amidst the turbulence of living to make ends meet, you do in fact make them meet. You have long since learned that frustration at, and grousing about, circumstances tender no assistance. Remain flexible and fluid through the upcoming events that befall you. If you face a situation that holds great consequence, your grace under pressure will see you through.

Possible Influencing Cards:
  Ace of Swords – watch overspending
  Devil – personal life is interfering with professional life
  Hanged Man – don't be too impatient
  Temperance – need for balance

Psychological Function: Manifestation and Formation
Quality: Passive
Regent: Uriel
Royal Star: Fomalhaut
Sabbat: Yule
Season: Winter
Suit: Pentacles
Temperament: Melancholic

Tetragrammaton: Heh
Time of Day: Midnight

Three of Pentacles

Alchemical Quality: Cold and Dry

Alchemical Symbol: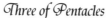
Animal Energy: Bear
(Introspection and Dreams)

Astrological Correspondence:
Mars ♂ in Capricorn ♑

Astrological Quadruplicity:
    Cardinal Zodiac (Aggressive) – ♑
    Capricorn

    Fixed Zodiac (Rigid) – Taurus ♂

    Mutable Zodiac (Passive) – Virgo ♍

Attribute: Physical
Blood Type: Type A
Character Trait: Hibernation
Colors: White, Black
Direction: North
Element: Earth
Elemental: Gnomes, The Spirits of Earth
Elemental King: Ghob
Esoteric Title: Lord of Material Works
Fundamental Force: Gravity
Gender: Feminine

Holy Creature: The Winged Bull

I-Ching: 16 – Enthusiasm,
Motivation, Inspiration, Encouragement
Key Phrase: "I Have"
Keyword: Mastery
Lunar Phase: New Moon
Magical Organ: The Body and Senses
Magical Phrase: Tacere, To Keep Silent
Matter: Solid

Meanings:

Upright:
Competence, craftsmanship, distinction and fame, doing it the right way or no way at all, employment, expertise, following instructions, holding yourself to a higher standard, innovative, job satisfaction, perfection, recognition, reward for a job well done, skill, status, strong work ethics, takes the initiative, teamwork, technical ability, visible results.

Reversed:
Conceit, creative dry spell, delays, inexperience, fraud, ignorance, jealousness, lack of ambition, loss of interest, miserliness, misrepresentation, missed opportunities, need a second opinion, need to try harder, not accepting constructive criticism, not having the needed tools for the job, pettiness, obstinacy, prejudice, sabotage, trouble at work, tunnel vision, wastefulness.

Musical Mood: "Best I Can" by Queensrÿche
Mythological Creatures: Giants and Elves
Numerology: 3 – Growth, enterprise, manifestation, unity, intuition
Phase of Life: The Elder
Physical Property: Solidity
Plane: Physical
Playing Card Suit: Diamonds

Possibility:

The skills you have acquired are ready to be put to use. Put your abilities on display for those that can assist you in the pursuit of a career in your craft. Diligent effort and attention to detail are the Attributes that you must apply to the project at hand. How you go about your business is just as noticeable and significant as your end results. You may well be in line for a promotion or a monetary reward for your efforts.

Possible Influencing Cards:

3 of Cups – need for teamwork
5 of Wands – unwillingness to cooperate
9 of Pentacles – not willing to accept outside help
Emperor – strong opposition
Wheel – more self confidence is needed

Psychological Function: Manifestation and Formation
Quality: Passive
Regent: Uriel
Royal Star: Fomalhaut
Sabbat: Yule
Season: Winter
Suit: Pentacles
Temperament: Melancholic

Tetragrammaton: Heh
Time of Day: Midnight

Four of Pentacles

Alchemical Quality: Cold and Dry

Alchemical Symbol:

Animal Energy: Bear
(Introspection and Dreams)

Astrological Correspondence:
Sun ☉ in Capricorn ♑

Astrological Quadruplicity:
   Cardinal Zodiac (Aggressive) – ♑
      Capricorn

   Fixed Zodiac (Rigid) – Taurus ♂

   Mutable Zodiac (Passive) – Virgo ♍

Attribute: Physical
Blood Type: Type A
Character Trait: Hibernation
Colors: White, Black
Direction: North
Element: Earth
Elemental: Gnomes, The Spirits of Earth
Elemental King: Ghob
Esoteric Title: Lord of Earthly Power
Fundamental Force: Gravity
Gender: Feminine

Holy Creature: The Winged Bull

I-Ching: 45 – Assembling or Gathering Together, Integration
Key Phrase: "I Have"
Keyword: Acquisition
Lunar Phase: New Moon
Magical Organ: The Body and Senses
Magical Phrase: Tacere, To Keep Silent
Matter: Solid

Meanings:

Upright:

Acquisitions, bull market, control, desire for power, financial security, gainful employment, generosity, gifts, fear of change, fear of loss, inheritance, keeping up with the Joneses, money management, movers and shakers, possessions, power through acquisition, protecting your territory, reluctance to take risks, solid investments, stability, upwardly mobile.

Reversed:

Avarice, bankruptcy, bear market, carelessness, defensive, delays, financial loss, grasping, hoarding, house of cards is collapsing, lack of initiative, miserliness, obsession with money, obstructions, oppositions, overprotective, overspending, paranoia, power hungry, problems in business or finance, refusal to share good fortune, stingy, suspicion, timidity.

Musical Mood: "Money" by Pink Floyd
Mythological Creatures: Giants and Elves
Numerology: 4 – Rest, inactivity, patience, stability, legal matters
Phase of Life: The Elder
Physical Property: Solidity
Plane: Physical
Playing Card Suit: Diamonds

Possibility:

It appears that money and material worth drive your heart, mind, and actions. As a result you have separated yourself from others, or they are separating themselves from you, because, although not unkind, you are less than generous, and find little time for non-monetary pursuits. Reluctant to entrust what you value in others, or delegate your responsibility, you have defined yourself as a team of one.

Possible Influencing Cards:

2 of Swords – inertia and stagnation
Hanged Man – budget cuts
High Priestess – consider all possible repercussions before acting
Moon – hidden agendas
Tower – don't be easily let by others
Wheel of Fortune – success is imminent

Psychological Function: Manifestation and Formation
Quality: Passive
Regent: Uriel
Royal Star: Fomalhaut
Sabbat: Yule
Season: Winter
Suit: Pentacles
Temperament: Melancholic

Tetragrammaton: Heh
Time of Day: Midnight

Five of Pentacles

Alchemical Quality: Cold and Dry

Alchemical Symbol:

Animal Energy: Bear
(Introspection and Dreams)

Astrological Correspondence:
Mercury ☿ in Taurus ♂

Astrological Quadruplicity:
  Cardinal Zodiac (Aggressive) – ♑
  Capricorn

  Fixed Zodiac (Rigid) – Taurus ♂

  Mutable Zodiac (Passive) – Virgo ♍

Attribute: Physical
Blood Type: Type A
Character Trait: Hibernation
Colors: White, Black
Direction: North
Element: Earth
Elemental: Gnomes, The Spirits of Earth
Elemental King: Ghob
Esoteric Title: Lord of Material Trouble
Fundamental Force: Gravity
Gender: Feminine
Holy Creature: The Winged Bull

I-Ching: 12 – Stagnation, ䷋
Powerless, Obstructed, Blocked
Key Phrase: "I Have"
Keyword: Poverty
Lunar Phase: New Moon
Magical Organ: The Body and Senses
Magical Phrase: Tacere, To Keep Silent
Matter: Solid

Meanings:

Upright:

Abandonment, bankruptcy, breakdowns, can't see the forest for the trees, despondency, destitution, disappointments, down and out, financial crisis, health problems, impracticality, legal problems, loneliness, loss of employment, loss of faith, obstacles, outcast, poverty, redundancy, rejection, self doubt, self pity, spiritual impoverishment, taking unnecessary risks, it is worse than you know, worry.

Reversed:

Accepting a hand up, adversity is ending, charity, coming in from the cold, deceptions, forgiveness, hard times coming to a close, hope, improper relationships, improved health, misconduct, new lease on life, new starts, renewed hope and faith, return of the prodigal son, sanctuary, sense of belonging and acceptance, spending wisely, squandering resources, welcoming the lost sheep back into the fold.

Musical Mood: "Nobody Knows You When You're Down and Out" by Eric Clapton
Mythological Creatures: Giants and Elves
Numerology: 5 – Changes, disruptions, instability, conflict, uncertainty
Phase of Life: The Elder
Physical Property: Solidity
Plane: Physical
Playing Card Suit: Diamonds

Possibility:

Although you have had a run of bad luck lately, what is crippling you is your self-pity. You feel as though others shun you because you aren't doing well, but it is your constant demand for sympathy that causes them to leave when they hear you coming. Your life has taken a turn for the worse, and there are those that are willing to help you get yourself back on your feet, but your obstinacy is blocking their efforts.

Possible Influencing Cards:

9 of Cups – better luck is coming
10 of Wands – no light at the end of the tunnel yet
Ace of Swords – credit is cut off
Lovers – miscommunications and misunderstandings
Tower – financial disaster

Psychological Function: Manifestation and Formation
Quality: Passive
Regent: Uriel
Royal Star: Fomalhaut
Sabbat: Yule
Season: Winter
Suit: Pentacles
Temperament: Melancholic

Tetragrammaton: Heh
Time of Day: Midnight

Six of Pentacles

Alchemical Quality: Cold and Dry

Alchemical Symbol:
Animal Energy: Bear
Introspection and Dreams)

Astrological Correspondence:
Moon ☽ in Taurus ♂

Astrological Quadruplicity:
  Cardinal Zodiac (Aggressive) – ♑
  Capricorn

  Fixed Zodiac (Rigid) – Taurus ♂

  Mutable Zodiac (Passive) – Virgo ♍

Attribute: Physical
Blood Type: Type A
Character Trait: Hibernation
Colors: White, Black
Direction: North
Element: Earth
Elemental: Gnomes, The Spirits of Earth
Elemental King: Ghob
Esoteric Title: Lord of Material Success
Fundamental Force: Gravity
Gender: Feminine

Holy Creature: The Winged Bull

I-Ching: 27 – Nourishing or Nutrition, Fulfillment, Feedback
Key Phrase: "I Have"
Keyword: Benevolence
Lunar Phase: New Moon
Magical Organ: The Body and Senses
Magical Phrase: Tacere, To Keep Silent
Matter: Solid

Meanings:

Upright:
Added bonuses, accomplishment, altruism, benevolence, charity, completion, empathy, fairness and equality, financial aid, generosity, gifts, gratification, helping your fellow man, kindness, material abundance, sharing the wealth, philanthropy, planning for the future financially, promotions, random acts of kindness, repaying a debt, rewards, solvency, sympathy.

Reversed:
Blind ambition, bribes, cheating, criminal activity, dirty money, dishonesty, dominance and submission, extravagance, fair weather friends, highway robbery, jealousy, loans come due, loan sharking, money owed, oppression, poor choices in friends, racketeering, refusal to help those in need, self centered behavior, selfishness, thievery, uneasiness, unfairness.

Musical Mood: "He Ain't Heavy, He's My Brother" by The Hollies
Mythological Creatures: Giants and Elves
Numerology: 6 – Home life, harmony, nostalgia, responsibility, reconciliation
Phase of Life: The Elder
Physical Property: Solidity
Plane: Physical
Playing Card Suit: Diamonds

Possibility:

It's important that you be seen as a compassionate and charitable person. Thusly you make your measured contributions to those that profess their need the loudest, drawing more attention to your gifts, even if they are not of greater need. To truly be of a charitable nature you must be willing to seek out those that are less boisterous and keep their needs in their pocket. The scale should favor the recipient.

Possible Influencing Cards:

5 of Swords – misrepresentation of finances
6 of Cups – contentment and happiness
7 of Cups – unrealistic financial expectations
Empress – all is well in your world
High Priest – avoid a condescending attitude
Star – perseverance is the key
World – material gain

Psychological Function: Manifestation and Formation
Quality: Passive
Regent: Uriel
Royal Star: Fomalhaut
Sabbat: Yule
Season: Winter
Suit: Pentacles
Temperament: Melancholic

Tetragrammaton: Heh
Time of Day: Midnight

Seven of Pentacles

Alchemical Quality: Cold and Dry

Alchemical Symbol:
Animal Energy: Bear
(Introspection and Dreams)

Astrological Correspondence:
Saturn ♄ in Taurus ♂

Astrological Quadruplicity:
    Cardinal Zodiac (Aggressive) – ♑
    Capricorn

    Fixed Zodiac (Rigid) – Taurus ♂

    Mutable Zodiac (Passive) – Virgo ♍

Attribute: Physical
Blood Type: Type A
Character Trait: Hibernation
Colors: White, Black
Direction: North
Element: Earth
Elemental: Gnomes, The Spirits of Earth
Elemental King: Ghob
Esoteric Title: Lord of Success Unfulfilled
Fundamental Force: Gravity
Gender: Feminine

Holy Creature: The Winged Bull

I-Ching: 39 – Obstacles or Impediment, Impasse, Barriers
Key Phrase: "I Have"
Keyword: Reflection
Lunar Phase: New Moon
Magical Organ: The Body and Senses
Magical Phrase: Tacere, To Keep Silent
Matter: Solid

Meanings:

Upright:
Better to make a slow nickel than a fast dime, calculated risks, clearing out of unwanted or unneeded items, considering the consequences of your actions, evaluating your progress, fear of success, finances are improving, gambles, investments, need for consistency, perseverance, progress, reflection and assessment, seeing the big picture, slow and steady wins the race, slow growth, working towards a goal.

Reversed:
Anxiety, bad gambles, complications, dead end street, depression, despair, disillusionment, financial insecurity, getting shortchanged, giving up too easily, impatient, inattention, inertia, irresponsibility, lazy, money troubles, not carrying your share of the workload, procrastination, refusing to learn from past mistakes, self pity, setbacks, shortcuts.

Musical Mood: "Paperback Writer" by The Beatles
Mythological Creatures: Giants and Elves
Numerology: 7 – Mystical, spiritual, dreams, discipline, struggles
Phase of Life: The Elder
Physical Property: Solidity
Plane: Physical
Playing Card Suit: Diamonds

Possibility:
It's important to concentrate on the details as you work towards your goal. However, when you are observing the progress so closely, the larger picture can be obscured. You must occasional step back and assess whether you are still on the desired course. A slow methodical effort will provide the desired results. Be patient as you approach the harvest, just because you are done does not mean the fruit is ripe.

Possible Influencing Cards:

9 of Cups – your hard work will be recognized
Empress – don't nitpick, don't stress the small stuff
Judgment – coming to a crossroads in life
Wheel of Fortune – trust in your intuition

Psychological Function: Manifestation and Formation
Quality: Passive
Regent: Uriel
Royal Star: Fomalhaut
Sabbat: Yule
Season: Winter
Suit: Pentacles
Temperament: Melancholic

Tetragrammaton: Heh
Time of Day: Midnight

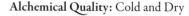

Alchemical Quality: Cold and Dry

Alchemical Symbol:
Animal Energy: Bear
(Introspection and Dreams)

Astrological Correspondence:
Sun ☉ in Virgo ♍

Astrological Quadruplicity:
   Cardinal Zodiac (Aggressive) – ♑
   Capricorn

    Fixed Zodiac (Rigid) – Taurus ♂

    Mutable Zodiac (Passive) – Virgo ♍

Attribute: Physical
Blood Type: Type A
Character Trait: Hibernation
Colors: White, Black
Direction: North
Element: Earth
Elemental: Gnomes, The Spirits of Earth
Elemental King: Ghob
Esoteric Title: Lord of Prudence
Fundamental Force: Gravity
Gender: Feminine

Holy Creature: The Winged Bull

I-Ching: 22 – Grace, Beauty, Acceptance, Celebration
Key Phrase: "I Have"
Keyword: Craftsmanship
Lunar Phase: New Moon
Magical Organ: The Body and Senses
Magical Phrase: Tacere, To Keep Silent
Matter: Solid

Meanings:

Upright:

Apprentice, attention to detail, craftsmanship, dedication, diligence, education to further your current success, focused effort, fulfilling employment, giving it that special touch, new line of work, perfecting your craft, perseverance is necessary, practicality, skill, talent, thriftiness, using advantage/risk reasoning, well-rounded, wise investments.

Reversed:

Avarice, cheating, conceit, cutting corners, dishonesty, dealings, embezzlement, feeling that the world owes you a living, financial problems, imposters and pretenders, insincerity, lack of preparation, laziness, misappropriated energy and skill, overly concerned with appearances, poor job performance, quantity not quality, vanity, second rate.

Musical Mood: "Taking Care of Business" by Bachman Turner Overdrive
Mythological Creatures: Giants and Elves
Numerology: 8 – Material progress, security, expansion, priorities, advancement
Phase of Life: The Elder
Physical Property: Solidity
Plane: Physical
Playing Card Suit: Diamonds

Possibility:

How many times do you have to duplicate a process to reach the point where you can't distinguish one result from the other? If you are truly committed to achieving respect and success in your chosen career, profession, or art, you will repeat your efforts as many times as it takes. Pride comes from achievement, and achievement requires more than completion, it requires that your pride raise the acceptable standard.

Possible Influencing Cards:

3 of Wands – telecommuting
4 of Cups – not payment enough attention to details
7 of Cups – lack of focus
7 of Wands – office politics
9 of Wands – perseverance is key
Fool – consider everything before acting
Hanged Man – seize the moment

Psychological Function: Manifestation and Formation
Quality: Passive
Regent: Uriel
Royal Star: Fomalhaut
Sabbat: Yule
Season: Winter
Suit: Pentacles
Temperament: Melancholic

Tetragrammaton: Heh
Time of Day: Midnight

Nine of Pentacles

Alchemical Quality: Cold and Dry

Alchemical Symbol:
Animal Energy: Bear
(Introspection and Dreams)

Astrological Correspondence:
Venus ♀ in Virgo ♍

Astrological Quadruplicity:
    Cardinal Zodiac (Aggressive) –
    Capricorn ♑

    Fixed Zodiac (Rigid) – Taurus ♂

    Mutable Zodiac (Passive) – Virgo ♍

Attribute: Physical
Blood Type: Type A
Character Trait: Hibernation
Colors: White, Black
Direction: North
Element: Earth
Elemental: Gnomes, The Spirits of Earth
Elemental King: Ghob
Esoteric Title: Lord of Material Gain
Fundamental Force: Gravity
Gender: Feminine

Holy Creature: The Winged Bull

I-Ching: 52 – Meditation or Calm, Tranquility, Stability
Key Phrase: "I Have"
Keyword: Independence
Lunar Phase: New Moon
Magical Organ: The Body and Senses
Magical Phrase: Tacere, To Keep Silent
Matter: Solid

Meanings:

Upright:

Accepting consequences for your actions, autonomy, comfort, confident in abilities, discipline, financial security, gambling wins, gifts, good health, inheritance, possessions, refinement, self sufficient, settlements, still haven't found what you're looking for, success, using talents wisely, wealthy but alone, well being.

Reversed:

Bad money management, barely making ends meet, clingy, corruption, feeling that the world owes you a living, guilty conscience, hasty decisions, ill gotten gains, integrity is being questioned, lacking in scruples and integrity, corruption, loss of friendship, overly dependent on others, pilferage, self indulgence, swindling, theft.

Musical Mood: "Independent Women" by Destiny's Child
Mythological Creatures: Giants and Elves
Numerology: 9 – Satisfaction, fulfillment, luck, complacency, just desserts
Phase of Life: The Elder
Physical Property: Solidity
Plane: Physical
Playing Card Suit: Diamonds

Possibility:

In order to achieve affluent self-sufficiency you must be self confident and relentless, while still remaining amiable and in control. It is not wise to be difficult to deal with, as a willingness to be flexible and accept compromise will forge associations that can be beneficial in the future. Sheathed power is much more useful than flailing it about, because a reputation for being rigid and unyielding will be hard to lose.

Possible Influencing Cards:

7 of Swords – resisting outside help
Chariot – firm control of your surroundings
Emperor – added responsibility is coming
High Priestess – avoid isolation
World – major changes

Psychological Function: Manifestation and Formation
Quality: Passive
Regent: Uriel
Royal Star: Fomalhaut
Sabbat: Yule
Season: Winter
Suit: Pentacles
Temperament: Melancholic

Tetragrammaton: Heh
Time of Day: Midnight

Alchemical Quality: Cold and Dry

Alchemical Symbol:
Animal Energy: Bear
(Introspection and Dreams)

Astrological Correspondence:
Mercury ☿ in Virgo ♍

Astrological Quadruplicity:
    Cardinal Zodiac (Aggressive) – ♑
    Capricorn

    Fixed Zodiac (Rigid) – Taurus ♂

    Mutable Zodiac (Passive) – Virgo ♍

Attribute: Physical
Blood Type: Type A
Character Trait: Hibernation
Colors: White, Black
Direction: North
Element: Earth
Elemental: Gnomes, The Spirits of Earth
Elemental King: Ghob
Esoteric Title: Lord of Wealth
Fundamental Force: Gravity

Gender: Feminine
Holy Creature: The Winged Bull

I-Ching: 45 – Assembling or Gathering, Integration, Blending
Key Phrase: "I Have"
Keyword: Legacy
Lunar Phase: New Moon
Magical Organ: The Body and Senses
Magical Phrase: Tacere, To Keep Silent
Matter: Solid

Meanings:

Upright:

Affluence, close knit, comfort, cooperation, financial security, inheritance, good advice, harmony and tranquility, heritage, influence, it's all good, life events, pampered, personal loyalty, prestige, privileged, prosperity, retirement, riches abound, the good life, old money, reputation, the whole enchilada, tradition, tranquil family life.

Reversed:

Burdened by responsibility, coddled, emotional baggage, family secrets, family squabbles, gambling, illness (parental or elder), insecurity, legal problems, loss, more money than sense, old grudges, resentments, skeletons in the closet, spoiled, theft, uncertainty, unmotivated, unstable finances, unwanted family obligations.

Musical Mood: "100 Years" by Five for Fighting
Mythological Creatures: Giants and Elves
Numerology: 10 – Completions, resolutions, beginning and/or ending of a cycle
Phase of Life: The Elder
Physical Property: Solidity
Plane: Physical
Playing Card Suit: Diamonds

Possibility:

Don't allow your family loyalty to come in to question. The great family tradition begins and ends with trust and devotion, and it must exist in both the darkness and the light. If you turn your back on your ancestry, and tradition, it could very well be your descendents that will be deprived of the strength and security that is only attainable in the sanctity of one's family. Take time to appreciate what your family means to you.

Possible Influencing Cards:

2 of Wands – investments
3 of Swords – financial worries
Devil – watch spending
High Priest – controlling through money
Sun – happiness and security
Wheel of Fortune – success in gambles

Psychological Function: Manifestation and Formation
Quality: Passive
Regent: Uriel
Royal Star: Fomalhaut
Sabbat: Yule
Season: Winter
Suit: Pentacles
Temperament: Melancholic

Tetragrammaton: Heh
Time of Day: Midnight

The Tarot Court

The Court Cards are included with the Minor Arcana; however, it is our opinion that they should be considered an Arcanum of their own. They are divided into four groups: Kings, Queens, Knights, and Pages. They can represent you and your feelings, people in your life, or situations.

The Court Cards can represent three different aspects in a reading – the qualities that the Querent is exhibiting, the qualities the Querent needs to acquire, or a situation described by the characteristics of the card. Because of this, we did not list possible card combinations in the keywords section. The Attributes, Element, Direction, Color and Season will follow the suit of the Court Card.

Kings are generally mature men over thirty, and can represent authority figures in your personal life, or situations where you have to deal with those in positions of power.

Multiples in a spread:
2 Kings – partnerships
3 Kings – social outing
4 Kings – powerful alliances
(business related)

Queens are generally mature women over thirty, and can represent women in positions of authority, or situations where powerful women are involved.

Multiples in a spread:
2 Queens – gossip and rumors
3 Queens – close female friendship, social outings
4 Queens – powerful alliance
(friendships or social ties)

Knights, or young adults, can be of either sex, and while they take on the characteristics of the Kings and Queens, they are not yet mature enough to reach the correct decisions all the time. A Knight can also indicate a situation where fresh energy is needed.

Multiples in a reading:
2 Knights – bonding
3 Knights – youthful social outing
4 Knights – testosterone overload, gang mentality

Pages are usually children or young people, and they are nearly always associated with messages, information and news coming into your life. A look at the Page's suit indicates what the message is about. A Page can be of either sex, although there are some schools of thought that see the Page as feminine only and the Knight as masculine only.

Multiples in a reading:
2 Pages – gossip
3 Pages – child oriented social outings
4 Pages – possible school or other educational system situations

The Court Cards may appear with other names as well, depending on the deck you are using. Some other names that may be used are:

For **Page**
Princess, Knave, Sage, Maiden, Place, Student

For **Knight**
Prince, Child, Reformer, Knower, Warrior, Graduate

For **Queen**
Matriarch, Gift, Oracle, Woman, Master

For **King**
Patriarch, Speaker, Sage, Man, Doctor

Page of Swords

The Swords

The Swords are typically presented as those people with dark brown to black hair, dark eyes, and olive skin, or associated with the Air signs of Libra, Aquarius, and Gemini.

Alchemical Quality: Hot and Wet

Alchemical Symbol: △
Animal Energy: Hawk (Observation and Clarity)
Astrological Correspondence: The Season of Spring

Astrological Quadruplicity:
   Cardinal Zodiac (Aggressive) – Libra ♎

   Fixed Zodiac (Rigid) – Aquarius ♒

   Mutable Zodiac (Passive) – Gemini ♊

Attribute: Intellectual
Blood Type: Type O
Character Trait: Restlessness
Colors: Yellow, Red
Direction: East
Element: Air
Elemental: Sylphs, The Spirits of Air
Elemental Counterchange: Earth of Air
Elemental King: Paralda

Esoteric Title: Princess of the Rushing Winds, Lotus of the Palace of Air, Empress of the Sylphs, Throne of the Ace of Swords
Fundamental Force: Electromagnetic
Gender: Masculine
Holy Creature: The Winged Man

I-Ching: 10 – Correctness or Conduct, Peach, Harmony, Magnanimous
Keyword: Analytical
Key Phrase: "I Think"
Lunar Phase: 1st Quarter Moon
Magical Organ: The Brain
Magical Phrase: Noscere, To Know
Matter: Gas

Meanings:

Upright:

Adaptability, daring, decisive, defensive, delays, detachment, dexterity, diplomatic, discerning, discriminating, energetic, grace, highly intelligent, inquisitive, intellectual development, intuition, keen, legal affairs, logic, mental challenges, messages by letter, negotiator, not the time for rash decisions, prodigy, quick thinking, strong willed, travel, truthful, unpredictable.

Reversed:

Always has an excuse, bad news coming, bratty behavior, busybody, calculating personality, cunning, danger, deceit, devious, false pretenses, gossip, health problems, hyperactive, inaction, misunderstandings, psychological abuse, remoteness, sarcastic, self-centered, spying, suspicious, too clever for his own good, vindictive.

Musical Mood: "She's a Rebel" by Green Day
Mythological Creatures: Gryphons and Pegasus
Phase of Life: The Child
Physical Property: Motion
Plane: Mental
Playing Card Suit: Spades

Possibility:

Having found sure footing upon rough terrain, you're braced and ready for what you are about to face. Although wary about what difficulty the future might present, you are nonetheless confident and willing, as this is the time and place to show your mettle. It is never wise to charge the unknown, so stand fast and observe while the mystery is revealed. Once the challenge is clear you can act effectively and efficiently.

Psychological Function: Thoughts and Ideas
Quality: Active
Regent: Raphael
Royal Star: Alderbaran
Sabbat: Ostara
Season: Spring
Suit: Swords
Temperament: Sanguine

Tetragrammaton: Vau
Time of Day: Dawn

Knight of Swords

Swords

Knight

Alchemical Quality: Hot and Wet

Alchemical Symbol:
Animal Energy: Hawk
(Observation and Clarity)

Astrological Correspondence:
Gemini

Astrological Quadruplicity:
   Cardinal Zodiac (Aggressive) –
   Libra

   Fixed Zodiac (Rigid) – Aquarius

   Mutable Zodiac (Passive) –
   Gemini

Attribute: Intellectual
Blood Type: Type O
Character Trait: Restlessness
Colors: Yellow, Red
Direction: East
Element: Air
Elemental: Sylphs, The Spirits of Air
Elemental Counterchange: Fire of Air
Elemental King: Paralda
Esoteric Title: Prince of the Chariot of the

Wind, Emperor of the Sylphs
Fundamental Force: Electromagnetic
Gender: Masculine
Holy Creature: The Winged Man

I-Ching: 1 – Creative Power, Cause, Strength, Decisive
Keyword: Assertive
Key Phrase: "I Think"
Lunar Phase: 1st Quarter Moon
Magical Organ: The Brain
Magical Phrase: Noscere, To Know
Matter: Gas

Meanings:

Upright:
Aggressive, ambitious, assertive, bravado, call to action, career minded, courage, determination, direct, diversity, emotionally distant, firm resolve, focused, idealistic, knowledgeable, leadership material, logical, passionate, perseverance, problem solver, protector and defender of the weak, swift changes, versatile, warrior.

Reversed:
Arrogance, blunt and opinionated, coldly logical, chaotic, cheater, covert operations, deceitful, detached, dishonesty, dominating, false bravado, hidden agendas, ill health, impassible, impatience, intolerance, intrigue, meanness, must win at any cost, overbearing, sly, spying, takes things too literally, tyranny, violent behavior.

Musical Mood: "Problem Child" by AC/DC
Mythological Creatures: Gryphons and Pegasus
Phase of Life: The Child
Physical Property: Motion
Plane: Mental
Playing Card Suit: Spades

Possibility:

For you, strategy is simple. Decide what is right and aggressively defend it with vigor and fortitude. Blessed with great acuity, you do not deal in emotion or sentiment, and you have no use for tact and diplomacy. With each onslaught you push harder, driven by the fear of the inevitable failure that lies somewhere before you. You must learn to temper your approach, as some goals cannot be reached in a single thrust.

Psychological Function: Thoughts and Ideas
Quality: Active
Regent: Raphael
Royal Star: Alderbaran
Sabbat: Ostara
Season: Spring
Suit: Swords
Temperament: Sanguine

Tetragrammaton: Vau
Time of Day: Dawn

Queen of Swords

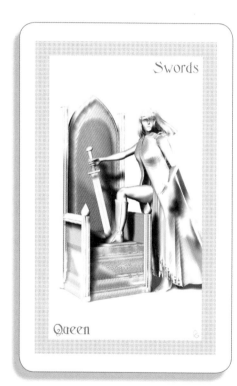

Alchemical Quality: Hot and Wet

Alchemical Symbol: △

Animal Energy: Hawk (Observation and Clarity)

Astrological Correspondence: ♎ Libra

Astrological Quadruplicity:
    Cardinal Zodiac (Aggressive) – ♎ Libra

    Fixed Zodiac (Rigid) – Aquarius ♒

    Mutable Zodiac (Passive) – Gemini ♊

Attribute: Intellectual
Blood Type: Type O
Character Trait: Restlessness
Colors: Yellow, Red
Direction: East
Element: Air
Elemental: Sylphs, The Spirits of Air
Elemental Counterchange: Water of Air
Elemental King: Paralda

Esoteric Title: Queen of the Thrones of Air, Queen of the Sylphs
Fundamental Force: Electromagnetic
Gender: Masculine
Holy Creature: The Winged Man

I-Ching: 20 – Contemplation, Perspective, Introspective, Observative
Keyword: Astute
Key Phrase: "I Think"
Lunar Phase: 1st Quarter Moon
Magical Organ: The Brain
Magical Phrase: Noscere, To Know
Matter: Gas

Meanings:

Upright:

Ambitious, astute, brutally honest, capable, charitable, childless, emotional detachment, excellent powers of observation, fair judgment, independent, needs no one's permission but her own, open minded, outspoken, perceptive, sadness, solitary, sorrowful, sterility, strong willed, suffers no fools gladly, widowed or divorced woman.

Reversed:

A bitch on wheels, angry, bitter, cold and calculating, demanding, finicky, formidable enemy, gossip, hidden agendas, hypercritical, ice water instead of blood in her veins, insensitive, intolerance, jilted lovers, judgmental, malicious, manipulation, narrow minded, sarcastic, spiteful, undermining, unforgiving, untrustworthy, vindictive.

Musical Mood: "I Am Woman" by Helen Reddy
Mythological Creatures: Gryphons and Pegasus
Phase of Life: The Child
Physical Property: Motion
Plane: Mental
Playing Card Suit: Spades

Possibility:

No stranger to sorrow, you have overcome emotional upheaval and grown from it. You are a survivor, but you don't think of yourself as such. That would imply a need for pity and you will have none of that. You do not consider honesty to be a flexible characteristic, and you are not easily fooled.

In the challenge you face ahead you must remember that humor, and your ability to laugh at yourself, can be the best tonic.

Psychological Function: Thoughts and Ideas
Quality: Active
Regent: Raphael
Royal Star: Alderbaran
Sabbat: Ostara
Season: Spring
Suit: Swords
Temperament: Sanguine

Tetragrammaton: Vau
Time of Day: Dawn

King of Swords

Alchemical Quality: Hot and Wet

Alchemical Symbol: △
Animal Energy: Hawk (Observation and Clarity)

Astrological Correspondence: ♒
Aquarius

Astrological Quadruplicity:
    Cardinal Zodiac (Aggressive) – ♎
    Libra

    Fixed Zodiac (Rigid) – Aquarius ♒

    Mutable Zodiac (Passive) – ♊
    Gemini

Attribute: Intellectual
Blood Type: Type O
Character Trait: Restlessness
Colors: Yellow, Red
Direction: East
Element: Air
Elemental: Sylphs, The Spirits of Air
Elemental Counterchange: Air of Air
Elemental King: Paralda

Esoteric Title: King of the Spirits of Air, Lord of the Winds and Breezes
Fundamental Force: Electromagnetic
Gender: Masculine
Holy Creature: The Winged Man

I-Ching: 9 – Restrained or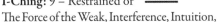
The Force of the Weak, Interference, Intuition, Preparing
Keyword: Decisive
Key Phrase: "I Think"
Lunar Phase: 1st Quarter Moon
Magical Organ: The Brain
Magical Phrase: Noscere, To Know
Matter: Gas

Meanings:

Upright:
Alert, ambitious, analytical, assertive, austere, balance, diplomatic, discipline with compassion, emotionally distant, ethical, fair, fierce, forthright, impartial, intellectual, intense, inventive, objective, powerful, private, professional, quick, rational, severe, somber, stern, strong leader, strict, supreme authority, wise.

Reversed:
Contemptuous, cruelty, demanding, disruption, distrustful, domineering, evil intentions, he acts as judge, jury and executioner, hypercritical, misuse of power, obstinate, overly cautious, prejudice, retribution and revenge, rigid, ruthless, sadistic, spiteful, suspicious, tyrant, underhanded, vengeful, vindictive, violence and abuse.

Musical Mood: "Demolition Man" by Sting
Mythological Creatures: Gryphons and Pegasus
Phase of Life: The Child
Physical Property: Motion
Plane: Mental
Playing Card Suit: Spades

Possibility:

When the proper interpretation of information and circumstance leads you to take appropriate action, then you have acted wisely. If you amass great amounts of knowledge and do nothing with it, you are a library. If you take action without comprehending the situation and what the possible outcomes of your efforts will be, you are imprudent. Authority serves the needs of the subjects; anything else is tyranny.

Psychological Function: Thoughts and Ideas
Quality: Active
Regent: Raphael
Royal Star: Alderbaran
Sabbat: Ostara
Season: Spring
Suit: Swords
Temperament: Sanguine

Tetragrammaton: Vau
Time of Day: Dawn

Alchemical Quality: Hot and Dry

Alchemical Symbol:

Animal Energy: Lioness
(Courage and Initiative)

Astrological Correspondence: The Season of Summer

Astrological Quadruplicity:
Cardinal Zodiac (Aggressive) – Aries

Fixed Zodiac (Rigid) – Leo

Mutable Zodiac (Passive) – Sagittarius

Attribute: Spiritual
Blood Type: Type B
Character Trait: Passion
Colors: Red, White
Direction: South
Element: Fire
Elemental: Salamanders, The Spirits of Fire
Elemental Counterchange: Earth of Fire
Elemental King: Djinn

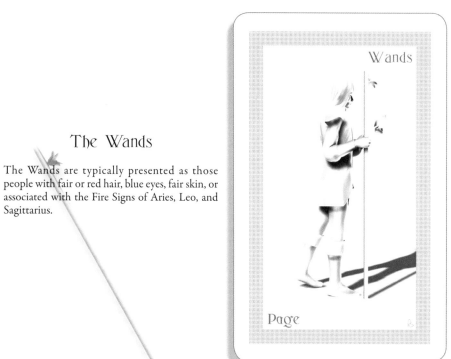

The Wands

The Wands are typically presented as those people with fair or red hair, blue eyes, fair skin, or associated with the Fire Signs of Aries, Leo, and Sagittarius.

Esoteric Title: Princess of the Shining Flame, Empress of the Salamanders, and Throne of the Ace of Wands
Fundamental Force: Strong
Gender: Masculine
Holy Creature: The Winged Lion

I-Ching: 43 – Resolution, 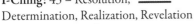 Determination, Realization, Revelation
Key Phrase: "I Will"
Keyword: Enthusiastic
Lunar Phase: Full Moon
Magical Organ: The Spirit
Magical Phrase: Velle, To Will
Matter: Energy

Meanings:

Upright:

Adventurous, bravura, charming, courage, daring, derring do, easily bored, energetic, enterprising, faithful, friendly and elegant, graceful, imaginative, innovation, joie de vivre, messages by phone, new ideas, opportunity for employment and growth, optimism, prankster, resourceful, seizing the moment, self assured and confident, youthful exuberance.

Reversed:

Arrogance, bad news, conceit, cruelty, easily distracted, feckless, hot tempered and reckless, inconsistency, indecisive, instability, legal problems, miscommunications, mood swings, negative responses, overly ambitious, pompous, rumors, secrets exposed, selfish, sore loser, spoiled, temper tantrums, unfaithful, unreliable, untrustworthy, vain and overly dramatic, worry.

Musical Mood: "Centerfield" by John Fogerty
Mythological Creatures: Dragons and Phoenix
Phase of Life: The Youth
Physical Property: Intensity
Plane: Spiritual
Playing Card Suit: Clubs

Possibility:

The fire that burns inside you has grown larger than you, and is more than you can contain. That is as it should be now that it is time to get out there and find out what the world holds for you. An opportunity belongs to no one, and must be taken with enthusiasm and desire. They can come in a word, without warning, and pass you by while you stop to tie your shoe. A message is forthcoming with news you want to hear.

Psychological Function: Energy and Desire
Quality: Immediate
Regent: Michael
Royal Star: Regulus
Sabbat: Litha
Season: Summer
Suit: Wands
Temperament: Choleric

Tetragrammaton: Yod ⟩
Time of Day: Noon

Knight of Wands

Alchemical Quality: Hot and Dry

Alchemical Symbol: △
Animal Energy: Lioness
(Courage and Initiative)

Astrological Correspondence:
Sagittarius ♐

Astrological Quadruplicity:
 Cardinal Zodiac (Aggressive) – ♈
 Aries

 Fixed Zodiac (Rigid) – Leo ♌

 Mutable Zodiac (Passive) – ♐
 Sagittarius

Attribute: Spiritual
Blood Type: Type B
Character Trait: Passion
Colors: Red, White
Direction: South
Element: Fire
Elemental: Salamanders, The Spirits of Fire
Elemental Counterchange: Fire of Fire
Elemental King: Djinn

Esoteric Title: Prince of the Chariot of Fire, Emperor of the Salamanders
Fundamental Force: Strong
Gender: Masculine
Holy Creature: The Winged Lion

I-Ching: 16 – Enthusiasm, 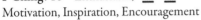 Motivation, Inspiration, Encouragement
Key Phrase: "I Will"
Keyword: Idealistic
Lunar Phase: Full Moon
Magical Organ: The Spirit
Magical Phrase: Velle, To Will
Matter: Energy

Meanings:

Upright:
Adventure seeker, ambition, bravura, business rival, change is imminent, charming, competitive, creative energy, enthusiasm, excitement, fun loving, future oriented, growth, inspiration, need to plan ahead, noble and gallant, noncommittal, optimistic, passionate, playful, positive attitude, possible travel by water, revolutionary, spontaneous.

Reversed:
Adrenaline junkie, argumentative, delays, egotism, hastiness, headstrong, hidden enemies, hot tempered, impatience, instigator, irresponsible, jealous, me first mentality, no self discipline, obstacles, opportunistic, promiscuous, pushy, quixotic, refusal to accept the natural flow of things, unable to finish what is started, unpredictable, unreliable, volatile, zero tolerance attitude.

Musical Mood: "Windmills" by Blackmore's Night
Mythological Creatures: Dragons and Phoenix
Phase of Life: The Youth
Physical Property: Intensity
Plane: Spiritual
Playing Card Suit: Clubs

Possibility:
It soon will become clear to you that the more you chase, the less you catch. Perpetually in an ebullient state with a need for constant stimulation you are always in motion, yet you make little or no progress towards accomplishment. The great passion that burns inside you will take you anywhere you want to go, but you still can only be one place at a time. Prioritize and aim your energy at what matters most.

Psychological Function: Energy and Desire
Quality: Immediate
Regent: Michael
Royal Star: Regulus
Sabbat: Litha
Season: Summer
Suit: Wands
Temperament: Choleric

Tetragrammaton: Yod ♪
Time of Day: Noon

Queen of Wands

Alchemical Quality: Hot and Dry

Alchemical Symbol: △
Animal Energy: Lioness
(Courage and Initiative)

Astrological Correspondence: ♈
Aries

Astrological Quadruplicity:
  Cardinal Zodiac (Aggressive) – ♈
  Aries

  Fixed Zodiac (Rigid) – Leo ♌

  Mutable Zodiac (Passive) – ♐
  Sagittarius

Attribute: Spiritual
Blood Type: Type B
Character Trait: Passion
Colors: Red, White
Direction: South
Element: Fire
Elemental: Salamanders, The Spirits of Fire
Elemental Counterchange: Water of Fire
Elemental King: Djinn

Esoteric Title: Queen of the Thrones of Fire, Queen of the Salamanders
Fundamental Force: Strong
Gender: Masculine
Holy Creature: The Winged Lion

I-Ching: 62 – Continuing or 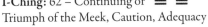 Triumph of the Meek, Caution, Adequacy
Key Phrase: "I Will"
Keyword: Passionate
Lunar Phase: Full Moon
Magical Organ: The Spirit
Magical Phrase: Velle, To Will
Matter: Energy

Meanings:

Upright:

Ambitious, businesswoman, confidence, courageous, creative, drama queen, dynamic, endurance, good money management, high energy, highly competitive, independent thinker, intuitive, loves an audience, organized, passionate, practical knowledge, protective, proud, stamina, temperamental, versatile, vibrant and outspoken, witty and fun.

Reversed:

Bitter, burnout, catty, controlling, demanding, egotistical, emotional blackmail, envious, extravagant, holding grudges, intolerant, jealous, long memory, malicious, manipulative, matriarchal, narrow minded, neurotic, out of control, overly strict or protective, prejudice, quick to anger, sarcastic, self indulgent, self-centered, shallow, twisted sense of humor.

Musical Mood: "Bitch" by Meredith Brooks
Mythological Creatures: Dragons and Phoenix
Phase of Life: The Youth
Physical Property: Intensity
Plane: Spiritual
Playing Card Suit: Clubs

Possibility:

Aggressive energy used for self-gratification is a negative force serving benefit to only the aggressor, and is often destructive to others. Although there are those that would describe your behavior as such, you are in truth a benevolent leader, serving the purpose of the community of life on Earth.

Your pride is deserved, but it is important to remember that if you judge, even those that judge you, then you will have fallen.

Psychological Function: Energy and Desire
Quality: Immediate
Regent: Michael
Royal Star: Regulus
Sabbat: Litha
Season: Summer
Suit: Wands
Temperament: Choleric

Tetragrammaton: Yod
Time of Day: Noon

King of Wands

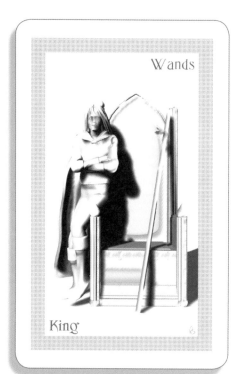

Wands

King

Alchemical Quality: Hot and Dry

Alchemical Symbol: △
Animal Energy: Lioness
(Courage and Initiative)

Astrological Correspondence:
Leo

Astrological Quadruplicity:
  Cardinal Zodiac (Aggressive) –
  Aries

  Fixed Zodiac (Rigid) – Leo

  Mutable Zodiac (Passive) –
  Sagittarius

Attribute: Spiritual
Blood Type: Type B
Character Trait: Passion
Colors: Red, White
Direction: South
Element: Fire
Elemental: Salamanders, The Spirits of Fire
Elemental Counterchange: Air of Fire
Elemental King: Djinn

Esoteric Title: Lord of Flame and Lightning, King of the Spirits of Fire
Fundamental Force: Strong
Gender: Masculine
Holy Creature: The Winged Lion

I-Ching: 34 – Great Power or Power of the Great, Opportunity, Breaking Free
Key Phrase: "I Will"
Keyword: Charismatic
Lunar Phase: Full Moon
Magical Organ: The Spirit
Magical Phrase: Velle, To Will
Matter: Energy

Meanings:

Upright:

Ambition, authoritative, bold, charismatic, charming, conscientious, considerate, creative, dashing, decisive, enthusiasm, entrepreneur, excellent communicator, forgiving, generous, innovation, inspiring, legal matters, loyalty, monogamous, motivation, optimistic, passionate, risk taking, spirited, strength, strong leader, The Boss, versatile, virility.

Reversed:

Aggressive, always needs an audience, arrogant, autocratic, bigoted, by any means necessary, con artist, condescending, demeaning, domineering, egotistical, everything to excess, fierce enemy, histrionic, impulsive, inflexible, intolerant, narrow minded, no attention to detail, pessimistic, prejudice, ruthless, self absorbed, self righteous, sore loser, undependable.

Musical Mood: "Man on the Silver Mountain" by Rainbow
Mythological Creatures: Dragons and Phoenix
Phase of Life: The Youth
Physical Property: Intensity
Plane: Spiritual
Playing Card Suit: Clubs

Possibility:

A normally unpretentious natural leader you have quite the passionate righteousness about you, and will shed your cloak of humility when you deem the situation warrants it. Sound in your beliefs of morality and ethics, you have a strong dislike for deceit and misuse of trust. You must learn to temper your impatience with those that can't keep your pace, or maintain the standards that you place upon yourself.

Psychological Function: Energy and Desire
Quality: Immediate
Regent: Michael
Royal Star: Regulus
Sabbat: Litha
Season: Summer
Suit: Wands
Temperament: Choleric

Tetragrammaton: Yod
Time of Day: Noon

Page of Cups

The Cups

The Cups are typically presented as those people with light to medium brown or blonde hair, hazel eyes, and medium skin, or associated with the Water signs of Cancer, Scorpio, and Pisces.

Cups

Page

Alchemical Quality: Cold and Wet

Alchemical Symbol: ▽
Animal Energy: Dolphin (Joy and Love)

Astrological Correspondence: The Season of Autumn

Astrological Quadruplicity:
　Cardinal Zodiac (Aggressive) – ♋ Cancer

　Fixed Zodiac (Rigid) – Scorpio ♏

　Mutable Zodiac (Passive) – Pisces ♓

Attribute: Emotional
Blood Type: Type AB
Character Trait: Healing
Colors: Blue-Green, Gray
Direction: West
Element: Water
Elemental: Undines, The Spirits of Water
Elemental Counterchange: Earth of Water
Elemental King: Nixsa
Esoteric Title: Princess of the Water and Lotus of the Palace of Floods, Empress of the

198

Nymphs and Undines, and Throne of the Ace of Cups

Fundamental Force: Weak
Gender: Feminine
Holy Creature: The Eagle

I-Ching: 41 – Decline or Decrease, Unknowing, Learning, Beginner
Key Phrase: "I Feel"
Keyword: Sensitive
Lunar Phase: 3rd Quarter
Magical Organ: The Heart
Magical Phrase: Audere, To Dare
Matter: Liquid

Meanings:

Upright:

Affectionate, artistic ability, birth of a child, creative, divination, dramatic, dreamy, emotional, fondness for animals, gentle, good news, hidden talents, imagination, intimate, introverted, loving, messages by spoken word, new beginnings, prefers to work alone, psychic, romantic dreamer, self awareness, sensitive, strong intuitions, thoughtful.

Reversed:

Arrested development, bad news concerning relationships, deception, easily led, escapism, impetuous, jealousy, lazy, lives for the moment only, melancholy, not rooted in reality, self absorbed, shallowness, slave to his affections, spoiled, substance abuse, susceptible to false flattery, tactless, unhappiness, untrustworthy, weak minded.

Musical Mood: "If We Were a Movie" by Miley Cyrus
Mythological Creatures: Merfolk and Hippocampus
Phase of Life: The Adult
Physical Property: Fluidity
Plane: Astral
Playing Card Suit: Hearts

Possibility:

You are about to embark on a new and daringly imaginative romance. If you are youthful and have had little time to experience love as of yet, there is a wonderfully enlightening relationship just ahead. If the excitement of being in love is something you remember from your past, or perhaps have continually held out hope to find, you are about to experience the sensations that have lived in your hopes and dreams.

Psychological Function: Emotions and Feelings
Quality: Receptive
Regent: Gabriel
Royal Star: Antares
Sabbat: Mabon
Season: Autumn
Suit: Cups
Temperament: Phlegmatic

Tetragrammaton: Heh
Time of Day: Dusk

Cups

Knight

Alchemical Quality: Cold and Wet

Alchemical Symbol:
Animal Energy: Dolphin (Joy and Love)

Astrological Correspondence: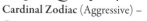
Pisces

Astrological Quadruplicity:
   Cardinal Zodiac (Aggressive) –
   Cancer

   Fixed Zodiac (Rigid) – Scorpio

   Mutable Zodiac (Passive) – Pisces

Attribute: Emotional
Blood Type: Type AB
Character Trait: Healing
Colors: Blue-Green, Gray
Direction: West
Element: Water
Elemental: Undines, The Spirits of Water
Elemental Counterchange: Fire of Water
Elemental King: Nixsa
Esoteric Title: Prince of the Chariot of the
Waters, Emperor of the Nymphs

Fundamental Force: Weak
Gender: Feminine
Holy Creature: The Eagle

I-Ching: 16 – Enthusiasm, ䷏
Motivation, Inspiration, Encourage
Key Phrase: "I Feel"
Keyword: Charming
Lunar Phase: 3rd Quarter
Magical Organ: The Heart
Magical Phrase: Audere, To Dare
Matter: Liquid

Meanings:

Upright:

Amiable, artistic, compassionate, eager to please, earnest, empathetic, hopeless romantic, idealistic, imaginative, kind, knight in shining armor, marriage proposals, need to express feelings, new love, Prince Charming, refined, romance, sensitive soul, sincere, story book romances, suave, sympathetic.

Reversed:

Conceited, deceptive, embezzlement, emotional manipulation, evasive, fake or fraud, false flattery, false promises, il-lusions, immature, infidelity, insincere, lazy, narcissistic, overactive imagination, pathological liar, reckless, seduction, substance abuse, sugar-coating the situation, temperamental, trickery, unreliable, weakness, wolf in sheep's clothing.

Musical Mood: "Hero" by Enrique Inglesis
Mythological Creatures: Merfolk and Hippocampus
Phase of Life: The Adult
Physical Property: Fluidity
Plane: Astral
Playing Card Suit: Hearts

Possibility:

Be mindful of stubbornness or foolishness in romance. If you are going to give of your heart, open your eyes and see whom you are giving it to. It might be that you are the one that is misleading you. Concern about your partner's view of the relationship might be preventing you from seeing your own view of it. A major step is just before you, as a marriage or a first weekend getaway together is about to be proposed.

Psychological Function: Emotions and

Feelings
Quality: Receptive
Regent: Gabriel
Royal Star: Antares
Sabbat: Mabon
Season: Autumn
Suit: Cups
Temperament: Phlegmatic

Tetragrammaton: Heh
Time of Day: Dusk

Cups

Queen

Alchemical Quality: Cold and Wet

Alchemical Symbol:
Animal Energy: Dolphin (Joy and Love)

Astrological Correspondence:
Cancer

Astrological Quadruplicity:
   Cardinal Zodiac (Aggressive) –
   Cancer

   Fixed Zodiac (Rigid) – Scorpio

   Mutable Zodiac (Passive) – Pisces

Attribute: Emotional
Blood Type: Type AB
Character Trait: Healing
Colors: Blue-Green, Gray
Direction: West
Element: Water
Elemental: Undines, The Spirits of Water
Elemental Counterchange: Water of Water
Elemental King: Nixsa
Esoteric Title: Queen of the Thrones of Water, Queen of the Nymphs and Undines
Fundamental Force: Weak

Gender: Feminine
Holy Creature: The Eagle

I-Ching: 61 – Inner Truth, Trusting, Wholehearted, Centered
Key Phrase: "I Feel"
Keyword: Intuitive
Lunar Phase: 3rd Quarter
Magical Organ: The Heart
Magical Phrase: Audere, To Dare
Matter: Liquid

Meanings:

Upright:

Artistically gifted, compassionate, emotional maturity, empathetic, enigmatic, fey, generous, good counselor, good mother and wife, healer, imaginative, intuitive, lover of the arts, loving, loyalty, mystery, nurturing, occult interests, otherworldly, poetic, psychic, sensitive, sentimental, spiritual, tender-hearted, unpretentious, visions and dreams.

Reversed:

Behind the scenes manipulator, cryptic, daydreamer, dishonesty, disorganized, emotionally unstable, escapism, fickle, frivolous, gullible, has a personal agenda, heartbreaker, hypersensitive, irrational, moody, not to be trusted, oblivious, perversity, secretive, secretly vindictive, self delusional, substance abuse, susceptible to flattery, unrealistic, unreliable, vanity.

Musical Mood: "She's Got a Way" by Billy Joel
Mythological Creatures: Merfolk and Hippocampus
Phase of Life: The Adult
Physical Property: Fluidity
Plane: Astral
Playing Card Suit: Hearts

Possibility:

Your sensitivity and instinctive ability to nurture may be needed to salve the wounds of someone you care about. Perhaps it is a child of yours, maybe a niece or a nephew. It could very well be an adult such as a spouse, lover, or just a friend. Certain intuitive feelings you are experiencing may not be as abstract as you are being led to believe. Trust in the psychic part of yourself and learn to accept what others dismiss.

Psychological Function: Emotions and Feelings
Quality: Receptive
Regent: Gabriel
Royal Star: Antares
Sabbat: Mabon
Season: Autumn
Suit: Cups
Temperament: Phlegmatic

Tetragrammaton: Heh
Time of Day: Dusk

Alchemical Quality: Cold and Wet

Alchemical Symbol:
Animal Energy: Dolphin (Joy and Love)

Astrological Correspondence:
Scorpio

Astrological Quadruplicity:
   Cardinal Zodiac (Aggressive) –
   Cancer

   Fixed Zodiac (Rigid) – Scorpio

   Mutable Zodiac (Passive) – Pisces

Attribute: Emotional
Blood Type: Type AB
Character Trait: Healing
Colors: Blue-Green, Gray
Direction: West
Element: Water
Elemental: Undines, The Spirits of Water
Elemental Counterchange: Air of Water
Elemental King: Nixsa
Esoteric Title: Lord of the Waves and Waters, King of the Hosts of the Sea
Fundamental Force: Weak

Gender: Feminine
Holy Creature: The Eagle

I-Ching: 34 – Great Power,
Breaking Free, Opportunity, Persevering
Key Phrase: "I Feel"
Keyword: Artistic
Lunar Phase: 3rd Quarter
Magical Organ: The Heart
Magical Phrase: Audere, To Dare
Matter: Liquid

Meanings:

Upright:
Calm, caring, chivalrous, compassionate, cool under fire, cultured, dignity, diplomatic, educated, empathetic, faithful, father figure, finds humor in even the bleakest situations, kind, lover and supporter of the arts, loving, reliability, responsibility, romantic, secretive, selfless, supportive friend, tactful, tolerant, trustworthy, virtuous, wise counselor.

Reversed:
Avoidance, con man, crafty, deceptive, despoiler of others, dishonest, double dealer, fraud, hypersensitive, immoral, jaded, jealous, lecher, manipulative, neurotic, power seeker, rogue, ruthless, scandal, seducer, self delusional, self indulgent, substance abuse, treachery, unscrupulous, untruthful, vanity, vice, violent tendencies.

Musical Mood: "Turn of the Century" by Yes
Mythological Creatures: Merfolk and Hippocampus
Phase of Life: The Adult
Physical Property: Fluidity
Plane: Astral
Playing Card Suit: Hearts

Possibility:

Sageness is found to be expressible in many different forms, and covers every known aspect of life. You have a particular area of knowledge or expertise that someone you know could benefit from. Sometimes wisdom passes through the emulation of a role model, so be aware of who might be learning by observing you. It's possible that you should step up, be the mentor to someone, and initiate exposure to the fine arts.

Psychological Function: Emotions and Feelings
Quality: Receptive
Regent: Gabriel
Royal Star: Antares
Sabbat: Mabon
Season: Autumn
Suit: Cups
Temperament: Phlegmatic

Tetragrammaton: Heh
Time of Day: Dusk

Alchemical Quality: Cold and Dry

Alchemical Symbol: ▽
Animal Energy: Bear
(Introspection and Dreams)

Astrological Correspondence: The Season of Winter

Astrological Quadruplicity:
    Cardinal Zodiac (Aggressive) – Capricorn ♑

    Fixed Zodiac (Rigid) – Taurus ♂

    Mutable Zodiac (Passive) – Virgo ♍

Attribute: Physical
Blood Type: Type A
Character Trait: Hibernation
Colors: White, Black
Direction: North
Element: Earth
Elemental: Gnomes, The Spirits of Earth
Elemental Counterchange: Earth of Earth
Elemental King: Ghob
Esoteric Title: Princess of the Echoing Hills, Rose of the Palace of Earth, Empress

The Pentacles

The Pentacles are typically presented as those people with white or dark hair, any color eyes or skin. They can also represent members of the dark-skinned races.

of the Gnomes, and Throne of the Ace of Pentacles
Fundamental Force: Gravity
Gender: Feminine
Holy Creature: The Winged Bull

I-Ching: 25 – Innocence, Spontaneous, Open, Impetuous
Key Phrase: "I Have"
Keyword: Practical
Lunar Phase: New Moon
Magical Organ: The Body and Senses
Magical Phrase: Tacere, To Keep Silent
Matter: Solid

Meanings:

Upright:

Articulate, childlike fascination, conscientious, curious about nature, deliberate, determination, educational opportunities, enthusiasm, financial opportunities, looking to the future, messages by email, IM, or text, open minded, paperwork and documents, practicality, pragmatic, respectful, responsible, setting reasonable goals, thrifty.

Reversed:

Bad news concerning money, busybody, conceited, degradation, depression, disorder, extravagant, ignorance, illogical, impractical, impatience, impudent, lack of respect, low self esteem, maladroit, materialistic, monotony, moody, nitpicking, not reading the fine print, overzealous, rebel without a clue, shallow, snobbish, spendthrift, wasteful.

Musical Mood: "I'm Going to Say it Now" by Phil Ochs
Mythological Creatures: Giants and Elves
Phase of Life: The Elder
Physical Property: Solidity
Plane: Physical
Playing Card Suit: Diamonds

Possibility:

You have reached a point in your life, a crossroads perhaps, where it is time to take stock in what you expect from yourself. What is to be the path of fulfillment for you is the question that lingers about you. Should you follow the road to academia, or become the apprentice of a tradesman? Is it the rewards that you enjoy, or maybe you are fond of the purposeful feeling that comes from the work? Either way, it's time to choose.

Psychological Function: Manifestation and Formation
Quality: Passive
Regent: Uriel
Royal Star: Fomalhaut
Sabbat: Yule
Season: Winter
Suit: Pentacles
Temperament: Melancholic

Tetragrammaton: Heh
Time of Day: Midnight

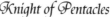

Knight of Pentacles

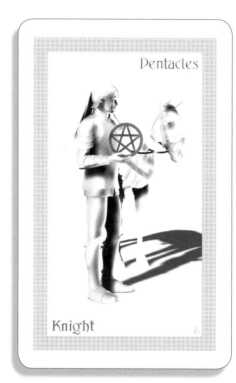

Alchemical Quality: Cold and Dry

Alchemical Symbol: ▽
Animal Energy: Bear
(Introspection and Dreams)

Astrological Correspondence: ♍
Virgo

Astrological Quadruplicity:
   Cardinal Zodiac (Aggressive) – ♑
   Capricorn

    Fixed Zodiac (Rigid) – Taurus ♂

    Mutable Zodiac (Passive) – Virgo ♍

Attribute: Physical
Blood Type: Type A
Character Trait: Hibernation
Colors: White, Black
Direction: North
Element: Earth
Elemental: Gnomes, The Spirits of Earth
Elemental Counterchange: Fire of Earth
Elemental King: Ghob
Esoteric Title: Prince of the Chariot of Earth,
Emperor of the Gnomes

Fundamental Force: Gravity
Gender: Feminine
Holy Creature: The Winged Bull

I-Ching: 19 – Promotion, ䷖
Action, Investment, Encounter
Key Phrase: "I Have"
Keyword: Accomplished
Lunar Phase: New Moon
Magical Organ: The Body and Senses
Magical Phrase: Tacere, To Keep Silent
Matter: Solid

Meanings:

Upright:
Boy scout, cautious, conscientious, dependable, down to earth, easy going, helpful, impassive, indifferent, industrious, kind to animals, loyal, nature and animal lover, patient, perseverance, practical and pragmatic, progress is being made, realistic, responsible, serious, stability, stoic, thorough, thoughtful, traditionalist, unwavering.

Reversed:
Apathy, boorish, dull, foppish, greed, impatience, instability, irresponsible, lack of progress, laziness, missed opportunities, money problems, no sense of humor, overly cautious and conservative, plodding, impractical, irresponsible, self satisfied, sense of entitlement, smug, stagnation, tunnel vision, unemployed, unimaginative, uninspired, unrefined.

Musical Mood: "Simple Man" by Lynyrd Skynyrd
Mythological Creatures: Giants and Elves
Phase of Life: The Elder
Physical Property: Solidity
Plane: Physical
Playing Card Suit: Diamonds

Possibility:

Gazing over the foundation you have put down and checking it against the plans you have set is where you find yourself, and now is a good time to compare where you are against where you expected to be. Temper your judgment on your efforts so far. Don't get down if it seems less than you expected just continue to apply yourself. If you are pleased so far you will need to be careful not to let it go to your head.

Psychological Function: Manifestation and Formation
Quality: Passive
Regent: Uriel
Royal Star: Fomalhaut
Sabbat: Yule
Season: Winter
Suit: Pentacles
Temperament: Melancholic

Tetragrammaton: Heh
Time of Day: Midnight

Queen of Pentacles

Pentacles

Queen

Alchemical Quality: Cold and Dry

Alchemical Symbol: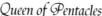
Animal Energy: Bear
(Introspection and Dreams)

Astrological Correspondence: ♑
Capricorn

Astrological Quadruplicity:
  Cardinal Zodiac (Aggressive) – ♑
  Capricorn

  Fixed Zodiac (Rigid) – Taurus ♂

  Mutable Zodiac (Passive) – Virgo ♍

Attribute: Physical
Blood Type: Type A
Character Trait: Hibernation
Colors: White, Black
Direction: North
Element: Earth
Elemental: Gnomes, The Spirits of Earth
Elemental Counterchange: Water of Earth
Elemental King: Ghob
Esoteric Title: Queen of the Thrones of
Earth, Queen of the Gnomes

Fundamental Force: Gravity
Gender: Feminine
Holy Creature: The Winged Bull

I-Ching: 46 – Advancement, Arising, Growth, Mobility
Key Phrase: "I Have"
Keyword: Productive
Lunar Phase: New Moon
Magical Organ: The Body and Senses
Magical Phrase: Tacere, To Keep Silent
Matter: Solid

Meanings:

Upright:

Bright, budget keeper, capable, close attention to details, down to earth, emotionally mature, environmentalist, experienced, fertile, flashy, fond of luxury, good business sense, good manager, hard working, intelligent, nature lover, practical, protective, provider, reliable, resourceful, thoughtful, well organized, wonderful hostess, works well with others.

Reversed:

Blames others for her mistakes, controlling, distrustful, dogmatic, elitist, fair weather friend, feels entitled, flighty, frivolous, gluttony, greed, insecurity, irresponsible, judges by visible wealth, loves gossip, materialistic, overly concerned with appearances, poor money management, pretentiousness, self loathing, snobbish, stingy, stubborn, two faced, vain, workaholic.

Musical Mood: "Material Girl" by Madonna
Mythological Creatures: Giants and Elves
Phase of Life: The Elder
Physical Property: Solidity
Plane: Physical
Playing Card Suit: Diamonds

Possibility:

It's time to let the better part of you come forward and be the person others can always look to for support and comfort, somebody out there needs that from you right now. You need to encourage others to realize the value of life, the beauty of nature, and that all things matter, great and small. Make a point of speaking on behalf of those that might be unable to speak for themselves. Let your voice be their voice.

Psychological Function: Manifestation and Formation
Quality: Passive
Regent: Uriel
Royal Star: Fomalhaut
Sabbat: Yule
Season: Winter
Suit: Pentacles
Temperament: Melancholic

Tetragrammaton: Heh
Time of Day: Midnight

King of Pentacles

Pentacles

King

Alchemical Quality: Cold and Dry

Alchemical Symbol: ▽
Animal Energy: Bear
(Introspection and Dreams)

Astrological Correspondence: ♂
Taurus

Astrological Quadruplicity:
   Cardinal Zodiac (Aggressive) – ♑
   Capricorn

   Fixed Zodiac (Rigid) – Taurus ♂

   Mutable Zodiac (Passive) – Virgo ♍

Attribute: Physical
Blood Type: Type A
Character Trait: Hibernation
Colors: White, Black
Direction: North
Element: Earth
Elemental: Gnomes, The Spirits of Earth
Elemental Counterchange: Air of Earth
Elemental King: Ghob
Esoteric Title: Lord of the Wild and Fertile
Land, King of the Spirits of the Earth

Fundamental Force: Gravity
Gender: Feminine
Holy Creature: The Winged Bull

I-Ching: 53 – Developing, Advance, Progress, Mobility
Key Phrase: "I Have"
Keyword: Grounded
Lunar Phase: New Moon
Magical Organ: The Body and Senses
Magical Phrase: Tacere, To Keep Silent
Matter: Solid

Meanings:

Upright:

Achievable goals, captain of industry, cautious, common sense, consultant, enjoys comfort and luxury, enterprising, father figure, good investments, manager, methodical, old school, open minded, patience, practical, professional, reliable, responsibility, school of hard knocks, slow to anger, solidity, sound advice, success, supportive, trustworthy, wealth.

Reversed:

Abusive, amoral, crude, dishonest, dull, exploitation, jealous, lack of business sense, lack of foresight, materialistic, misuse of power, obsessed with wealth or acquiring possessions, offensive, opinionated, quick to anger, resistance to change, roué, ruthless, shallow, spendthrift, status conscious, violent temper, vanity, vulgar.

Musical Mood: "Pastime With Good Company (The King's Ballad)" By HRM King Henry VIII
Mythological Creatures: Giants and Elves
Phase of Life: The Elder
Physical Property: Solidity
Plane: Physical
Playing Card Suit: Diamonds

Possibility:

You have already discovered that the conservative approach is the better choice, and now is not the time to call in to question the lessons you have long since learned. Be a patient administrator of fiscal matters and never lose sight of what it is that financial security protects. Always keep your commitments and be true to your word, there is always the right thing to do in every decision you face.

Psychological Function: Manifestation and Formation
Quality: Passive
Regent: Uriel
Royal Star: Fomalhaut
Sabbat: Yule
Season: Winter
Suit: Pentacles
Temperament: Melancholic

Tetragrammaton: Heh
Time of Day: Midnight

12
Advanced Tarot Work

Tarot can be added into your rituals as a wonderful tool for creative visualization. Be sure to choose a deck where the symbolism speaks directly to you. Your choice of card or cards should be directly related to that which you wish to accomplish. You should choose cards that not only portray that which you desire, but also evoke strong feelings. For example, if your goal is marriage, then the Two of Cups may be a good choice to aid in your visualizations. New job? Try the Three of Pentacles. Strength to leave an abusive relationship? The Eight of Cups epitomizes that strength. However, unless you are actually out there dating, checking the want ads, or making preparations to get out of that bad situation, all the magick in the world isn't going to help you. In other words, you have to make the effort to help yourself in order to ask for help from the Divine and receive it.

Also, two small bits of advice – One, do not ask for more than you truly need. Selfish actions such as that tend to come back to haunt you when least expected. And two, always and without exception remember the laws of Karma and Free Will. Here's a little poem to help you keep these in mind:

Ever mind the Rule of Threes – times three my acts return to me
This lesson well I must learn – I only get that which I earn.

As in forming a question to ask the cards, remember to keep the focus on yourself and what is within your power to change.

There are many books with wonderful Tarot spells in the bookstores and libraries. However, the strongest spells are those you write yourself. After all, who better knows your wants and needs than you? It doesn't have to rhyme, although rhyme in itself is a form of magick and lends a sense of purpose to the ritual. Don't despair if you are unable to put words together in perfect prose; if you are sincere in your words, this is all you truly need.

You can place the cards directly on your altar if you choose, or make photocopies of the cards and plaster them all over your space as a constant reminder of your desires. Put them in your purse or wallet, on the wall next to your desk if that is acceptable in your office, in your car, or anywhere where you can get a visual reminder of what it is you want.

Along with the cards on your altar, you may wish to arrange gemstones or herbs, or light incense whose fragrance corresponds with your need. Poppets or small pouches in a dizzying array of available materials can be made to carry along in a pocket, containing stones, herbs and cards to help you see yourself realizing your goals. For example, a Love Poppet could contain the above-mentioned Two of Cups, a piece of rose quartz, a pinch of rosemary and an acorn for luck. We would again stress that in order to preserve your Tarot deck, make a photocopy of the card you choose, or even better, draw it. Creativity is of the utmost importance – do what feels right to you, and don't worry about making mistakes. It is your spell, your visualization, and if you feel that it is done correctly, then it surely is.

13
Herbs *and* Fragrances

This is a partial, and by no means all-inclusive, list of herbs and fragrance, along with their associated metaphysical properties. If you do decide to use some of these in your readings or rituals, we strongly urge you to do research first on the herb(s) you wish to use.

Some of the herbs listed (such as mistletoe and mandrake among others) are poisonous to humans and/or animals and should not in any manner, fashion or form or under any circumstances be ingested!
There are many good herb manuals at your local bookseller, your local library, as well as sites on the Internet. It is much better to be safe than sorry; take the time to arm yourself with knowledge about the herbs you intend to use.

Herbs are best when grown yourself; this way you can be assured of freshness and purity. If growing them yourself presents a problem, there are always alternatives. Many websites now offer herb by mail service, and there is always the grocery store in case of herbal emergency. Look around you for some of the more common – while you may not be able to find the elusive rowan in your area, you may find a lucky acorn or two from a neighborhood oak.

You'll notice when going through the table that many herbs have numerous properties. The properties are not listed in any particular order; you can choose which aroma is most pleasing to you and will achieve the desired result. For example – one of the least appealing fragrances to us is anise. Therefore, if we are being plagued with bad dreams, we are not limited to one choice to rid ourselves of them. We could choose Chamomile, Lavender, Catnip or Thyme. It is simply a matter of personal preference.

Note: You'll see several herbs here with the association of exorcism. This is not to equate it with driving out the devil; its function is to banish negative or hostile energy.

Acacia – intuition, protection
Acorn – Fertility, luck, money, wisdom
Agrimony – restful sleep, protection
Allspice – money, luck, healing
Almond – prosperity, wisdom
Aloe – luck, protection
Amarantha – love, self-image, marriage
Ambergris – love
Angelica – visions, healing, protection, exorcism
Anise – protection, purification, restful sleep
Apple – immortality, healing, love, fertility
Asafoetida – protection, exorcism, banishing, purification

Basil – wealth, exorcism, love, protection
Bay – protection, purification, strength, fertility, healing
Bayberry – money, prosperity

Benzoin – prosperity, cleansing
Bergamot – money, prosperity
Bistort – fertility, intuition
Blackberry – stress relief, cleansing
Borage – courage, wisdom, intuition
Bladderwrack – invocations, intuition, protection, money
Bloodroot – protection, love, cleansing
Broom – divination, protection, cleansing

Cactus – protection
Calamus – protection, money, healing, luck
Camphor – divination, healing, cleansing
Caraway – protection, healing, intuition
Cardamon – love
Carnation – healing, protection, strength
Catnip – love, happiness, divination, restful sleep
Cedar – healing, money, protection, cleansing
Celery – intuition, cleansing
Chamomile – restful sleep, money, love, fertility
Cinnamon – money, protection, self-image, love, intuition
Cinquefoil – love, money, healing, wisdom, protection
Citron – healing, intuition
Clove – love, money, exorcism, protection
Clover – money
Comfrey – money, protection, safe travel
Copal – spirituality, love, cleansing
Coriander – healing, love, wisdom, understanding
Corn – protection, cleansing, luck
Cumin – love, marriage
Cotton – luck, protection, healing
Cypress – healing, protection, luck

Damiana – visions, love
Dandelion – divination, luck, money

Deerstongue – intuition
Dill – love, lust, protection, money, fertility
Dragon's Blood – exorcism, protection, love

Echinacea – healing
Elder – protection, exorcism, prosperity, healing
Endive – love
Eucalyptus – healing, protection
Eyebright – intuition

Fennel – healing, protection, cleansing
Fig – love, fertility, divination
Flax – intuition, protection, healing, money
Frankincense – spirituality, protection, exorcism, breaking bad habits

Galangal – healing, money, protection, intuition
Gardenia – love, healing, fertility, cleansing
Garlic – luck, healing, protection, exorcism
Geranium – love, fertility, healing, protection, calming
Ginger – love, success, money, breaking bad habits
Ginseng – love, protection

Hawthorn – fertility, happiness, communication
Hazel – fertility, protection, luck
Heather – luck, protection
Heliotrope – wealth, healing, exorcism
Hibiscus – divination, love
Holly – luck, protection
Honeysuckle – protection, money, intuition
Hops – healing, restful sleep
Horehound – exorcism, healing, protection, creativity
Hyacinth – love, protection
Hyssop – protection, cleansing

Iris – cleansing, wisdom

Ivy – protection and healing

Jasmine – money, love, romance
Juniper – love, healing, exorcism, protection
Lavender – divination, spirituality, love, protection, restful sleep

Lemon – love, protection, cleansing, self image
Lemon Verbena – love, cleansing
Lilac – love, protection
Lily – protection, platonic love
Lily of the Valley – intuition, happiness
Lime – protection (particularly good in working environments), love, healing
Mace – confidence, intuition
Mandrake – money, protection, love, healing, fertility
Maple – love, happiness, stability
Marigold – protection, intuition, self image, communication, wisdom
Marjoram – money, protection, healing, love
Mint – healing, safe travel, protection, exorcism, money
Mistletoe – love, communication, confidence
Mugwort – intuition, healing, protection
Mulberry – protection
Mustard – fertility, protection
Myrrh – protection, exorcism, healing
Myrtle – fertility, love
Nettle – healing, protection, exorcism
Nutmeg – healing, money, love, monogamy

Oak – protection, money, stability, understanding
Olive – protection, fertility, healing
Onion – exorcism, healing, protection, money
Orange – money, divination, luck, love

Orchid – love
Orris – love, protection, divination

Pansy – love
Parsley – cleansing, protection
Patchouli – money, fertility, peace
Peony – exorcism, protection
Pepper – grounding, stability
Peppermint – love, healing, intuition, protection
Periwinkle – intuition, money, protection, love
Pincushion Flower – protection, aid in selling or renting real estate
Pine – fertility, protection, exorcism, healing, prosperity
Plumeria – Love
Pomegranate – fertility, wealth, luck, happiness
Poppy – restful sleep, fertility, love, money, luck
Purslane – restful sleep, love, protection, love

Raspberry – love, protection
Rice – rain, money, fertility, protection
Rose – love, protection, luck, healing, intuition
Rosemary – love, intuition, protection, exorcism, cleansing
Rowan – healing, intuition, protection
Rue – exorcism, healing, love

Saffron – love, healing
Sage – wisdom, protection
Sandalwood – spirituality, exorcism, protection, healing, grounding
Sarsaparilla – love, money
Skullcap – divination, intuition
Spearmint – intuition, healing, love
Star Anise – intuition

Strawberry – fertility, love, luck, self-image
Sunflower – fertility, happiness, wisdom

Tarragon – healing, protection, divination
Thistle – exorcism, protection, healing
Thyme – intuition, healing, love, restful sleep
Tobacco – healing, purification

Valerian – restful sleep, cleansing, protection, love
Vanilla – love, peace
Vetivert – love, luck, money
Vervain – love, cleansing, money, healing
Violet – love, protection, healing, peace

Willow – love, protection and healing
Wintergreen – prosperity, healing, wisdom
Witch Hazel – protection
Wormwood – protection, love, intuition

Yarrow – love, exorcism, intuition, courage

14

Gemstones

There are many ways to acquire gemstones. Many semi-precious stones can be found in arts and craft stores. There are places throughout the world that allow open gemstone mining, offering the chance to dig for raw rubies, emeralds, diamonds, etc. for a nominal fee. And then there is the Internet, where nearly any manner of stone can be found and delivered directly to you.

Charging your gemstones for use is a relatively simple matter. Leave them on your windowsill to be lit by the full moon, or wash them in blessed water. Carry them with you so that they attune themselves to your personal vibrations and request that they assist you in your workings. We have assembled a partial list of gemstones here for reference:

Agate – repels negative energy, unites emotion with logic, balance
Amazonite – helps to bring clarity of mind, aids in communications
Amber – healing, aids in creative visualization, attracts positive energy
Amethyst – promotes psychic ability, heightens intuition, opens channels
Apatite – promotes psychic ability, heightens intuition, opens channels

Aquamarine – promotes tolerance, aids in communications
Aventurine – promotes psychic ability, healing
Azurite – promotes psychic ability, heightens intuition, opens channels

Bloodstone – strength, courage, prosperity

Carnelian – strength, endurance, happiness
Cat's Eye – promotes serenity, intuition and awareness
Charoite – promotes healing and understanding
Chrysocolla – stress relief, healing, strength
Crystal (Quartz) – healing, repels negativity, promotes psychic ability, heightens intuition, all purpose stone
Citrine – aids in creative visualization, confidence, willpower
Coral – protection, healing, wisdom

Diamond – strength, endurance, and energy

Emerald – prosperity, stability, harmony

Fluorite – promotes tranquility, harmony

Garnet – personal power, energy, strength

Hematite – grounding, repels negativity

Jade – wisdom, harmony, tranquility, prosperity
Jasper – energy, strength, positive energy
Jet – grounding, balance, repels negativity

Lapis Lazuli – promotes psychic ability, heightens intuition

Malachite – healing, prosperity, repels negative energy
Moonstone – promotes psychic ability, heightens intuition, opens channels
Mother of Pearl – protection, wealth, serenity

Obsidian – protection, grounding, repels negativity
Onyx – protection, grounding, stress reduction
Opal – promotes intuition, lucid dreaming, prosperity

Pearl – faith, integrity, wisdom
Peridot – happiness, contentment, joy
Pyrite – energy, grounding, repels negativity

Rhodonite – balance, serenity
Rose Quartz – love, healing, serenity
Ruby – protection, courage, prosperity

Sapphire – promotes psychic ability, communication, serenity
Snowflake Obsidian – repels negativity, grounding, balance
Sodalite – aids in communication
Sunstone – courage, strength, happiness

Tanzanite – promotes psychic ability, heightens intuition
Tiger Eye – prosperity, strength, courage
Topaz – creativity, prosperity, repels negativity
Tourmaline – self-confidence, balance, heightens intuition
Turquoise – protection, healing, prosperity

15
Color Correspondences

One of our favorite books is "*My Many Colored Days*" by Dr. Seuss (Text copyright © 1996 by Dr. Seuss Enterprises, L.P.) As the title would imply, it's a very simple book about how different colors make you feel different ways. When doing a reading or ritual of any kind, you may wish to include the additional facet of color in the form of candles, tablecloths, curtains, or clothing to give it additional focus and symbolism. Color has long been a mainstay of candle and knot magicks, attributing specific meanings to a specific color.

Colors have also been associated with the Chakras. The Chakras are literally defined as the seven spiritual centers of the human body, and their colors are those of the rainbow:

The **First, or Root, Chakra** is located at the base of the spine, and is considered the Grounding Force, connecting the body to the physical plane. This is the Chakra of Health and Prosperity, and the color associated with this Chakra is Red.

The **Second, or Sacral, Chakra** is located in the groin area, and governs Sexuality. This is thought to be the resting place of the Serpent Goddess Kundalini, and the color associated with it is Orange.

The **Third Chakra** is located in the Solar Plexus, and rules the Ego. This is where the body's metabolism is located, and the color associated with this Chakra is Yellow.

The **Fourth Chakra** is located over the heart, and is in fact referred to as the Heart Chakra. This center governs Love and Compassion, and its color is Green.

The **Fifth Chakra** is located in the throat area, and is the Chakra of Communication and Self Expression. Blue is the color associated with this Chakra.

The **Sixth Chakra** is located between the eyebrows, and is considered to be the Third Eye Center. Psychic Awareness and Understanding stems from this Chakra, and the color associated is Indigo.

The **Seventh Chakra** is the Crown Chakra, and brings the earthbound body in contact with the higher consciousness. The color for this Chakra is Violet, although it is also described as being brilliant White with Violet overtones.

A partial list of color correspondences is included here:

Aqua: Balance, Harmony

Beige: Calming

Black: Banishing, Binding, Breaking Free from Bad Habits and Addictions, Crone Magick, Empowerment, Meditation, Mourning, Protection, Repelling Negativity, Samhain, Shapeshifting, Strength, Success, Vision, Wisdom

Blue: The Fifth Chakra – Astral Projection, Calm, Changes, Counsel, Creativity, Devotion, Element of Water, Femininity, Good Fortune, Guidance, Happiness, Harmony, Healing, Hidden Knowledge, Honor, Hope, Inner Light, Inspiration, Justice, Loyalty, Meditation, Opening Blocked Communications, Patience, Peace, Prophetic Dreams, Protection, Psychic ability, Reassurance, Self Assurance, Sincerity, Sleep, Spiritual Inspiration, Thoughtfulness, Tranquility, Truth, Understanding, Wisdom

Bronze: Career Promotions, Love and Passion, Positive Relationships, Successful Negotiations

Brown: Animal Healing, Balance, Common Sense, Concentration, Conservation, Increasing Decisiveness, Finding Lost Objects, Friendship, Attracting Money, Grounding, Healing, Hex Breaking, Home Matters, Financial Success, Influence, Intuition, Justice, Lost Objects, Material Increase, Nurturing, Peace, Permanence, Practicality, Protection of Household, Family, Familiars and Pets, Retribution, Special Favors, Stability, Study, Success, Talent, Telepathy

Copper: Career Growth, Career Strategy, Money Goals, Professional Growth, Success in Business, Wealth

Dark Blue: Calming, Communication, Creativity, Healing, Loyalty, Patience, Persuasion, Purification, Sincerity, Truth

Dark Green: Ambition, Fertility, Wealth

Gold: Abundance, Attraction, Confidence, Creativity, Financial Gains, Happiness, Longevity, Luck, Luxury, Perfection, Prosperity, Strength, Virility, Vitality, Wealth

Green: The Fourth Chakra – Abundance, Ambition,

Balance, Beauty, Clairvoyance, Element of Earth, Environment, Fertility, Finance, Good Fortune, Good Luck, Growth, Harmony, Healing, Hidden Knowledge, Hope, Independence. Judgment, Money, Nature, Nurturing, Peace, Personal Goals, Physical Healing, Prosperity, Psychic Ability, Psychic Protection, Recovery, Rejuvenation, Self Assurance, Self control, Spiritual Power, Success, Tree, Herb, and Plant Magick, Wisdom

Grey: Balance, Diffusion, Neutrality

Indigo: The Sixth Chakra – Artistic Talent, Change, Clairvoyance, Deep Thought and Reflection, Focus, Imagination, Insight, Intuition, Mysticism, Psychic Ability, Stability, Understanding, Vision, Wisdom

Lavender: Delicate, Dignity, Elegance, Femininity, Grace, Intuition, Knowledge, Spiritual Shields
Light Blue: Balance, Compassion, Dreams, Harmony, Healing, Mental Clarity, Protection, Purity, Serenity, Tranquility
Light Green: Financial Aid

Magenta: Attraction, Change, Exorcism, Intuition, Life Purpose or Path, Magnetism, Quick changes, Spiritual Healing, Vitality
Maroon: Exorcism, Healing
Orange: The Second Chakra – Abundance, Action, Adaptability, Ambition, Attraction, Authority,

Business Success, Business Goals, Career Goals, Change, Charm, Confidence, Control, Creativity, Encouragement, Energy, Good Fortune. Good Luck, Happiness, Health, Investments, Justice, Kindness, Legal Matters, Mental Clarity, Optimism, Personal Strength, Power, Property Deals, Prosperity Resourcefulness, Stimulation, Strength, Success, Warmth

Peach: Compassion, Gentle Strength, Joy, Understanding
Pink: Affection, Calmness, Caring, Delicacy, Emotional Healing, Emotional Love, Femininity, Friendship, Good Will, Happiness, Harmony, Healing, Honor, Maturity, Morality, Nurturing, Peace, Relationships, Romance, Romantic Love, Self Improvements, Service, Spiritual Awakening, Spiritual Healing, Sweetness, Tenderness, Truth, Unity, Youth
Purple: Ambition, Awareness, Beauty, Business Success, Clairvoyance, Courage, Creativity, Financial Rewards, Hidden Knowledge, Idealism, Independence, Inner Strength, Inspiration, Intuition, Judgment, Manifestation, Mysticism, Peace, Power, Psychic Ability, Psychic Protection, Purification, Royalty, Sacred, Self Assurance, Self Esteem, Sensitivity, Spiritual Power, Spirituality, Success, Wisdom

Red The First Chakra – Aggression, Assertiveness, Career Goals, Competition, Conflicts, Courage,

Determination, Driving Force, Element of Fire, Energy, Enthusiasm, Fast Action, Fertility, Health, Heat, Independence, Love, Lust, Masculinity, Menstruation, Passion, Physical Desire, Physical Strength, Potency, Power, Represents the Mother Aspect of the Triple Goddess, Self Confidence, Self Love, Sex, Sexual Attraction, Survival, Vibrancy, Victory, Vigor, Vitality, Will, Will Power
Royal Blue: Healing, Increasing Influence, Independence, Insight, Laughter, Loyalty

Sea Green: Calming, Emotional Healing, Protection
Silver: Astral Energies, Banishing Negativity, Clairaudience, Clairvoyance, Communications, Creativity, Cycles, Dreams, Emotional Stability, Female Power and Energy, Inspiration, Intuition, Joy, Lunar Matters, Protection, Psychic Abilities, Psychic Protection, Psychometry, Purity, Rebirth, Reincarnation, Serenity, Spiritual Purification, Stability, Telepathy, The Goddess, Vision
Silver Blue: Deep Wisdom, Intuition, the Moon

Turquoise: Awareness, Brotherhood, Changes, Creativity, Femininity, Honor, Humanity, Idealism, Intellectual and Intuitive Insights, Meditation, Originality, Renewal, Self Discipline

Violet: The Seventh Chakra – Astral Projection, Banishing Negativity,

Ab...
Powe...
Sentime...
Spiritual...
Strength, Su...

White: A Balanc...
Astral Travel, Aura...
Calmness, Clairvoya... ...ng,
Consecration, Devotio... ...ination,
Exorcism, Happiness, Healing,
Higher Self, Inspiration, Meditation,
Peace, Protection, Psychic Awareness,
Purification, Purity, Serenity, Sincerity,
Spiritual Enlightenment, Spiritual
Strength, The Maiden Aspect of the
Triple Goddess, Tranquility, Truth,
Wholeness (May be substituted for any
color candle)

Yellow: The Third Chakra – Attraction, Balance, Change, Charisma, Charm, Cheerfulness, Clairvoyance, Clarity, Comfort, Communication, Concentration, Confidence, Courage, Creativity, Happiness, Harmony, Heath, Imagination, Inspiration, Intelligence, Joy, Knowledge, Learning, Logic, Memory, Overcoming Mental Blocks, Persuasion, Progress, Remembrance, Repels Negative Energy, Self Esteem, The Sun, Vigor, Visualization, Vitality, Wisdom

Resources and Recommended Reading

Abraham, Sylvia. *How to Read the Tarot.* St. Paul, MN: Llewellyn Publications, 1994.

Alexander, Skye. *The Everything Tarot Book: Reveal Your Past, Inform Your Present, and Predict Your Future.* Avon, MA: F+W Publications Company, 1999.

Amberstone, Ruth Ann and Wald. *Tarot Tips (Special Topics in Tarot).* St. Paul, MN: Llewellyn Publications, 2003.

Amberstone, Wald and Ruth Ann. *The Secret Language of Tarot.* San Francisco, CA: Red Wheel/Weiser, LLC, 2008.

Andrews, Ted. *Animal-Speak: The Spiritual & Magical Powers of Creatures Great & Small.* St. Paul, MN: Llewellyn Publications, 1996.

Arrien, Angeles. *The Tarot Handbook: Practical Applications of Ancient Visual Symbols.* New York, NY: Penguin Putnam, Inc., 1997.

Ashcroft-Nowicki, Dolores. *Your Unseen Power: Real Training in Western Magic.* Louisville, CO: Sounds True, Inc., 2006.

Blum, Ralph. *The Book of Runes.* New York, NY: St. Martin's Press, 1982.

Boyer, Janet. *The Back in Time Tarot Book: Picture the Past, Experience the Cards, Understand the Present.* Charlottesville, VA: Hampton Roads Publishing Company, Inc., 2008.

Buckland, Raymond. *Signs, Symbols & Omens: An Illustrated Guide to Magical & Spiritual Symbolism.* St. Paul, MN: Llewellyn Publications, 2003.

Bunning, Joan. *Learning the Tarot: A Tarot Book for Beginners.* Boston, MA: Red Wheel/Weiser, LLC, 1998.

Butler, Bill. *Dictionary of the Tarot.* New York, NY: Schocken Books, 1975.

Campion, Nicholas. *The Ultimate Astrologer: A Simple Guide to Calculating and Interpreting Birth Charts for Effective Application in Daily Life.* Carlsbad, CA: Hay House, Inc., 2002.

Carroll, Wilma. *The 2 Hour Tarot Tutor: The Fast, Revolutionary Method for Learning to Read Tarot Cards in Two Hours Without Memorizing Meanings!* New York, NY: Berkley Publishing Company, 2004.

Connolly, Eileen. *Eileen Connolly's Tarot: The First Handbook for the Master.* Van Nuys, CA: Newcastle Publishing Company, Inc., 1996.

Connolly, Eileen. *Tarot: A New Handbook for the Apprentice.* Van Nuys, CA: Newcastle Publishing Company, Inc., 1979.

Connolly, Eileen. *Tarot: The Handbook for the Journeyman.* Van Nuys, CA: Newcastle Publishing Company, Inc., 1987.

Crowley, Aleister, *The Book of Thoth: A Short Essay on the Tarot of the Egyptians Being the Equinx Volume III No. V.* Boston, MA: Red Wheel/Weiser, LLC, 2005.

Crowley, Aleister. *777 and Other Qabalistic Writings of Aleister Crowley.* Boston, MA: Red Wheel/Weiser, LLC, 1986.

Crowley, Aleister. *Tarot Divination.* Boston, MA: Weiser Books, 1976.

Cunningham, Scott. *Cunningham's Encyclopedia of Magical Herbs.* St. Paul, MN: Llewellyn Publications, 1985.

Decker, Ronald. *A Wicked Pack of Cards: The Origins of the Occult Tarot.* New York, NY: St. Martin's Press, 1996.

Donaldson, Terry. *The Tarot Spellcaster.* Hauppauge, NY: Barron's Educational Series, Inc., 2001.

Douglas, Alfred. *The Tarot: The Origins, Meaning and Uses of the Cards.* London, UK: Penguin Books, Ltd., 1972.

Dubats, Sally. *Natural Magick: Inside the Well-Stocked Witch's Cupboard.* New York, NY: Kensington Books, 1999.

Eason, Cassandra. *Complete Guide to Tarot: Everything You Need to Know Including Spreads, Card Analysis, and Divination.* Berkeley, CA: Ten Speed Press, 1999.

Fenton, Sasha. *Secrets of Chinese Divination: The Ancient Systems Revealed.* New York, NY: Sterling Publishing Company, 2001.

Gad, Irene. *Tarot and Individuation: A Jungian Study of Correspondences with Cabala, Alchemy, and The Chakras.* Berwick, ME: Nicolas-Hays, Inc.

Garen, Nancy. *Tarot Made Easy.* New York, NY: Fireside, 1989.

Gillentine, Julie. *Tarot and Dream Interpretation (Special Topics in Tarot).* St. Paul, MN: Llewellyn Publications, 2003.

Graves, Robert. *The White Goddess: A Historical Grammar of Poetic Myth.* New York, NY: Farrar, Straus & Giroux, 1966.

Gray, Eden. *Mastering the Tarot: Basic Lessons in an Ancient Mystic Art.* New York, NY: Signet/Penguin Books, 1973.

Greenaway, Leanna. *Simply Tarot.* New York, NY: Sterling Publishing Company, Inc., 2005.

Greer, Mary K. and Little, Tom. *Understanding the Tarot Court (Special Topics in Tarot).* St. Paul, MN: Llewellyn Publications, 2004.

Greer, Mary K. *Tarot for Your Self: A Workbook for Personal Transformation.* Franklin Lakes, NJ: New Page Books, 2002.

Greer, Mary K. *The Complete Book of Tarot Reversals (Special Topics In Tarot).* St. Paul, MN: Llewellyn Publications, 2002.

Hollander, P. Scott. *Tarot For Beginners:*

An Easy Guide to Understanding & Interpreting the Tarot. St. Paul, MN: Llewellyn Publications, 1995.

Japikse, Carl. *Exploring the Tarot*. Canal Winchester, OH: Ariel Press, 1989.

Jette, Christine. *Tarot for the Healing Heart: Using Inner Wisdom to Heal Body and Mind*. St. Paul, MN: Llewellyn Publications, 2001.

Kelly, Dorothy. *Tarot Card Combinations*. Boston, MA: Red Wheel/Weiser, 1995.

Konraad, Sandor. *Classic Tarot Spreads*. Atglen, PA: Schiffer Publishing, 1985.

Lawrence, D. Baloti. *Tarot: 22 Steps to a Higher Path*. Stamford, CT: Longmeadow Press, 1992.

Lewis, Anthony. *Tarot Plain and Simple*. St. Paul, MN: Llewellyn Publications, 1996.

Macgregor, Trish and Vega, Phyllis. *Power Tarot: More Than 100 Spreads That Give Specific Answers to Your Most Important Question*. New York, NY: Fireside, 1998.

Mangiapane, John. *It's All In The Cards: Tarot Reading Made Easy*. New York, NY: Sterling Publishing Co., Inc., 2004.

McCoy, Edain. *Past-Life and Karmic Tarot (Special Topics in Tarot)*. St. Paul, MN: Llewellyn Publications, 2004.

McCormack, Kathleen. *Tarot Decoder: Interpret the Symbols of Tarot and Increase Your Understanding of the Cards*. Hauppauge, NY: Barron's Educational Series, Inc., 1998.

McCormack, Kathleen. *The Tarot Workbook: An IQ Book for the Tarot Practitioner*. Hauppauge, NY: Barron's Educational Series, Inc., 2002.

Michelsen, Teresa C. *The Complete Tarot Reader: Everything You Need to Know From Start to Finish*. St. Paul, MN: Llewellyn Publications, 2005.

Murphy, Joseph. *Secrets of the I-Ching*. New York, NY: Penguin Putnam, Inc., 1999.

Nichols, Sallie. *Jung and Tarot: An Archetypal Journey*. Boston, MA: Red Wheel/Weiser, LLC, 1980.

Olmstead, Kathleen. *The Girls Guide to Tarot*. New York, NY: Sterling Publishing Company, 2002.

Ozaniec, Naomi. *Teach Yourself Tarot*. Lincolnwood, IL: NTC/Contemporary Publishing, 1998.

Ozaniec, Naomi. *The Element Tarot Handbook: An Initiation into the Key Elements of the Tarot*. Rockport, MA: Element, Inc., 1994.

Parker, Julia and Derek. *Parker's Astrology – The Definitive Guide to Using Astrology in Every Aspect of Your Life*. London, UK: Dorling Kindersley Limited, 1991.

Paxson, Diana L. Taking Up the Runes: A Complete Guide to Using Runes in Spells, Rituals, Divination and Magic. Boston, MA: Red Wheel/Weiser, 2005.

Peach, Emily. *Understanding & Using Tarot*. New York, NY: Sterling Publishing Company, Inc., 1984.

Place, Robert M. *The Tarot: History, Symbolism, and Divination*. New York, NY: Penguin Group, Inc., 2005.

Pollack, Rachel. *Seventy-Eight Degrees of Wisdom: A Book of Tarot*. London, UK: Thorsons/HarperCollins Publishers, 1980.

Pollack, Rachel. *The Complete Illustrated Guide to Tarot: How to Unlock the Secrets of the Tarot*. New York, NY: Random House, Inc., 1999.

Pollack, Rachel. *The Tarot of Perfection*. Prague, Czech Republic: Magic Realist Press, 2008.

Porter, Tracy. *Tarot Companion: An Essential Reference Guide*. St. Paul, MN: Llewellyn Publications, 2000.

Regardie, Israel. *The Golden Dawn: The Original Account of the Teachings, Rites & Ceremonies of the Hermetic Order*. St. Paul, MN: Llewellyn Publications, 2002.

Renee, Janina. *Tarot Spells*. St. Paul, MN: Llewellyn Publications, 1990.

Seidman, Richard. *The Oracle of Kabbalah: Mystical Teachings of the Hebrew Letters*, New York, NY: St. Martin's Press, 2001.

Seuss, Dr. *My Many Colored Days*. New York, NY: Dr. Seuss Enterprises, LP, 1996.

Shine, Norman. **Numerology:** *Your Character and Future Revealed in Numbers*. New York, NY: Fireside, 1995.

Sorrell, Amy Max and Roderic. *The I-Ching Made Easy: Be Your Own Psychic Advisor Using the World's Oldest Oracle*. New York, NY: HarperCollins

Publishers, 1994.

Tyson, Donald. *Portable Magic: Tarot is the Only Tool You Need*. Woodbury, MN: Llewellyn Publications, 2006.

Von List, Guido. *The Secret of the Runes*. Rochester, VT: Destiny Books, 1988.

Waite, Arthur Edward. *The Pictorial Key to the Tarot: Being Fragments of a Secret Tradition under the Veil of Divination*. Stamford, CT: US Games Systems, Inc., 2001.

Wang, Robert. *The Qabalistic Tarot: A Textbook of Mystical Philosophy*. York Beach, ME: Samuel Weiser, Inc., 1983.

Watters, Joanna. *Tarot for Today: Use the Insights of the Cards to Gain Clarity and Direction in Your Life*. London, UK: Carroll & Brown Publishers Limited, 2003.

Whitaker, Hazel. *Numerology: A Mystical, Magical Guide*. Sydney, Australia: Lansdowne Publishing, 1998.

Wilhelm, Richard; Baynes, Cary F.; Wilhelm, Hellmut; Jung, C.G. *The I-Ching or Book of Changes*. Princeton, NJ: Princeton University Press , 1967.

Zell-Ravenheart, Oberon. *Grimoire for the Apprentice Wizard*. Franklin Lakes, NJ: New Page Books/Career Press, 2004.

—. *The American Heritage® Science Dictionary*. Houghton Mifflin Company. Houghton Mifflin Company, 2002. (All rights reserved.)

Index

224